To Corinna~

May you be lavished with God's love in all areas dear to your heart — writing, family, and God.

~Julie Rogers

To Corinne,
May each day be lavished
with lots of love to
all over — your writings
your work and
family and food

Best wishes

THE GIFT
of SOCIAL ANXIETY

Julie Rajnus

The Gift of Social Anxiety: Finding Rest in God's Grace

© 2016 by Julie Rajnus

Malin, Oregon

All rights reserved. No part of this book may be reproduced in any form by any electronic or mechanical means including photocopying, recording, or information storage and retrieval without permission in writing from the author.

Book Website

www.julierajnus.com

Email: mail@julierajnus.com

ISBN-13: 978-1517105280

ISBN-10: 1517105285

Edited by Scott Philip Stewart, Ph.D.

Book and cover design by Julie Rajnus

Cover border design "Sketchy Leaves" provided by Freepik.com

Dedication

For You, my dearest love.
I believe in You, Your character,
Your love, Your goodness, Your grace.
You are everything that I am not.

Contents

Section I: The Journey

1. My Pitiful Story 11
2. What is Social Anxiety? 23
3. A Floppy Foundation 39

Section II: The Corpse

4. The Brain: Welcome to the Circus 59
5. The Autism-Sensory Connection 77
6. Pills, Plants, and Food 97

Section III: A New Creature

7. A Brand New Me (and You) 121
8. The Top Twelve Rules 147
9. Safety Behaviors & PEP 169

Section IV: Counseling-The good, Bad, & Ugly

10. My Strange Thoughts and Behavior 183
11. Committed (and Not to a Mental Institution) ... 205
12. More in the Tool Box 219

Conclusion

13. Extra Mini-Gifts 233

    References 241
    Appendix 263
    Index 267

SECTION I
The Journey

    Every journey starts somewhere. This one begins with the word "No!" As innocent little babies, we are slowly introduced to the world of good and bad, right and wrong, correct and incorrect. The rules. Some of us grow up to be overachievers—big rule-followers. Others among us become rebels, yelling "No!" right back most of our lives. No matter how the journey unfolds, the ending is always the same for both those who conform and those who rebel: The rules catch up to us.

    And that's just when the journey starts to get fun because God designed the rules to be broken.

1

My Pitiful Story

aked

    My bedroom is an oasis in this foreign land. It is surely the coziest place in the world. Heavy burgundy drapes block out the sunbeams so not a solitary dust mote can be seen floating about. The bedspread is a rich brocade the color of milk chocolate, something right out of a castle (though I live in a modest enough home). The light is low, the temperature perfect, all sounds muffled. A wax warmer perfumes the air with the scent of lilacs. My bedroom is my sacred place of retreat. It is where I go to write, pray, nap….

    One thing can destroy all this coziness: Nightmares. Night terrors, to be precise. I have had the same dream, over and over again, for the last 10 years. It is as real as the black-and-white words on this page. It is always the same, down to the finest detail.

    Here it is…

In the darkness, I see the lens of a video camera embedded in the bedroom wall. I am horrified. A tiny red light is flashing, indicating live recording. I always sleep in a nightgown, and as I sleep it tends to get twisted up around my waist while the blankets and sheets migrate down to my feet. As a result, in sleep I am vulnerable, exposed from the waist down. This means the video camera in the wall was recording me in a nearly naked state.

In my dream I understand somehow that the recordings are for sick, perverted purposes. Malevolent eyes are watching me in real time, ogling my nakedness; judging and exposing. My place of cozy retreat, of rest and peace, has become the seat of shame and horror. Although I understand that there is no erasing the images once captured, I am driven mindlessly to rip the camera out of the wall.

I spring out of bed, in true night-terror form. I fumble about in the darkness, trembling with adrenaline, until I finally manage to flip on the bedroom light. This wakes up my tired husband. He always blinks, covers his eyes, and speaks softly.

"Go back to bed," he says. "It's just the nightmare." He says it with such gentleness and familiarity that even through my panicked haze a tiny piece of reality clicks.

Just to be sure, I peer hard at the wall again and discover that where I had previously seen that blinking red light ... there is nothing. Just a smooth bedroom wall—no peep hole, no camera lens— lit up harshly in the dead of night. Relief cascades over me as I begin to swim up and out of the nightmare. I awake from what I thought was wakefulness.

Then, of course, comes the icy tingling sensation in my lips. This familiar warning sign demands that I get my head down, immediately. I shut off the light and quickly collapse into bed, now wide awake. I try desperately to slow my breathing and heart rate. It's no use; it always ends up out of my control anyway. In a tidal wave of nausea, I am overwhelmed with the urge to vomit and use the bathroom, all at the same time. Minutes pass as I endure violent contractions of abdominal pain, my face icy cold and pouring sweat. I fade in and out of consciousness, mind spinning, praying broken prayers. If I compare this experience to childbirth (which I have survived twice) and a heart procedure (which I have survived once) ... it feels worse. Much worse.

After what seems like hours, yet is only minutes, the misery fades. My face stops tingling. I am aware and able to think again. Anticlimactically, I gather the covers around me and fall sickly back to sleep. The next morning I will have a headache and feel like I've had a bout with the flu.

For many years, this nightmare has occurred at least once a month. Something about the vivid dream, combined with jumping up from a dead sleep, causes my body to go into shock. It is technically called vasovagal syncope (a relatively harmless, though unpleasant, form of fainting). It involves a dramatic blood pressure drop along with a pooling of blood in the lower extremities. The brain, starved of oxygen, goes into emergency shutdown. I once fainted in the bathroom and bruised my temple on the toilet. Another time, my terrified young son found me motionless on the living room floor.

Why does a video camera in my sleep inspire such terror? What ungodly thing lives at the root of my fear? Is there a message here that I am failing to understand?

Though the dream's meaning should have been obvious, I have only just now—after more than 40 years of living—begun to understand it. My greatest fear has become crystal clear. The video camera is not just a camera. It represents a judgmental eye, staring at me, exposing me. And therein lies the root of my torment, the cause of my reoccurring dream: I am deeply afraid of being seen.

Like Adam and Eve in the Garden of Eden, I am hiding in shame and nakedness. I am constantly scrambling to cover myself for fear that anyone who got a glimpse of the real me—the naked truth of me—would surely reject me. Looking back, I now recognize I have kept myself carefully hidden for much of my life. I have hidden both from God and from other people.

Writing this book is an act of worship. It is the only true expression of gratitude I can give to God. After years of hiding, I am ready to be known. I am ready to expose the real me because in doing so I expose the amazing nature of grace. If God can give me—the real, dirty, messy, naked me—the riches of His love and acceptance, then He can extend them to virtually anyone.

Let me introduce to you the person I have tried for so long to hide … the real me.

IN HIDING

I had one of those lovely, content childhoods that are hard to come by these days. My parents were (and still are) loving, nurturing, and sweetly supportive. I grew up with lots of farmland to roam, animals to play with, fresh-baked chocolate chip cookies to eat, and a little brother to adore. No family is perfect, but mine was about as close as they come.

My parents say I had a sensitive temperament from the moment I entered this world. My mother recalls me crying and getting sick to my stomach nearly every day before preschool. I used to hide behind her legs and peek out cautiously when faced with unfamiliar people or situations.

As I grew older, people frequently commented on my quietness. Though my family accepted my shyness as a unique part of me, others found it unusual. I dreaded being the center of attention, and yet, ironically, my extreme quietness seemed to draw attention. The harder I tried to shrink, the more attention I attracted.

I began to hate my shyness. To cope, I forced myself to act more outgoing than I was—in hopes of garnering less attention. Hiding became a habit. One method of hiding was to become an excellent rule-follower. If there were rules, I obeyed them. If there weren't rules, I created them. I came to believe that good behavior earned a certain measure of invisibility.

After I married and had children, I became heavily involved in church activities. Even though I preferred solitude, I wanted to please God and serve others. It was not easy overcoming my natural shyness, but I wanted a place in the family of God—a place of belonging, value, and purpose. So I did what everyone else was doing, with naïve gusto. Somehow a new rule began to form within my heart: By doing good things for God, I please Him.

One day, after dropping both children off at school, I rushed to make it to my women's Bible study. As I drove, I realized with startling clarity that I was absolutely miserable. I wanted to go home and crawl into my bed. The scenery blurred around me, and I longed to be still and quiet. I was dead tired, over-stimulated, and stretched too thin. I should have been anticipating joy in fellowship with others, but it all seemed so draining.

I feared judgment for not attending. Perhaps the ladies would think I was backsliding or losing my devotion to God. And what would God think? Did I love rest and solitude more than I loved Him? Above all, I did not want to displease Him. I did not want to break any of His rules. I felt hopelessly trapped. So I drove on.

This scenario replayed itself a dozen times. My discontent with life grew, stemming largely from a lack of energy to perform. Little things, like greeting the other moms at school, became exhausting. I woke up each morning oppressed with the list of duties required for the day and no energy to accomplish them. I began making mistakes (like sending my daughter to school one day in the wrong uniform). Mistakes brought self-condemnation. Soon, the only thing I truly looked forward to was sleep.

Eventually, physical exhaustion drove me to see a doctor. Apart from a slight thyroid issue, I was (to my great disappointment) quite healthy. In fact, the doctor suggested that my low energy might be a symptom of depression. She handed me a depression assessment. With a shaky hand I checked off multiple symptoms on the list: fatigue, lack of appetite, loss of pleasure, excessive guilt. I marveled at how fitting the symptoms were, while instantly dismissing the idea of clinical depression. Depression was a spiritual problem. How could I, being a Christian, have a spiritual problem like depression? It was shameful.

The doctor gave me a sample antidepressant medication to take home, which I later stuffed in a drawer. I now had more questions than answers. I was not only exhausted but troubled as well. What if I was depressed? I certainly felt as if God was displeased with me. I had no zest for life, no joy, no contentment. Was there some hidden sin that was causing God to reject me? A rule I had somehow failed to follow?

I had heard other Christians recommend prayer, forgiveness, spiritual growth, quiet time with God, Bible reading, biblical thinking, thankfulness, increased faith, and worship as cures for hopelessness. So, for the next few weeks, I redoubled my efforts in all of these things. And then I waited expectantly for God to provide relief.

Nothing.

When no reprieve came, I began to view myself as lazy and condemned. I knew the rules for joy and peace, but they were not working. Surely God was ignoring me, refusing to help or answer or intervene in any way. He was judging me, condemning me, but for what, specifically?

By the end of the school year I was nearly non-functional. I was so tired that I cried whenever I was alone. I had constant chest pain and difficulty drawing a deep breath. I just could not get enough oxygen, as if I was slowly smothering. Perhaps I was suffering from asthma or heart problems. *Surely this is what hell feels like,* I thought—a drawn out, torturous sensation of suffocation.

When trying to fall asleep, my body remained so tense that I had to consciously unclench my thigh muscles, biceps, and hands. I tried to find a sleep position in which breathing was less shallow and taut. Usually, this meant lying on my stomach, which eased some of the tension in my diaphragm.

Then, after fitfully falling asleep, I would wake up precisely one hour later. I would pace our home, uneasy, praying for protection. My joints and bones ached, and my throat was chronically sore. My appetite was nonexistent.

I had reached a place of brokenness—spiritually, emotionally, and physically. I began to fantasize about escape. Life was too hard and utterly joyless. Though I refused to overtly contemplate suicide because I was unable to bear the pain it would bring my family, the idea of simply disappearing entered my fantasy life. And, always, I was painfully aware that I had no legitimate reason for my misery. I was just tired. Numb.

I dropped out of most social and church activities. I made excuses about being too busy, determined to hide my inner turmoil. I gave in to my desire for quiet and rest. But now it seemed too late. Even solitude could not revive me.

I did nothing but sit on the couch all day. I did not even have the energy to talk. My exuberant, joyful children must have been so confused. A billion bubbly questions, which I often only answered with a tired shake of my head. I was overwhelmed with guilt.

The doctor's words echoed in my mind: "...symptoms of depression..."

Finally, I reached a crossroads. It went against everything I held dear…privacy, quietness, and the avoidance of undue attention. But I was wretched and tired of being miserable. I was getting worse and desperately needed help.

It took all the courage I had, but I finally asked for public prayer at my church. I sobbed and sobbed as the elders and my husband huddled in a circle and prayed for me. This was my last hope. I could not continue living life with such a deep weariness and lack of joy. *God, help me.* I publicly humbled myself, and allowed others to see that I was in deep pain. As difficult as it was, I was also relieved to expose the real me. I vaguely recall someone praying for "a spirit of Jezebel" to come out of me, but I was too distraught to care.

I went home from church realizing that this was it. I had put the last of my lingering faith in today's public healing prayer. I had done all I could, and now God must do His part. Things had to get better. I was completely broken and thus was counting on Him.

To my astonishment, absolutely nothing changed.

The exhaustion, the trouble breathing, sleeping, eating…all of it remained exactly the same. I became utterly hopeless, angry towards God, and sure I had been abandoned. The Bible said I only needed faith the size of a tiny mustard seed to move mountains. I had placed all the faith I had in Him and yet I could still barely lift myself off the couch. Where was God when I needed Him?

I gave up. I remembered then those antidepressant samples the doctor had given me. There were religious rules (largely of my own making) against taking antidepressant medication—and, beyond that, against needing them. At that point, however, the rules no longer mattered. I was done trying. Crying and hopeless, I pulled out the package and swallowed the first pill in defeat. Then I wept for hours, until I fell into a dull sleep. Done.

For weeks, I barely hung on, dutifully taking my little blue pill each day. Those pills became a symbol of my failure as a Christian. I was too miserable to care.

Weeks later, as my husband and I were watching television together, a funny commercial came on. To my surprise, I found myself laughing at it. The sound of my own laughter startled me. I think it may have startled my husband, too. It had been months since I had laughed. It was subtle, such a small thing. But it was the first, memorable sign of change. Recovery.

Eventually, my appetite returned, my chest pain eased, and sleep became refreshing again. Energy seeped back into my life. The dark cloud gently and gradually lifted. I was astounded.

I recall the pleasure of feeling the car air conditioning on my skin on a hot summer day. Physical, emotional, and spiritual pleasure had been absent in my life for months, and I marveled at this simple experience. I had done nothing spiritual to earn this new healing—not prayer, not church activities…nothing.

As physical health returned, I still had to put back the pieces of my soul. What did all this say about God? Medication? Depression? Faith? I had always believed depression was rooted in spiritual causes and failures. I had believed it could only be relieved through spiritual means. I had begged God for spiritual assistance, but it had not come. I had pursued every spiritual rule I knew (prayer, Bible reading, worship, etc.) and none had made even the tiniest difference. No matter what I tried, my body betrayed me... fatigue, sleep, appetite, breathing. I felt as though I had absolutely no control, spiritual or physical, over any of it.

As I recovered, I found a new, easy joy in my relationship with God. Perhaps instead of abandoning me, He had been gently teaching me through this season of suffering. Maybe, I began to think, being a Christian was less about obeying rules and more about the One who had obeyed them all on my behalf.

I had a million questions for Him, such as, "Am I the only Christian who has ever experienced clinical depression?" And then, "OK, then, am I the only Christian who needed medication in order to recover from it?"

I began researching these topics, in my Bible and online. First, I discovered that many, many others—Christian or not—had suffered in a pattern identical to mine. Those classic symptoms of anxiety and depression (i.e., exhaustion, chest pain, insomnia, loss of appetite) are experienced the world over. I was most certainly not alone. That is a sad fact, but it came as a relief to me.

Second, I discovered that there is no biblical ban on taking medication—not on aspirin, not on insulin, not on antidepressants. I had created that rule or absorbed it from others. I was comforted by this verse, "Every good gift and every perfect gift is from above, and comes down from the Father of lights, with whom there is no variation or shadow of turning" (James 1:17, NKJV). The context of these verses is discerning the source of sin and temptation. God is a giver of good things (not evil things, such as sin and temptation). He did not give me clinical depression. But He certainly provided a way out. If antidepressant medication helped restore my well-being, could I not simply consider it a good gift from Him?

While medication treated the physical aspects of depression, God did some spiritual healing as well. He opened my eyes to the true meaning of grace. His love for me was never based on what I can do (or how well I do it). He was not waiting in judgment, ready to condemn. He has always been completely aware that I am a sinner, through and through. He knew I would never be able to obey enough rules to earn His love (whether they are His good rules or the not-so-good-ones I create). I don't have to become invisible to avoid His judgment. He loves me through Jesus Christ. Period.

Exposed

During this time period, I had stayed home from church often. I was focused on resting, rebuilding, and recovering. It was also uncomfortable because although people at church knew vaguely that I had been suffering, no one knew the details, and I was ashamed to talk about medication with anyone.

Just as I had feared God's judgment, so I remained deeply afraid of other people's judgment. Eventually, however, I worked up the courage to speak with our pastor. He was extremely compassionate and understanding. Just opening up to one person and not receiving judgment felt as if a weight had rolled off my shoulders. It was a mirror of God's grace, passed from one human to another.

My pastor asked me to speak at our church about my experience. I was terrified. This would require me to be completely transparent and undisguised with my church family. I would have to talk about mental illness and medication. Depression. All eyes on me. Exposed.

After much prayer and deliberation, I found that my gratitude to God outweighed my fear of being judged. Though I still felt rather fragile, I agreed to share my story. My objective for the night was to underscore God's grace. Try as I might, I had been unable to earn God's love, and it was only when I gave up trying that grace came. That is the very nature of grace.

Many of my church family were shocked to learn how deeply I had suffered. Many in the audience who cared about me wept, wishing they could have helped. Of course, there was no way they could have because I had carefully hidden my pain. That night I was open, vulnerable, and genuine as never before in my life. The little girl who always hid behind her mother's dress stepped out…tentatively.

Unfortunately, there was fallout from my night of genuine sharing. Within days, I noticed that other women at church were treating me differently, avoiding me. I was perplexed, and when I asked about it, a wrenching truth was unveiled: Some people believed I had taught a false teaching. They believed—just as I once had—that depression was a spiritual problem and that only spiritual avenues of healing were acceptable. The religious rules dictated that prayer, Bible reading, personal goodness, church fellowship/attendance, and faith were acceptable means of healing depression. Antidepressant medication skirted those rules and was thus a sinful way out.

A popular book was circulating among Christians at that time that warned against the influences of the spirit of Jezebel in church. I recalled hearing those words—"spirit of Jezebel"—as the elders in church prayed over me. I began to put the pieces together and realized that a select few members of my church family believed I had this spirit of Jezebel. Another church member confirmed that indeed a few people believed this. According to the book, this meant I was hiding moral corruption. In fact, I had the potential to destroy the church through false teaching, flattering of the pastor, sexual enticements, and a victim mentality.

I was hurt, ashamed, embarrassed, and angry, and I felt suddenly alone. I, who was once afraid of being judged for being overly quiet, now faced judgment of a far more serious nature. I became the focus of increasingly negative attention. I received letters, emails, and phone calls from church members attempting to correct my faulty theology about depression, suffering, and medication. A huge debate erupted in our church over the sinfulness of antidepressant medication.

I went back into hiding.

Our church would eventually experience a wrenching split over this matter—among other issues. A core group of leadership, however, was extremely generous with love and support for us. I will never forget their acts of kindness, home visits, and sacrifice of energy and time. They extended grace...unearned and unconditional love. Others simply could not get past the idea of using medication to treat depression—and they were not gentle in their disapproval. In their religious system, I was a rule-breaker. I was no longer a sister or a valued member of their family.

We left the church and lost many friendships. I had wanted the church to be a hospital during my recovery, but it had been a place of judgment instead. I tasted the difference between religion and Christ-like love. Religion is all about rules and even creates rules where none exist (don't touch, don't taste, don't handle! Colossians 2:21-23). In contrast, genuine Christ-like love is unearned. We are not members in God's family based on our goodness or rule-following. We are members based on the goodness of God, and the beautiful way Jesus obeyed every rule.

It would be a very long time before we set foot in a church again. Religion had left a bad taste in our mouths. Thankfully, God is in the heart-healing business, and in a few years we found a new church family to grow up in.

In the meantime, I tried to wean myself off of antidepressant medication. Perhaps I had learned enough about God's grace and grown enough spiritually to avoid falling into the pitfalls of depression again. I was also now deeply impassioned about helping other Christians through mental health challenges. I went back to college to pursue a master's degree in Human Services counseling. I wanted to do my very best to extend grace to others like me—the flawed.

To my surprise, after going off medication, I found myself regularly flirting with a relapse. Whenever I made a commitment to something people-oriented (i.e., job, ministry, etc.), the physical symptoms of depression would eventually return. First, I would grow emotionally numb. Then exhaustion would creep in. Soon I was yearning for sleep, irritable, unhappy. Without medication, the physical symptoms of anxiety washed back over me and were unbearable. So I was forced to go back on medication and drastically readjust my lifestyle. In spite of spiritual growth and a deeper understanding of God's grace, it seemed I just could not overcome the physical trend towards depression without medication.

ACCEPTANCE

In one of my final terms of graduate school, I completed a research paper on social anxiety. I read through hundreds of studies on introversion, temperament, shyness, and social phobia. I felt deep compassion for those suffering from social anxiety and recognized myself in many of their stories.

I had always known that my extreme introversion made certain things challenging. But I had not realized how deeply various personality traits affected virtually every part of my life. I almost never answer the phone. I dread going to the post office. I shop awkwardly, using a grocery cart as a physical shield. I never go to social events by myself unless I can do so anonymously. And those are the *little* things—the little things that many people with social anxiety experience. The bigger things, such as the frequent combination of social anxiety and depression, also fit my life story.

I reexamined my depressive cycles. Each one was precipitated by intense social involvement. Could the draining effect of being with others have led to my bouts of depression? Church activities, taking my children to school, working a desk job, and ministry events—each has a strongly social component. Each one eventually led to depressive symptoms (fatigue, burnout, etc.). It takes a lot of energy to hide inherent shyness, to fit in with my idea of "normal." I had many rules for social interaction. I just could not seem to follow them. I often felt like a social misfit. Somehow, I had veered away from grace once again and was still trying to earn love (from God and man).

A light bulb came on. I had worked so hard to hide the parts of me I dislike (i.e., my shyness, quietness, introversion). Deep in my core, I believed I could eventually reshape myself into someone more worthy of love. Or, even better, God would change me into someone He could really love.

What if I believed that God Himself was the One who decreed I would be a quiet person? What if I believed that God knew what He was doing when He formed me—even the parts of me I despise? What if…He had never been trying to change me at all? What if He wanted me to simply rest? What if I learned to rest from all my good deeds and rules and expectations? What if all the rules just fell away…?

With six years of my life invested in preparing to become a counselor, I now faced a crossroads. My imaginary, perfect me would have been fabulous at counseling. The real me simply did not have the energy, the will, or the desire to spend that much time with other people. I care deeply for people, but I am neither an eloquent speaker nor a skilled listener. In other words, I am not a counselor.

To compensate for my social weakness, I (long ago) developed the ability to communicate in writing. Journaling, letter writing, emails… I have relied heavily on these tasks to cultivate relationships with God and others. Being able to write my thoughts, rather than verbally or socially communicate them, was birthed out of weakness but eventually became an effective way to love. For me, it is a joyous and natural way to express affection.

In the weeks after completing graduate school, a grace-based truth emerged like a butterfly from its wrinkled cocoon. My path shifted from counseling to writing. And, suddenly, my life's journey began to all make sense. This is what God had designed me for all along. No more hiding, no more trying to be someone else. I am free to be me at last, secure in the unconditional love of God.

That is how I have arrived at this project, *The Gift of Social Anxiety*. Social anxiety causes tremendous suffering, but it also points to the deep longing we all have for grace. We all want to truly be ourselves and be loved for who we are. We want to stop trying so hard to change. We want to stop being tormented by all the social rules that we regularly fail to obey. We just want rest.

This yearning for rest is the gift social anxiety provides. And grace, through Jesus, supplies the answer:

> Come to Me, all you who labor and are heavy laden, and I will give you rest. Take My yoke upon you and learn from Me, for I am gentle and lowly in heart, and you will find rest for your souls. For My yoke is easy and My burden is light (Matthew 11:28-30, NKJV).

In the pages that follow, I have organized all (or as much as I could get my hands on) of the information about social anxiety that exists. I am capitalizing on the hard work of others: scientists, therapists, theologians, pastors, and disciples. To them, I give my fierce gratitude. Without their hours of dedicated research, caring practice, diligent Bible study, and earnest seeking after God, this text would be devoid of useful material. Throughout the ages a lot of rules have been applied to social behavior. Some are good rules, ordained by God (i.e., love one another). Some are oppressive rules, created by man (i.e., avoidance is bad). None of these rules provides the rest we are looking for. A rule cannot provide rest but only demands work.

I think back to my recurring nightmare. The camera lens is turned on me, viewing me at my most vulnerable. I am trembling, fearful of judgment. Critical eyes are on me. The camera zooms in on my nakedness, exposing my raw reality in high definition for all to see and judge.

But grace alters the view. It is as if a soft-view lens has been inserted, allowing the camera to only see Jesus in the viewfinder. No longer able to focus on my imperfections, the camera sees only the perfect image of Jesus. There is no need to hide because Jesus is all there is to see. Let the cameras roll, because my nakedness is covered. I need not fear judgment of any kind. I am free.

Since the first writing of this chapter, my camera nightmare never occurred again.

* * *

REFLECTION

1. Can you identify your greatest weakness?

2. In what way does Christ's power rest in your area of weakness?

3. Do you try to hide your flaws, or do you openly disclose them?

4. What are the dangers associated with revealing your flaws to others?

5. What are the possible benefits to God's Kingdom in sharing your weaknesses?

6. Read 2 Corinthians 12:7-10. How does Paul handle his weakness?

2

WHAT IS SOCIAL ANXIETY?

Social Anxiety is, by definition, an intense fear of human interaction. Social interactions tend to leave us feeling like…well, like we're real losers. Here's how blogger Susan Kay describes herself:

> If you are like me, your anxiety started somewhere in the womb and branched into all kinds of afflictions around the age of five. I was fearful of bees, stray dogs, loud noises, cameras, telephones, hallways, the toaster and generally anyone who did not share my gene pool...
>
> I suffer from... social anxiety accompanied by random panic attacks, dissociative episodes and I was a pastor's wife. Stir that up, shake it vigorously and you'll have enough nuclear material to take us into the next millennium.[1]
>
> There is a common thread underlying social anxiety. *Extreme. Fear.*

---

1 Kay, Susan. 2013. [Blog]. Posts Tagged Social Anxiety. http://www.anxiety-master.com/tag/social-anxiety/

Not ordinary fears, such as feeling nervous before a musical performance, job interview, or important meeting. Nearly everyone has experienced discomfort in these high-pressure social situations. This type of anxiety falls within the normal range of human experience. This is *not* the stuff of Social Anxiety Disorder (SAD).

For those of us with SAD, the fear of a given social situation is so intense as to be crippling. In contrast to a manageable sense of nervousness, SAD could be likened to hitting a brick wall of fear. Only those who have experienced this type of intense anxiety truly understand its baffling severity.

Social anxiety causes us to perceive ourselves as if from the eyes of a harshly judging audience, with social expectations that are impossible to meet. Although we understand that the judgment of others should not make or break our happiness, we are incapable of escaping the fiery expectation of judgment. The first, ironclad rule of social anxiety is this: **fear judgment**. The expectation of harsh judgment and a deep sense of unworthiness are central to social anxiety.

Specific physical symptoms of social anxiety include: blushing, sweating, reduced eye contact, heart racing and palpitations, trembling, difficulty concentrating, and fear of fainting (Stein and Stein 2008, 1115). We may experience a dry throat and mouth, difficulty swallowing, and muscle twitches (Richards 2014b). Physical symptoms may progress to a full-blown panic attack, resulting in tachycardia (racing heartbeat) and breathlessness (Stein and Stein 2008, 1117). We are acutely aware that the symptoms are not in proportion to the situation. Still, there is a sense of helplessness at preventing or controlling these physical reactions. It is as if our body has a mind of its own.

> **Rule #1**
>
> THOU SHALT FEAR JUDGMENT

> **Rule #2**
>
> THOU SHALT CONTROL THY BODY

The second rule of social anxiety is this: **master one's body**. We should be able to stop sweating, blushing, and trembling, right? Wrong. This is not a bad rule, just completely unachievable. It's like commanding someone to set his heart rate to exactly 82 beats per minute. No higher, no lower. Ready, set, go! And good luck.

When social anxiety is severe enough to greatly decrease one's quality of life, it is considered a mental disorder and diagnosed as SAD. The American Psychiatric Association (APA) lists the following symptoms in its diagnostic definition of SAD (2013; Table 1).

SOCIAL ANXIETY DISORDER SYMPTOMS

1.	A persistent fear of at least one social situation.
2.	Any exposure to the feared situation provokes anxiety (sometimes leading to a panic attack).
3.	The person recognizes his or her fear is unreasonable.
4.	The person engages in avoidance of feared situations. If the situation can't be avoided, it is endured with intense discomfort.
5.	Avoidance or anxiety symptoms cause marked disruption of school, work, social, relationship, or routine functioning.
6.	Symptoms are of an enduring nature, typically lasting longer than 6 months.
7.	Substance abuse or medical illness is not to blame for the person's fear or avoidance.

Table 1. Source: APA, 2013

Clearly, it is not just negative attention that causes social fear. Even positive attention, such as winning an award, is a real head-trip for us (Weeks, Heimberg, and Rodebaugh 2008, 52). Disappearing seems to be the comfort zone for most of us with SAD. Anything that brings us "into the light" is uncomfortable. This is why some triggers for social anxiety are obvious while others make you scratch your head (see Table 2).

COMMON TRIGGERS

Making small talk	Attending a meeting or party	Having a visible injury/deformity
Taking a test	Public speaking	Musical or athletic performance
Writing in public	Eating in public	Participating in gym class
Shopping	Meeting with any authority figure	Carpooling
Dancing	Direct eye contact	Using a public restroom
Talking on the telephone	Attending church	Having a photo taken

Having vehicle serviced	Going to the post office	Checking in to a motel
Meeting someone new	Returning an item to the store	Buying fuel at a gas station
Activity with a friend	Chance meeting with an acquaintance	Being the center of attention (i.e. a surprise party)
Sitting in front of crowded room	Reading out loud	Entering or leaving a crowded room
Going to the library	Answering a question in class	Asking for help/directions
Going on a date	Going to a medical office	Attending a family reunion
Attending a Bible study	Walking into the workplace	Being observed while working
Receiving an award	Receiving praise	

Table 2. Triggers

OUR ELITE, YET SIZABLE, CLUB

Imagine a church pew that seats 10 individuals. How many sitting in the pew are likely to have social anxiety? Probably none because going to church is a difficult activity for most socially anxious people. Yet, SAD happens to be one of the most prevalent of mental health disorders in existence. Out of 10 people, at least one will experience SAD at some point in life (Kessler et al. 2012, 169–184).

*about **13%** will experience **SAD***

A large survey found that SAD was such a common disorder that only major depressive disorder, alcohol abuse, and specific phobias occurred more often (Kessler et al. 2005, 593-602). As many as 13% of people 18 to 64 years old will experience social anxiety disorder during their lifetime (Kessler et al. 2012, 174). That translates into over 40 million Americans.

Of those, about 77% probably identify as Christians (Newport 2012). Now, I am not that great at math. But my son helped me, and that adds up to more than 31 million American Christians who may experience SAD! That means that a huge portion of the church is potentially tormented by social anxiety, silently and needlessly ashamed. Those 31 million people are like me: isolated, different, subnormal. And we may nev-

31 million Christians

er see them, or hear from them, because they are not in the places most people go to.

Oh, but we need them.

SAD is not only incredibly common, it also starts at a very young age. In fact, SAD has an earlier onset than all other anxiety disorders (Seedat 2013, 192). Some behavioral markers begin in infancy. The uber-fussy baby, the baby who startles at every noise, the baby who needs the blankie to be just the same every night... These babies are at a higher risk of developing SAD (several studies cited in Weeks 2014). Many (but not all) of these highly reactive, highly sensitive infants seem to have an inborn tendency towards social anxiety.

What would be the very worst, most inconvenient, simply terrible time for a mental disorder to emerge? How about puberty? According to the Anxiety and Depression Association of America website, the usual age of onset of SAD is 13 years old[2]. So right about the time when hormones are rushing, bodies are changing, and life is turned upside down...SAD blooms.

In fact, an onset after the age of 25 years is very uncommon (Seedat 2013, 192). It nearly always hits early. A childhood or adolescent diagnosis of SAD is associated with loneliness, poor mood, poor social functioning (Beidel et al. 2006, 51) and increased victimization by bullies (Storch et al. 2005, 447-48;). SAD also interferes with education, making dropping out or failing a grade more likely (Stein and Kean 2000, 1612). In all ways, SAD makes survival of the teenage years just about as hard as we can imagine.

> **The very worst, most inconvenient, simply terrible time for a mental disorder... puberty**

When SAD arrives, it proceeds to do as much robbing and stealing as possible. Compared to all other psychiatric disorders, SAD is among the top-five most debilitating (Alonso et al. 2004, 44). SAD messes up job and relational functioning. Individuals with SAD reported less satisfaction with most life domains, including work, self-esteem, home lives, friendships, relationships with family, and romantic relationships (Eng et al. 2005, 149, 153). Romantic, friend, and family relationships tend to be markedly impaired (Ruscio et al. 2008).

SAD undermines church and community relationships. The goal of SAD is to get us alone, afraid, and most importantly, condemned. Unaccepted. This is the tragedy for the Christian church. Christianity highly values a sense of community and interconnectedness. Christians were designed to have extraordinary love for

> **IT robs and steals**

---

[2] http://www.adaa.org/social-anxiety-disorder

one another (John 13:35). When fear hinders connection, the church is crippled.

The following quote expresses one young woman's struggle with social anxiety and church activities:[3]

> As a teenager I was very involved in my youth group. I went on mission and camp trips and such. I had a couple of friends I felt comfortable with, but in general, it was difficult for me to feel connected to people. I have only recently realized my SA (social anxiety). I always just called myself shy or quiet... As I got older it became harder to assimilate. I tried a few 20's church groups, but the social activities made me very uncomfortable. I especially hated the Bible study groups in which people were expected to pray out loud and discuss their viewpoints to the group. I remained faithful in my relationship to the Lord, but going to church fell by the wayside because it caused me so much anxiety. I wasn't afraid of meeting people, so much as I was afraid of the expectations that would be put on me. Next, I'd be pressured into joining a ministry, another study group, etc. that would require me to enter more social situations.

Christians feel a particular sense of failure when SAD prevents us from loving others. This has been the heartbreak of my life. I know that loving others is a truly good and biblical rule. I want to do so in tangible ways. But I am often afraid. Rule number three for the socially anxious has haunted me most of my Christian life: **love others perfectly.** Unfortunately, this beautiful and profound rule is...completely unachievable.

Rule #3

THOU SHALT
LOVE PERFECTLY

SAD is associated with an overall lowered quality of life (Wittchen et al. 2000). People with SAD are less employed, less productive, and less satisfied with their income (Stein and Kean 2000). When it comes to trying to make it in this world, the easiest way to say it is SAD is BAD.

Let me give you a list of my previous jobs: beverage hostess at the Apple Peddler, fry cook at Wendy's, mat cutter in an art gallery, secretary at a medical clinic...and several others in a similar vein. Guess how long I lasted at these jobs? Never years, sometimes months, usually weeks. I am one of those pitiful persons who cannot hold down a job. I cannot even begin to describe how draining working with

---

[3] Lostinparadise, April 2008, forum post on "Christianity - Going to Church" *Social Anxiety Support Forum*, http://www.socialanxietysupport.com/forum/f38/christianity-going-to-church-37213/#post551040

the public is for me. And not because the public is a bunch of idiots and weirdos (though that might be true a certain percentage of the time). It was really just...me. And several other millions like myself.

Approximately 21.9% of those with SAD have attempted suicide (Katzelnick et al. 2001, 2004). This may be one of the strongest indicators of just how severe the experience of social anxiety can be. The hard rules of social anxiety can render us utterly hopeless. As I mentioned before, I teetered on the edge of just wanting to disappear. Forever. But without hurting anybody. Thankfully, no plan I ever considered included all those elements.

According to Al Hsu, author of *Grieving a Suicide: A Loved One's Search for Comfort, Answers and Hope*, suicide occurs among Christians at roughly the same rate as non-Christians (2013). Hsu's own father killed himself after suffering from a stroke and clinical depression. He is not alone. Every 15 minutes someone in the United States commits suicide.

The devastating impact of SAD is partly due to the extra baggage it brings. Anywhere from 62.9% to 90.2% of individuals with SAD report another mental health disorder (Ruscio et al. 2008). The higher the number of individual fears (i.e., writing in public, using a public restroom), the more likely the individual is to have another disorder. More rules equate to a heavier burden. SAD is frequently seen along with depression (Ohayon and Schatzberg 2010, 241) and bipolar disorder (Merikangas et al. 2007, 547). For me, social anxiety and depression are the very best of terrible friends.

In spite of its severity, more than 80% of those who suffer from SAD will never receive any treatment for it (Grant et al. 2005). This makes so much sense. Why would someone who is deathly afraid of people seek out...people—even helping people? Most of us are just not falling for that. For those of us who do seek treatment, it is usually after a stunning 15 to 20 years of symptoms!

**80%
never seek treatment**

The percentage of people who do not seek treatment is likely even greater for members of the Christian faith given the additional stigma of spiritual failure. No Christian wants to be known as a failed rule-follower, even though in truth that should be a major part of our identity. Because we are. Yet, admitting to having social anxiety is acknowledging a great and terrible defeat: "Rather than love others, I fear them."

An obvious reason that most people don't seek treatment is difficulty with stressful social interactions. Going to see a doctor, therapist, or counselor and sharing intimate personal information is very stressful for us. Researchers state that SAD individuals tend to speak softly, avoid eye contact, and offer only surface answers in a medical setting (Stein and Stein 2008, 1116-17). Frankly, I would rather have my teeth pulled than go tell a strange authority figure about what a loser I am.

The reason for such reticence is embarrassment about symptoms, fear of being judged, and a discomfort with authority figures (all central features of social anxiety). We perceive anyone who might be considered a rule-judger (authority figure) as particularly intimidating. We must. Appear. Normal.

When people with SAD are forced to engage in a social situation, they often utilize safety behaviors as a means of coping (Plasencia, Alden, and Taylor 2011, 666). These safety behaviors include avoiding eye contact, limiting speech, and attempting to hide one's genuine self (in order to avoid criticism or judgment). To put on this "act," we must tightly monitor and control our behavior, expending a large amount of energy to present a somewhat artificial self. Hiding is exhausting. This is the essence of rule number 4: **hide all flaws.** This rule entered the world when Adam and Eve tasted the forbidden fruit in the Garden of Eden and immediately hid in their shame. Hiding in shame continues today. Ironically, safety behaviors tend to backfire in SAD (discussed more in chapter 9).

> **Rule #4**
>
> THOU SHALT
> HIDE ALL FLAWS

A large number of people who begin treatment for SAD drop out before completion. In one study, 85% of those who initiated treatment never followed through (Coles et al. 2004, 379). For those brave enough to receive treatment (involving psychotherapy or medication), approximately 40%-48% did not improve significantly (Leichsenring et al. 2013, 765). Thus, nearly half of the patients who had the guts to show up for treatment did not get any better—at least not better enough to measure! This does not mean that treatment is worthless—only that a secret ingredient is often missing. We will get to that later.

Research into factors that help or hurt treatment is ongoing. Even those who receive treatment, and benefit from it, still rarely reach a normal quality of life (Eng et al. 2005, 153). It is as though we are destined to never quite achieve freedom from, or fulfillment of, all the rules inherent to SAD.

For unknown reasons, SAD tends to occur at a higher rate for females (Ohayon and Schatzberg 2010, 238). Of the two genders, however, men are more likely to seek treatment. Thus, females with social anxiety are at a significantly increased risk of remaining untreated (Hollander and Bakalar 2005, xii). Most people with SAD are like me: female and treatment-avoiding.

HIDE AND SEEK IS OUR FAVORITE GAME

Avoidance happens to be the key marker of social anxiety. Hiding is what breathes life into SAD. Researchers state, "Persons suffering from SAD typically either avoid the feared situations or endure them with intense anxiety or distress, leading to significant functional impairment" (Talati et al. 2013, 75). "Suffering through" a stressful social interaction can be so miserable that individuals with SAD often resort to avoidance. Church functions such as Bible studies, retreats, and even traditional Sunday services are all designed to foster relationships, both with God and with one another. Unfortunately, these are the very events those of us with SAD find unbearable to engage in and, thus, avoid.

Some socially anxious people (though not all) crave relationships. They wish to be known, yet find it terribly painful when they are known... and then rejected. Thus, social interactions are inherently risky. Once we have been burned (maybe only once or twice), fear begins to outweigh the potential benefits of revealing ourselves. Like an onion, our genuine inner core becomes covered in more and more layers. Ironically, even our fake self will eventually be rejected. This is what humans do to one another.

Most traditional counseling methods consider avoidance a maladaptive way to cope with fear. So many of us feel quite guilty about our avoidance habits. Staying home from church or a party is considered personally sinful. There is a chronic breaking of internal rule number 5: **face all fears.** Failure becomes a guilt-ridden habit. And even though we know better, we just cannot seem to find any viable alternatives. Nobody wants to be miserable all the time.

> **Rule #5**
>
> THOU SHALT FACE FEARS

A MODERN FAD?

Well, not really. Social fear has existed for a very long time. Moses is described in the Bible as having a fear of public speaking related to "a slow tongue" (Exodus 4:10, NKJV). The Bible is not clear about the cause of Moses' problem. Some theologians think he was a stutterer; others believe he was simply afraid of public speaking. In any event, God asked Moses to be a public speaker on His behalf. Moses argued with God repeatedly about this, based firmly on his own human shortcomings and his social anxiety (fear of the people).

Moses presented four arguments to God against becoming a public leader. First, he stated (paraphrased; Exodus 3-4), "I'M A NOBODY!" God responded by saying He would be right there beside Moses at all times. Second, Moses argued, "I HAVE NO AUTHORITY!" God graciously revealed His name, sort of a Secret Password that nobody else knew. Third, Moses cried out, "THE PEOPLE WILL REJECT ME!" In response, God granted Moses the ability to perform miracles so that the people would have no doubt

Social Anxiety in the bible

that Moses was intertwined with God's power. Fourth, Moses argued, "I HAVE NO SKILLS!" God reassured Moses, telling him He would provide the perfect words for Moses to speak. For every human shortcoming Moses provided, God responded with "Trust in Me. I will do the real work Myself." God already knew Moses was a nobody, had no authority, would be rejected, and lacked skills. It just wasn't about Moses.

Incredibly, after four arguments, and four reassurances from God (Moses was talking face to face with GOD!), Moses remained unconvinced that God had chosen wisely. He overestimated his own role and underestimated God's role in the proposed plan. (I do this all the time!) Ultimately, Moses pleaded with God to come up with a replacement, which is perhaps the first biblical example of social avoidance: *I'm not going. Find someone else!*

God was angry. When reading these passages, I always missed the real reason God was upset. He was not angry that Moses was weak or socially anxious. God already knew exactly who Moses was (and who he wasn't). God was offering Moses an identity that was completely enmeshed with His own. He was saying, in effect, "I will do everything for you. Do you believe it?"

Moses did not believe it.

This is a foreshadowing of the work of the cross. Moses could only see his own flawed humanness. In fact, he was so focused on his own failings that he could not rest and just let God be God. Moses could not comprehend a relationship with God that depended solely on God's goodness and disregarded human weakness. If a Bible hero made this mistake, why wouldn't we?

To humor Moses, God provided a social security blanket in the form of Moses' brother, Aaron. Aaron was supposed to be the replacement public speaker. But as it turned out, Aaron never did speak for Moses. Moses did it all.

In the end, Moses went on to play a pivotal role in God's plan. Throughout the Bible we find that human weakness *never* alters the will of God. Indeed, God's loving plans often require human weakness to provide startling contrast to His own incredible power and holiness.

Moses was not the only person in history to have felt socially inadequate. We social misfits have always had company. Over 2,400 years ago, the Greek physician Hippocrates observed cases of extreme shyness, social avoidance, and anxiety.[4] It was not until the early 1900s, however, that psychologist Pierre Janet first used the term social phobia (Heimburg et al. 1995, 3). Janet was referring to an intense fear of being watched while writing or speaking. For nearly another 50 years, social phobia was a forgotten topic that garnered almost no interest or study.

During the 1950s, the mental health community began to study

---

[4] http://socialanxietydisorder.about.com/od/overviewofsad/a/history.htm

phobias more actively.[5] Approximately 30 years later, the APA granted social phobia its own diagnostic criteria. The terms social phobia and Social Anxiety Disorder are currently considered interchangeable.

The scientific study of social anxiety did not begin in earnest until about the turn of the 21st century. To put that into perspective, Air Jordan tennis shoes, cell phones, and Seinfeld have been around longer than scientists have been formally researching social anxiety. So while social anxiety itself has been around for a very long time—millennia—its scientific study is still in its infancy. There is still so much to learn about how social anxiety affects the body, and vice versa.

All in all, social anxiety has likely existed pretty much forever. Recall that fear was first introduced into a social relationship (between man and God) in the Garden of Eden. It was also at this point that judgment became a threat. The result was avoidance, shame, fear, and relational separation. *Voila!* Social anxiety.

> **Since Adam and Eve first ate the forbidden fruit**

THE DREADED PERSONALITY DISORDER

When it comes to mental health disorders, a personality disorder is the one diagnosis nobody wants. A personality disorder tends to come on early, stay strong, and affect all areas of thinking and behavior (Tillfors and Ekselius 2009, 26). Individuals with personality disorders are generally so inflexible in their patterns of behavior that they experience significant life problems (APA 2013).

Avoidant Personality Disorder (APD) was introduced to the diagnostic scene at roughly the same time as SAD (Tillfors and Ekselius 2009, 25). The simplest way to describe APD is to call it the biggest, baddest case of SAD on the planet. Some professionals argue that it may be a completely different animal from SAD, but nobody is sure yet. What we do know is that APD shares many features with SAD.

Individuals with APD have the strictest, harshest rules for defining relationship success, and achievement remains elusive. Of all the personality disorders, APD is recognized as one of the most common (Torgersen, Kringlen, and Cramer 2001, 590-596) and disabling (Tillfors and Ekselius 2009, 31).

Traits associated with APD include: social inhibition, feelings of inadequacy, hypersensitivity to negative evaluation, despair, social dread, shrinking, risk aversion, joylessness, and rigidity (Lynam et al. 2012, 471). The individual with APD is extremely fearful of humiliation and others' judgment. Fear of rejection is

> **The biggest, baddest case of SAD**

---

5 Ibid.

so intense that it prohibits nearly all attempts at relationship forming. Loneliness and a craving for friendship are common in APD.

A 26-year-old describes her APD in this way:

> I can interpret many things as rejection. I'm constantly afraid everyone will turn against me one day and hate me for the rotten person I am. I find many social situations "dangerous," and I'm always afraid disapproval and rejection are waiting around the corner. Any criticism wounds me deeply, though I know there's such a thing as constructive criticism, which I try to take stoically.[6]

AVOIDANT PERSONALITY DISORDER

1.	Low self-esteem, sees self as socially inept, unappealing, inferior, feelings of shame and inadequacy.
2.	Unrealistic standards for behavior, leading to reluctance to pursue goals, take risks, or try new activities.
3.	Preoccupation with, and fear of, criticism or rejection.
4.	Only engages in relationships when certain of being liked.
5.	Reticence in social situations, avoidance of social interactions.
6.	Avoidance of intimate relationships.
7.	Lack of enjoyment in life experiences.
8.	Feelings of nervousness, tenseness, panic; often the result of social situations.
9.	Personality impairments are long lasting and extend to most situations.
10.	The impairments are not due to substance abuse or a general medical condition.

Table 3. Source: APA, 2013

Individuals with APD frequently disregard their own needs and "find it difficult to stand up for themselves" (Gilbert and Gordon 2012, 114). They would do just about anything to avoid conflict. They feel inept, inferior, and different from others, with chronically low self-esteem (Lynum, Wilberg, and Karterud 2008, 474). They are so easily swayed by others that they can become unassertive pushovers.

Severe depression commonly occurs along with APD (Sanislow,

---

[6] Flatley, Angel. 2012. Blog post entitled, "Avoidant Personality Disorder." https://themirthofdespair.wordpress.com/2012/10/14/avoidant-personality-disorder/

Bartolini, and Zoloth 2012, 260). Symptoms of APD tend to be longstanding and present in nearly every social situation. APD is a tremendous, heart-breaking burden.

Research on APD is lacking. One team of researchers hypothesized that individuals with APD avoid things because they are new (Huppert et al. 2008, 447). This fear of novelty translates into a dislike for trying new foods, reading a book by a new author, or engaging in a new sport. They have rigid rules for self-protection and yet are imprisoned within their own boundaries.

Traditional treatment methods for SAD and APD are generally the same. One notable difference between the two is that individuals with APD tend to show greater levels of improvement early in treatment (Huppert et al. 2008, 446). This is likely due to the greater severity of APD, leaving more room for substantial improvement.

Who, or What, Can We Blame?

The causes of both SAD and APD are currently the subject of much study. Researchers are just now beginning to swing more towards genetics as the biggest influencer in SAD (Isomura et al. 2014, 6). Our physical makeup is a critical factor behind the symptoms of SAD.

Those ultra-smart researchers are currently digging into causes such as genetics, temperament/personality, neurological factors, endocrine factors, family environment, thought-patterns, and more. The standard model of social anxiety includes both physical (body) and psychological (thinking/belief) factors.

This actually lines up just right with a biblical worldview. First, all people are born with human, fallible bodies. It should come as no surprise when the physical body malfunctions, triggering many of the symptoms of social anxiety. Second, beliefs are critical in a biblical worldview—so critical that what we believe determines our eternal destiny. So it is not surprising to find that they are also critical in maintaining social anxiety. Our beliefs about self, others, and God will, categorically, either worsen or alleviate the impact of social anxiety.

It is clear that SAD is heavily influenced by man-made rules. Some examples of man-made rules are: blushing is bad, stuttering is bad, introversion is bad, shyness is bad. Beyond man-made rules, an even heavier burden for many is an inability to observe the good, God-created rules (such as loving one's neighbor). When those with social anxiety fail at even the good rules, harsh self-judgment and condemnation often floods in. The Bible gently teaches that condemnation and rule-obeying is *not* the way to freedom. We will explore that (which is to say, grace) in its wonderful entirety throughout the next chapter.

The Only Test You'll Ever Love

An assessment is a list of rules that either qualify or disqualify one for an official label. I know labels are not popular, but I personally love them! I think assessments are valuable because they organize weaknesses in a precise, understandable way. For example, I fit all the defining rules for the label of social anxiety. Thus, I can predict (to some degree) how my weaknesses will play out here on Earth. I know, pretty confidently, that I will never ask my husband if we can go on a reality TV show. Cameras, people, and mass judgment. Those things are *not* me. And I know why. I understand that much about me. That's why I like labels. I honestly wish I could go around sticking labels on other people, so I could instantly understand them. Apparently, that's frowned upon.

One thing a label does not do is define our entire identity. I am not just socially anxious. I am first and foremost a treasured daughter of God. My identity covers a whole lot more than just my weaknesses. But I like predictability, and a label does a pretty good job of predicting future behavior.

If we require labels on food, why not humans?

One of the most popular assessment tools for measuring social anxiety in adults is the **Liebowitz Social Anxiety Scale** (LSAS). It is considered by many to be the gold standard for assessing social anxiety, and is available online at no charge (http://www.socialanxietysupport.com/disorder/liebowitz/). A score of 55 or above indicates social phobia. I completed the test with gusto (and a score of 94).

What if you take the assessment, and fail? Or pass? I'm not sure which, but let's say you seem to have elements of social anxiety. Making an appointment with a familiar primary care provider is considered a logical first step, though it will be really intimidating for someone with SAD.[7] If a close friend or family member is available, please utilize their social support.

At the first appointment, the primary care provider will ask pertinent questions and then provide referrals as needed. Visit http://www.mayoclinic.org/diseases-conditions/social-anxiety-disorder/basics/preparing-for-your-appointment/con-20032524 for a list of typical questions at a first visit.

And, if you have the courage to seek help, I am completely in awe of you.

Whatever you do, please keep reading this book! I want you to be thoroughly encouraged and heart-wrenchingly loved before you do anything. That is what grace is about to do.

* * *

---

[7] Mayo Clinic Staff. n.d. "Social Anxiety Disorder (Social Phobia): Preparing for Your Appointment." http://www.mayoclinic.org/diseases-conditions/social-anxiety-disorder/basics/preparing-for-your-appointment/con-20032524

REFLECTION

1. Do you recognize yourself (or someone you love) in the list of SAD or APD symptoms?

2. If so, which symptom is the most troubling?

3. What situations tend to trigger discomfort?

4. Have you ever experienced the sensation that your body "has a mind of its own"?

5. Read 1 Corinthians, chapter 2. Paul begins by listing his faults: poor communication, weakness, fear, and trembling. But he quickly switches his attention from himself to the power of God. How could this pattern be helpful for someone with social anxiety?

3

A Floppy Foundation

"*How bad* is the deterioration? If you think you'll be removing large portions of your foundation by brushing away loose concrete, you may want to have a professional look at it since the foundation is supporting your house. It's generally not a good idea to have 'holes' in your foundation, for obvious reasons."

~Community Forum, Bobvila.com[1]

Ancient, derelict buildings fascinate me. When I spot one, I stare longingly. The more dilapidated the structure is, the more thoroughly and instantly I fall in love with it.

A few miles from our home is an abandoned three-story colonial masterpiece. Clearly over 100 years old, its once white paint is now a peeling, dirty gray. The roof shingles have rotted, and most are scattered across

---

[1] WallyV, 2001. Forum post at http://www.bobvila.com/posts/11358-help-basement-walls-are-crumbling?page=1

the yard like dandruff. The third-story attic window is busted out, a gaping open mouth with birds flitting freely in and out. Last summer I drove past and saw more than 30 turkey vultures perched in the home's ghostly poplar trees. It is exactly what one would imagine a "haunted house" to look like.

Image 1: Abandoned home in Merrill, Oregon. © 2013, Julie Rajnus

Each time I drive by, I see this lonely skeleton of a house and visualize what it could be, given the proper care. I imagine what it was long ago… probably a warm, luxurious sanctuary for an affluent family in the early 1900s. A place where meals were cooked, children laughed, and Christmas presents were torn open. A home that saw love of every variety, husbands romancing wives, children adoring pets, and grandparents spoiling grandchildren.

I have tried to persuade my husband to buy it so that we (or more accurately, I) could restore it. Deep in my heart, though, I know it would be a foolish purchase. I am reminded of the 1988 comedy *The Money Pit* (Giler). In the movie a young couple buys a grand home with the notion of remodeling it. As the title infers, however, the house had serious, and expensive, problems that went deep below the surface.

At one point, Walter (played by Tom Hanks) falls through the upstairs' floorboards. His upper body is sandwiched upstairs while his legs dangle through the downstairs' ceiling…for hours. The situation does not improve from there. The remodeling process goes so badly, in fact, that the couple ends up nearly divorced and bankrupt. Thus, whenever I am considering any remodeling project I always try to imagine myself dangling between floors. I don't want to be a Walter.

In that magnificent old house near my neighborhood, deep cracks are visible in the stone chimney, running all the way from the third floor to the foundation. I can only imagine what state the actual foundation is in, buried deep beneath ground. Each year it freezes and thaws, expands and shrinks, crumbles and cracks, slowly absorbed by the earth around it. And all the while it is supporting three stories of architecture.

And this is the crux of the issue. If the foundation is cracked, shifted, or unstable, no amount of surface restoration will restore the house to its former glory. Walls painted tastefully and wooden floors skillfully refinished will create eye-pleasing beauty. But if the foundation is not firm, the whole thing is likely to come crashing down. At that point, all efforts at restoration will have been a complete waste of time and money—not to mention dangerous.

God is in the business of restoring people. I believe He is particularly drawn to the lonely, isolated, and suffering. That restoration process begins with a strong, solid, immovable foundation. There is only one solid foundation on which to build anything: the good news of Jesus Christ. "For no other foundation can anyone lay than that which is laid, which is Jesus Christ" (1 Corinthians 3:11, NKJV). That good news is grace. The message of grace is so important that one of the original disciples said, "I have determined not to know anything among you except Jesus Christ and Him crucified" (1 Corinthians 2:2, NKJV). So the truth is: you and I do not need to know anything except what the message of Jesus was and is.

I thought I had the foundation for this book down pat. I have been a Christian for more than 20 years. My understanding of grace consisted largely of this: God would someday let us live in Heaven with Him, through Jesus. Great. Super, super great! But… how about now? What do I do with my social anxiety now?

When I was doing research on specific treatments, I wanted to throw my computer across my bedroom. Not because the treatments were bad, but because they had never worked for me. I have the rare privilege of knowing just about every social anxiety treatment technique or method out there. I have studied them. I have tried them. They sort of helped. Then they didn't. And nothing really changed. Reading about even newer, greater techniques just made me feel…sad. Helpless. Defeated.

During this time, my husband and I went out to dinner with his sister and brother-in-law. My brother-in-law asked me what I was writing about. I thoughtfully took a bite of my taco salad before replying.

"I'm writing crap," I told him, matter-of-factly. "I would like to rename my book 'This is Crap.'" They thought I was kidding. Of course,

I wasn't. Luckily my in-laws usually forgive me for using Christian cuss words. Even luckier, the domain name for thisiscrap.com was already taken.

All of this to say… Something needed shifting in my perspective. Something really big. Otherwise, I had the uncanny feeling I was providing meaningless methods…methods that had never worked for me. And according to most statistics, these methods also do not work for almost half the people who courageously show up for treatment.

> **meaningless methods, without the power**

So I quit writing for a few weeks. I did a lot of discouraged praying and pondering. Like a little child, I spent hours asking myself (but really, asking God) "Why? But why? Why is that? Why don't we get better? Why don't these very smart and often truth-based techniques fail to do what they promise?"

Very slowly, a shift began to take place. God met me right in the midst of my questions…and answered. My heart (my actual physical heart—I am not making this up) began to tingle. Pieces of the puzzle…of God's mysterious plan, snapped together in high-def perfection. And with each new piece, the burning sensation of hope grew stronger.

After 20 years as a Christian, I had a life-altering, bone shaking experience with grace. And nothing has been the same since.

God provided three different people in my time of need. Each one happens to be an expert in his or her field. I shall call them **The Three Witnesses.** Like courtroom experts, they all testified to the same thing, but in incredibly different ways. What they said was powerful, infused with His Spirit. And to this day I have yet to actually meet any of them. And no, these are not famous Bible characters. These are human beings living and breathing today.

The three witnesses did not speak to me about God's grace…at least not audibly. But they did record their knowledge…in books. The Bible says, "…By the mouth of two or three witnesses every word shall be established" (1 Corinthians 13:1, NKJV). Even books can be witnesses. If you don't believe me, check out the Bible.

Witness #1: What Are Rules For?

Let me set the scene. I am in my cozy bedroom with a computer on my lap, as always. I have just finished reviewing a mountain of research on Cognitive Behavioral Therapy. My heart feels like it's made out of lead because I see the truth in the therapy techniques. I just cannot see how to do them. Isn't that the real problem? We can see the rules for health and wellness, but we feel powerless to perform them. Frustrating!

Then, I stumble across a treatment manual called *ACT with Faith, Acceptance and Commitment Therapy for Christian Clients: A Practitioner's Guide* (Ord, 2014). It was intriguing. I had heard of Acceptance and Commitment Therapy (ACT) before, but only as a secular model. Ingrid Rhea Ord's book is designed to teach counselors how to let God's grace drive improvement. It leaves the responsibility for growth in God's hands.

One of the first steps to recovery is understanding the role of rules in our lives. Why did God create rules? What do rules really do? Ord states: "In general, verbal rules enable humans to avoid bad consequences, without having to experience them first-hand. Hence a child learns how to cross a road safely without having to be run over by a vehicle first" (2014, 37).

So rules are protective. They show us the safest way to proceed. If you want to have the most peaceful, fulfilling, contented life possible while here on earth…aim for the rules. God knew what He was doing when He laid them out. When you inspect every rule God ever created, you will find that someone or something is being protected. Protection is a part of love (1 Corinthians 13:7).

But that's not all rules do. The Bible says the rules were also created to be a teacher. And what do they teach? Listen to this amazing, astounding, breathtaking verse in Galatians:

> Therefore the law was our tutor to bring us to Christ, that we might be justified by faith. But after faith has come, we are no longer under a tutor (Galatians 3:24-25, NKJV).

The rules protect, but even more importantly, they **teach.** The rules teach us that we need Christ. And Christ's message is unconditional love from God. If a + b = c, that means the rules teach us that we need love that is not based on our performance. Love that is completely independent of obeying rules. Wait, what? The rules teach us that we don't need rules?

It goes something like this: "Humans, look, here's perfection." During His time on earth, Jesus said such things as be perfect (Matthew 5:48), be extremely righteous (Matthew 5:20), even one wrong word will lead to condemnation (Matthew 12:37), sell all your things to buy righteousness (Matthew 19:21). Basically, Jesus invented the rules, explained the rules, expanded the rules, and then proceeded to fulfill the rules. He was perfect.

So the rules teach me what a perfect human looks like: Jesus. And if I am honest, I look nothing like Jesus. When Jesus said to turn the other cheek, I had both hands balled into fists. When Jesus said, "Forgive them because they know not what they do" I already had my Taser charged and ready to go. He is *so much better* than I am.

And yet… He always knew I was far below Him. God always knew I would fail at the good rules. He is not surprised that I am a human without godlike qualities. In fact, that was His message. He loves me anyway.

The rules of good and bad teach us what supreme goodness is. And supreme goodness is God. When we look into the law we see God. When we look into the law we do not receive the power to do good or be God. The rules measure our good and evil behavior with amazing accuracy. And we always fail. Always. That is actually really good news.

> ## Gospel In a Nutshell
>
> Adam and Eve ate the forbidden fruit. The fruit opened their eyes to who they were, compared to the perfection of God. They were horrified. Thus began a very long journey of humans working hard in order to become more like God (through the Law, i.e. rules). Fail, fail, fail.
>
> Then, God Himself came to earth to show humans what a perfect human really looked like. He said, "You're not even close. How about I give you credit for My perfection. There will be no more comparisons between you and I. In My eyes, you are now perfect. Forever more. Let's live!"

The rules take our temperature. And if the thermometer is working correctly, it reveals that we are sick. We need a doctor. We will never, ever, ever, ever, ever (emphasis on *ever*) get well on our own. God designed the rules to be broken by humans to reveal how much we cannot earn love. Yet it is there...for the taking.

Still, rules end up being used in a far different manner, especially in religious communities. Ord writes:

> Rule-governed behaviour is very significant in the lives of Christians, especially those who spend time in Christian communities. Guilt, self-judgment and condemnation are, ironically, characteristic of many Christians who have approached me for help, and seem, perhaps, to be an unfortunate side-effect of belonging to these communities (2014, p. ix).

The rules do not just reveal that *we* are sick and in need of a doctor. They reveal that everyone, from the pastor to the janitor, is in the same sorry state of illness. Problems come when we forget that we are all in the same typhoid-laden boat. We compare our sickness to someone else's and either feel better or worse. But the illness is fatal, no matter what.

Once we understand the role of rules, and the fact that we are helpless to be anything but rule-breakers, we should experience a great big feeling of relief. All of a sudden, our only hope is in God's unconditional love. Our performance or rule-obeying becomes insignificant in the light of the fact that everything is a gift of love—and a gift of course is unearned—from God.

I'll cover more of Ord's grace-based counseling techniques in a later chapter. For now, I had finished her book with my curiosity piqued. I had made the connection that my always-present pressure to perform (obey rules) was...well...useless. I was not designed with the capacity to obey rules perfectly.

But I still had some questions. What about spiritual growth? Was I to just stop putting any effort into "being good"? That just doesn't make sense. So I did what any good writer with unanswered questions does: I surfed Facebook.

WITNESS #2: QUIT RELIGION, QUIT TRYING

Based on a friend's random Facebook post, I made an online purchase of Blaise Foret's book, *It Is Finished: Why You Can Quit Religion and Trust in Jesus* (2014). Fast forward six hours and I was unable to stop reading. Foret is a passionate Christ-follower who has made some people *re-allllly* uncomfortable. One of the things he writes about is the fact that Jesus came to destroy religion. Not form a new one. He came to destroy it. That is, of course, threatening to many religious people. Jesus was threatening, too.

None of this was really that new to me. I remember reading about the Pharisees and Sadducees in the Bible. Yes, they were powerful religious leaders who worked to take Jesus down. But I had always read a lot of "trying harder" into the New Testament too, even in Jesus' words. And so I was always trying harder. And trying harder was killing me. It has been killing all of us since...well, forever.

The thing with social anxiety is that we try very, very hard when we are with people. We try hard to seem acceptable, normal, interesting, etc. We put so much effort into trying that we are unable to enjoy others or allow them the possibility of enjoying us. Those rules I just finished writing about? Yeah, we are enslaved to them because we are trying so hard to *do* them.

The people who listened to Jesus found His standards to be impossibly high. Some walked away sad, hopeless. Some were offended. Many were angry. Jesus came and set the bar higher than it had ever been. Even higher than when Moses presented the Ten Commandments. Olympic gold levels.

Religion says try harder.

Yet, strangely, I do not see "try harder" in the message of the cross. God took on the ultimate in human evil, a torturous physical death. And then He rose from human death to prove He was God. And, finally, He explained it all as an act of unconditional, unearned love. Because He is the very essence of perfect love. *Nowhere* in that is the message that I must try harder to obey the rules.

Foret brings us back to the beauty of Jesus' message by recommending the following: "The best thing you can do is give up. Yes, give up. Quit" (Foret 2014, p. 19). Um...*what?* What about getting closer to God, growing to be more like God?

Sitting in my bedroom, my excitement growing...a light began to dawn. So the point of God's walking around on earth as a human was to show us what perfection looks like? And not to be an example we should be constantly comparing ourselves to or using all our willpower to copy?

Religion, in pretty much any flavor, is a set of rules designed to get one closer to God or godlikeness. Rules, rules, rules. In Islam, it is paramount to wage a holy war (jihad) against personal weaknesses (Caner 2005). Most forms of Buddhism are based on the idea that all personal desires (which only cause suffering) must be obliterated. The foundation of Hinduism is that life is a continuous chain of reward and punishment (reincarnation/karma). We humans have always liked to use the rules as stepping-stones. Religion requires a lot of work. And I don't know about you, but I am really tired.

At their root, nearly all religions aim at achieving some measure of godlikeness (even Christianity carries this risk). The serpent whispers to our hearts, "Do this, and you will be more like God." The "do's" may differ from religion to religion. Some might say "do more good," "do more peacemaking," "do more witnessing," "do more family time," "do more patience," "do more miracles," "do more rituals," "do more sacrifice," "do more loyalty," "do more obedience," "do more service." The list is endless, and none of the "do's" produce the perfection of God.

All humans want to be like God. Even those who don't believe in God

It's not just religion that appeals to our desire to be like God. The secular world also says do, do, do. "Achieve more success," "get more money," "get more popularity," "get more love," "do more controlling," "get more power," "achieve more beauty," and "gain more possessions." God is all-successful, all-powerful, all-loving, unimaginably beautiful, and already owns everything. We want what He has, to be who He is because the desire to be like God is hardwired into our DNA. It is woven into every avenue of human activity.

The message I had somehow always heard was: "You're not good enough as you are. You've got a lot of growing to do. Being like Jesus is what you should be aiming for." This is what I heard because I was stuck in rules. I was stuck trying to be like God. And all along, God was saying...you never will be. Let Me gift that to you.

My favorite part of Foret's book is when he references the book of

Recipe for peace: add nothing

Galatians. And reading Galatians with a fresh perspective...Fried. My. Eyeballs. Paul was reprimanding the early Christians for turning the gospel into something it was not. How had they tweaked the gospel? Jesus said, "It is Finished." The early believers said, "Let's just add one more little thing." Let's make God's work a little more finished*er*. Christians today are still falling for the lie that says... just a little bit more than Jesus is what's needed. That often comes in the form of self-improvement. *If I can just change and grow spiritually, then God and I will truly be besties.* Nein! God's work on the cross made us best friends forever.

So how much effort should I put into obeying the good rules? I find that question is...well...no longer relevant. I find myself wanting to put all my effort into *believing* this amazing, unconditional love from God is real and mine. And resting in His love, His goodness, His perfection.

The idea of complete rest is *sooo* appealing. When I imagine pure contentedness, I am sitting on a cold, mildly stormy beach in Oregon. I am watching gray waves break while the wind blows my hair gently. Perhaps there are even a few raindrops falling. I see the ocean's vastness and it makes me feel small. Which makes God so big. And above all...I am still. I am at rest. I am safe. This was the hope I inhaled from Foret's book. Rest.

Now all my effort goes into BELIEVING rather than doing

WITNESS #3: WHERE'S THE POWER?

As soon as I finished Foret's book, I did an online search for the word "grace." I was beginning to feel like I was really onto something. That's how I stumbled upon Eddie Snipes' book *Abounding Grace: Dispelling Myths and Clarifying the Biblical Message of God's Overflowing Grace* (2013). At the time, the entire book was available online—and free. There's nothing better than online and free.

Snipes basically reiterated all the key points that were burning a hole in my heart. He also highlighted the fact that all things are provided as a gift from God. Our faith, our ability to do good, everything.

> "Everything in the Christian life is received through the grace of God. Anyone who loses sight of this truth falls into performance based religion and a false merit system" (Snipes, 2013, p. 23).

And the Bible says,
"For who makes you differ from another? And what do you have that you did not receive? Now if you did indeed receive it, why do you boast as if you had not received it?" (1 Corinthians 4:7, NKJV).

This kind of makes the idea of "personal holiness," well, laughable coming from a human. And spiritual growth...almost effortless? God's responsibility? The only good things about us, and in us, are given as gifts from God. Everything else is like the dirt we were made from.

If all this grace talk was true, how had I missed the totality of it for years? How had I returned again and again to rules and self-pressure. How could this be biblical, when I had studied the Bible for hours and hours and never got it?

Right about here.... I paused to go through the Bible again. It's all well and good when humans write books about stuff. (Did you know that somebody wrote a book called *Reusing Old Graves?* For real). In any case, humans are humans, and God is the only One I really trust.

I read through the entire New Testament. Twice. I looked up many of the original Greek words. I studied the hard verses. There are verses that say, "Do this." But I had been misreading these verses as rules for being a good Christian rather than what flows out from being filled with God's unconditional love. All the pressure is on Him! Now *that* idea shoots a hole right into the heart of social anxiety.

Here's how the Bible puts it (and every time you see the word law, think rules):

> ...a man is not justified by the works of the law but by faith in Jesus Christ, even we have believed in Christ Jesus, that we might be justified by faith in Christ and not by the works of the law; for by the works of the law no flesh shall be justified (Galatians 2:16, NKJV).

It is all about Jesus, who said:

> You search the Scriptures, for in them you think you have eternal life; and these are they which testify of Me. But you are not willing to come to Me that you may have life (John 5:39-40, NKJV).

At this point, the tingling in my heart had turned into all out euphoria. I was convinced. The cover of my heart had been peeled away, and the truth dawned that I am, at this moment, and forever more, truly perfect in God's eyes. Even if I didn't pray today, or go to church on Sunday, or attend social events often. Yes, those are all good things. But they are not what have given me the unconditional love of God. That, my friends, was all Jesus.

> **I normally prefer boring. Grace is not that.**

Now, I am not what one would call a "charismatic" type of Christian. I prefer order. Calm. Predictability. Gentle, if any, emotion. Well, I literally stumbled around for three weeks in a haze of joy. I can only describe it as the high of being drunk (not that I would know that from experience, Mom), only 1,000 times better.

I clearly should not have been driving. I'm pretty sure I glowed. I laughed a lot. I cannot explain why it took me 20 years to understand such a simple truth and specifically how it applied to social anxiety. But once I got it… everything changed.

Translated into very basic terms, God's grace means I am free to be exactly who I am. I am shy, quiet, socially anxious, oversensitive, and often put up a public facade. Eh, it's enough. I am enough. I need add nothing to the supreme work of Jesus Christ. Nothing. That is where the power is.

A Bigger Picture

Although I had seen God's grace as a free ticket into Heaven, I missed everything it meant for me today. In practical, everyday ways. I had built my faith on a rather floppy foundation. My vision of God's love and forgiveness was way too thin.

The rules are good. But I was never meant to achieve them. Religion was not going to help, either. All power to do good comes from God. The burden rests on Him. What a relief I feel.

He decides who we are in Him. He brings it to pass. He uses circumstances, people, blessings, and tragedies to strengthen us, grant us courage, and provide rest. He does all the work.

I read through well-known Bible stories with a fresh, grace-based perspective. Moses brought the people official rules, written in stone, known as the Ten Commandments (Exodus 20). The people agreed enthusiastically to obey all the rules, wildly overestimating their own abilities and goodness (Exodus 24:3). They promptly failed, quite spectacularly, to obey the rules and did exactly what they had pledged not to do (Exodus 32:1).

When we examine carefully the stories of Cain, Moses, Noah, David, and Job we find a very clear picture emerging. Humans are humans. Moral failure is guaranteed. Human heroes are not heroes after all. We really are not like God when it comes to goodness and perfection. And all humans are the same. There are no superstars. Not even me, and I put on a really good show.

So we use the law as it was meant to be used: as a teacher. It points out our flaws. It highlights God's perfection. We misuse the law when we use it as a measure of our merit. Galatians 5:4 states, "You have become estranged from Christ, you who attempt to be justified by law; you have fallen from grace" (NKJV). Christ is enough.

> **Failure is guaranteed. So is unconditional love.**

Please do not mistake what I am saying here with a big word Bible scholars like to use: antinomianism. **Antinomianism** (in my amateur paraphrase) is the belief that all the good laws and rules have been removed by grace. In other words, let's have orgies and get drunk and do dope…because Jesus has our sin covered anyway.

Jesus addressed this directly, "Do not think that I came to destroy the Law or the Prophets. I did not come to destroy, but to fulfill" (Matthew 5:17, NKJV). Laws and rules are good and reflect the loving nature of God. If you want to see the devastation of a world without laws, watch the movie *"The Purge."* (But don't let your kids watch it because, *zoweee*, that's a scary movie). God's law is good, the very highest kind of good. It displays His own perfection. But as good as rules are, they do not provide the power for doing good. That's what grace is for.

> Anti-gnomianism: the belief that garden gnomes are evil, creepy, and tacky.

So the rules come first. They display what perfect love looks like. Here's how it works: We fail at the rules. We crave love anyway. We get that love, through Jesus. With God's love comes power.

The missing ingredient in my life, and in many treatment strategies, was power. Supernatural power. And that power is provided through faith in the unconditional love of God towards us. Do I really believe God loves me through His message at the cross? Do I believe that His love never wavers and is completely independent of me? Yes, I do! That, my friends, is life-changing, out-of-my-control power. I need only believe it. The love is always there. The power is always there. The more I believe it, the more it gives *me* power.

The mysterious nature of grace makes anything possible. Does God want me to tackle public speaking? Well, that is only going to happen if He creates in me a genuine desire to do it and provides the necessary courage. If He does not provide those things, I am not wasting my time on it. That kind of living (relying totally on God) is such a relief.

THE BAD NEWS

Yes, there is bad news... but it's probably not what you think. This isn't the part where I attach some strings to the good news of Jesus. *Buuuuut*, I do have some bad news for us Christians. Here goes: Because humans are humans, Christianity can look a lot like a religion rather than a relief. "Do this...and earn that." This is bad news for an exhausted world. This idea returns the responsibility for achieving true goodness to human effort rather than to God's gift alone.

Undiluted Christianity is the only belief system in the entire world that is not based upon good deeds, rules, or special requirements. Literally every person, of every faith, race, ethnicity, economic level, sexual orientation, social skill level, etc., is invited to receive instantaneous new spiritual life...through Jesus Christ. Humans are merely humans, yet all are invited into the family of God. Now *that* is different.

Many have argued that if we rely on God's grace alone, without at least some emphasis on doing good deeds, it will lead to sinful abandon. In fact, isn't grace an argument for becoming a notorious rule-breaker? Paul had to answer this very question in Romans 6. His response was, "Certainly not!" In modern English, "Aw, hell no!"

It is a strange mystery that when there is no more requirement to fulfill all the rules...breaking the rules loses its allure (see Romans 7:7-11). We become so filled with the wonder of God's love that it naturally overflows to those around us. With God's unconditional love, we find ourselves loving what *He* loves. Rules cannot do that. And I am so glad.

For us socially anxious people, adding rules for thoughts and behaviors is not going to help. Our only solution is to move beyond the rules. We can only do that through the message of Jesus, which means that we can go into every social situation knowing we are perfectly accepted by the One who matters most. Whether we obey or break the rules of social behavior. Jesus fulfilled all the rules for good social interactions.

I'M DEAD

One important thing I always missed about the death of Jesus was... what's the point? Why did God have to endure torture? How does that relate to me, today, as I sweat and tremble and blush at Walmart?

A lot of Bible scholars will throw out words such as sacrifice, blood atonement—blah blah blah. I do not mean to be irreverent, but those words are not meaningful to me. Those things are not in my realm of daily experience (though they were in Bible times). Still, there are two really big points that smack me in the face about Jesus' death on the cross and subsequent resurrection.

1. It proved that He really was God. He was a human, and He was murdered. But it was not permanent. Um... that's pretty crazy. So His death was a proof of identity: Human/God. If He was telling the truth about that, He was obviously telling the truth about everything else.

2. He said something highly unusual about His death. He said it counted as my death. The rotten me that could never live up to the rules... died. And in exchange, I get a new identity that is... well... perfect. As a chronic perfectionist, that's really good news. If I'm already perfect in God's eyes, I no longer have to try so hard to improve myself. The socially anxious me that I cannot stand...is dead for all intents and purposes. Dead.

Here's how the Bible describes the death of Jesus (and us):

Or do you not know that as many of us as were baptized into Christ Jesus were baptized into His death? Therefore we were buried with Him through baptism into death, that just as Christ was raised from the dead by the glory of the Father, even so we also should walk in newness of life. For if we have been united together in the likeness of His death, certainly we also shall be in the likeness of His resurrection, knowing this, that our old man was crucified with Him, that the body of sin might be done away with, that we should no longer be slaves of sin. For he who has died has been freed from sin (Romans 6:3–7, NKJV).

My heart's cry (along with millions of others throughout history) is, "I can't do it! I can't live up to all the rules. I can't judge good and evil, and find myself on the side of good! I always come up short compared to God, no matter how hard I try. God alone is like God, and I cannot even come close. Jesus, I want to substitute Your life for mine. I want to live as though everything You did was my work. I want my old self, the failed rule-follower, to die with You on the cross. And I want the new me, who gets credit for all You've done, to rise up instead" (see Romans 10:9, 10). And guess what? Wish granted.

> The word "abide" means to stay still. Rest.
> See John 15:4

So now life becomes a journey of comprehending just how loved and accepted we are, through Christ. It is no longer about striving to become more and more like God. It is about resting in His love and His goodness... Sweet rest. Jesus has become our rest (Hebrews 4). This rest is not just a day of the week (like a Sabbath day), but an entire way of life.

More than Restoration

How about a real-life illustration of how God sees us humans, through grace? Job (from the Bible) was a very blessed man. Job was the most moral of all humans, capable of more righteousness than any other person of his time. God said this about Job: "there is none like him on the earth, a blameless and upright man, one who fears God and shuns evil" (Job 1:8b, NKJV). Job knew the rules. Job was about as good as it gets when it comes to humans obeying the rules.

Though we often read the book of Job as an example of how to endure through tough times, it is actually a radical story of human failure. God invited Satan to test Job, in order to reveal Job's character. God already knew Job's human nature, but Job was about to learn it for himself. We see this same sort of testing by the serpent in the Garden of Eden. God allowed it, because He knew the end of the story. He knew that human failure was guaranteed, but used it as an opportunity to display His unconditional love.

Satan went right to work on Job. He created a vast amount of suffering in Job's life. At first, Job stayed strong, remarkably so for a mere human. But as the suffering continued, Job fell. Even the most righteous man on earth had no real understanding of God. He began to question God. God's powerful response was to remind Job that he was very different from Himself. Job was the created one, not the Creator.

Job: a radical story of human failure.

As God pointed out the differences between Himself and Job, Job was struck to the core. He greatly regretted doubting God's character, and said, "I have heard of You by the hearing of the ear, but now my eye sees You. Therefore I abhor myself, and repent in dust and ashes" (Job 42:5-6, NKJV). Job, like Adam and Eve, was filled with shame at the innate differences that separate God from mere human beings.

And here is the most amazing part of Job's story: God did not punish Job's fall. Instead, God restored everything Satan stole from Job, including his health, his wealth, and his family. Not only did God restore, He multiplied! Job 42:12, "Now the Lord blessed the latter days of Job more than his beginning" (NKJV). Job had earned God's cursing but was graciously given unexpected and unearned blessings instead. This is grace.

God tested Job, and Job failed. An angry, vengeful humanlike god would have allowed Job to die in his failure and misery (and Adam and Eve as well). But the loving nature of God is very different from the nature of man. He is merciful, gracious, and faithful…regardless of human failures. He is supremely aware of the nature of these humans He created. God allowed Satan to provide Job with a limited time of suffering and doubt, knowing that Job would fail to be faithful. Given the proper circumstances, each one of us will fail. God's love is not dependent on our faithfulness. He is faithful whether we are or not.

And why? What is the purpose of this entire story of mankind, from beginning to end? I believe it is to display how precious God's undeserved love is. We need it. He gives it. He is far above us. We are far below Him. Yet He treasures us. This is grace.

THE ROAD SIGN TO GRACE

Thus, in light of the grace of God, social anxiety becomes a gift. It highlights all the ways in which we fail at achieving the perfection of God. We really stink at rules. That path leads nowhere. Social anxiety shuts down our efforts to be perfect, and reroutes us to grace. And grace is the sparkling centerpiece of all things beautiful. The good rules have all been fulfilled, but not by us. God-like character is obtained, but solely as a gift.

We must take the message of God (Jesus' death and resurrection) very seriously. We are not God. We need His unearned love. Without it, we are choosing comparison of ourselves to Him as the Final Answer. We humans cannot win that game.

If you believe the words in this chapter to be true, you are a blessed member of God's family. Believing in the factual, genuine, gracious love of God (displayed in the human form of Jesus) seals the gift of grace. "For I am not ashamed of the gospel of Christ, for it is the power of God to salvation for everyone who believes…" (Romans 1:16, NKJV). It saves us from eternal separation from God. It also saves us from ourselves, right now.

The foundation for this book took a big hit. Originally, it was going to read something like this: How Jesus, plus a fair amount of work, can help you live with social anxiety. That was a pretty thin foundation, and would not have withstood much pressure. The new and improved foundation is a lot sturdier, and is (I don't mean to brag)…frankly, perfect. Grace. Grace is everything.

When it comes to restoration, a house does not restore itself. A house is just a house. Restoration depends solely on a skilled Restorer. Unearned love is the foundation, and God is the Master Builder. Incredibly, God not only restores the house. He transforms it into a mansion far greater than it was in the beginning. He makes something new from the skeleton of the old. The house does none of the work. It simply waits expectantly. This is grace.

* * *

Reflection

1. What is the message of Jesus, in one paragraph?

2. What role are rules designed to play in our lives?

3. Can failure be considered a good thing?

4. Where does the power for change come from? What is your part?

5. Did the message of grace stir something new and exciting in your heart?

6. Are you ready to embark on a journey of freedom and rest? What would that look like?

Section II
The Corpse

God created us in His own image…but formed us out of dirt. It was our dirt-like nature that died on the cross with Jesus. In effect, we now have two identities to choose from: the Old Us (made of dirt and now dead) or the New Us (perfect in Christ). Only one of these is our real identity. The other is just a counterfeit.

This section explores facets of our old, dead self. Unfortunately, we humans will carry around this corpse until all things are fulfilled. Thus, the next few chapters will read a bit like an autopsy. Who has not had the joy of dissecting a formaldehyde-soaked bullfrog just for the pleasure of seeing how everything works? Our old human nature may be dead, but it is still wonderfully interesting.

4

THE BRAIN: WELCOME TO THE CIRCUS

Ah... **the brain.** It is an amazing organ. If you are reading these words, you probably have one. The brain plays a central role in every facet of well-being. It is a highly complex and proficient organ, constantly morphing as humans learn and grow (DeWitt 2009). Weighing in at three pounds, it is engaged in sending and receiving electrical signals perpetually via neurons (brain cells). The adult brain has approximately 100 billion neurons, and each neuron can make tens of thousands of silent, instant electrical connections. This equals an estimated maximum number of electrical neuron fires of 20 quadrillion per second. That's more traffic than downtown Los Angeles, New York, Tokyo, and every other city on Earth at rush hour. And that's all happening *inside your head!*

Like most city drivers, the speed of these electronic connections vary greatly. Some can travel as slow as 1 mile per hour (think tortoise), or as fast as 268 miles per hour (similar to a jet airplane; Stanford University

2007). Sometimes slow is good for making connections, and sometimes fast is good.

There is no greater masterpiece in the universe. As one neuroscientist stated, "I believe nothing provides greater testimony than the brain to how we are 'fearfully and wonderfully made'" (DeWitt 2009). Humans will spend centuries studying this amazing organ, which God created in one wondrous flash. I mean, think about the fact that we are electrical beings. Running on electricity, people. Marvelous!

The brain is an area of the physical domain (i.e., the flesh) that is prone to disease, aging, and malfunction. The flesh is weak. Humans have limited control over much of our brain activity…a very tiny amount compared to perfect control. Jesus had perfect control because He was God in a human body. Our brains are more dysfunctional than that.

Dysfunctional brain activity really amps up social anxiety. Injuries to the brain have been shown to initiate social anxiety symptoms. The following is a true story:

> A normal, outgoing 17-year-old boy was hit by a car while riding his bicycle (Chaves et al. 2012, 884-885). The boy had no history of shyness. One year after the accident, however, he began to experience intense social fears. His anxiety was so bad that he began skipping school and avoiding friends. He was eventually diagnosed with SAD.
>
> **Normal boy hit by car. Bam... social anxiety.**
>
> Doctors decided to do a brain scan on the boy. What they saw was a bony growth compressing the boy's frontal lobe (Chaves et al. 2012, 884). Apparently, brain injuries sometimes produce extra bone growth after the initial trauma (known as an intradiploic hematoma). The bone had grown haphazardly and pressed into the boy's brain. The only neurological symptoms of the bony growth were the boy's new social anxieties. The boy underwent neurosurgery to remove the bony structure. Within six months, his social anxiety symptoms began to ease.

Clearly, the brain is a massive contributor to social anxiety. Even mild traumatic brain injuries double the risk of developing social anxiety (Bryant et al. 2010, 317). A mild traumatic brain injury is defined as a trauma that results in a loss of consciousness for less than 30 minutes. You get bonked in the head, and you pass out for a bit, and then, *wham*, you develop social anxiety (sometimes… not every single time, of course, in case you were worried!).

So even mild head traumas have the capacity to disrupt mood, emotions, and sociability. Researchers believe this is because most brain injuries happen in the front regions of the brain, where neural networks related to emotion (especially fear) are located.

And then there are genes. Williams Syndrome is a genetic disorder that is present at birth caused by deletions on chromosome 7q11.23 (Meda, Pryweller, and Thornton-Wells 2012). The symptoms include cardiovascular problems, developmental delays, learning disabilities, and an excessively social personality. People with Williams Syndrome are often overly (and inappropriately) friendly with strangers, due to unusual brain development. Scientists believe this hypersociability may be due to brain structural differences in the amygdala, insula, and orbitofrontal cortex. Those particular brain regions also play a role in social anxiety.

Williams Syndrome =too social

Fragile X syndrome (FXS) is the behavioral opposite of Williams Syndrome. It is a genetic disorder characterized by intellectual disabilities, poor eye contact, extreme shyness, and hyperarousal.[1] A core feature of FXS is social withdrawal. Individuals with FXS find strangers to be generally a scary bunch (Williams, Porter, and Langdon 2014, 145). They are also more likely to use social avoidance tactics. Researchers have found evidence of altered amygdala volume and reduced activity in key brain areas in FXS (Lightbody and Reiss 2009, 346-47). These brain areas are directly related to social behavior and fear.

Fragile X =not social

Thus, a number of brain factors are (at least partly) uncontrollable in social anxiety. For the first time in history, we are able to use space-age machines to see inside the human brain in action. We are peeping Toms into our own brains, where many mysteries reside. I love this so much that I am working out the logistics of fitting a functional magnetic resonance imaging (fMRI) machine into my living room.

Researchers recently compared the brains of SAD patients to those of healthy people (Frick et al. 2014, 330–335). Based on functional and structural brain imaging alone, researchers were able to identify which patients had SAD. It seems the brain is the smoking gun. In the near future, it is likely that a diagnosis of SAD will be made just through pictures of the brain (rather than old-fashioned symptom descriptions). I find that so cool that I might carry around a picture of my odd and amazing brain, just as proof.

Clear brain differences

For the rest of this chapter, I'm going to use a lot of illustrations. I just really like illustrations. Nobody said I couldn't make one chapter look like a graphic novel. You're welcome.

---

[1] See https://www.nichd.nih.gov/health/topics/fragilex/conditioninfo/Pages/common-symptoms.aspx for a complete list of symptoms.

THE FEAR CIRCUIT (CIRCUS)

Part of the brain commonly known as the fear circuit consists mainly of the amygdala, insula, anterior cingulate, and prefrontal cortex (Brühl et al. 2014, 2). Got all that? OK, when I was trying to imagine all this, I pictured a circus. There are a lot of sideshows at the circus. It takes several different circus acts to pull the whole circus off. If you went to the circus and all you got to see was an amygdala setting itself on fire you might go home disappointed. But the number of circus acts in the brain are practically endless. Let's begin...

AMYGDALAE: THE SPICY ALMONDS

The brain structure most frequently studied in SAD is the amygdala. The amygdalae (plural for amygdala) are two small, almond shaped structures deep within the brain. The Greek word amygdala is translated *almond*. The amygdalae seem to run a little hot in SAD. Imagine two spicy little almonds as the Grand Conductors of the fear circus.

These amygdalae receive input from all of the senses.[2] They are integral in initiating fear, aggression, and other intense emotions. So the sense organs (eyes, ears, nose, etc.) send messages to the amygdalae. Then the amygdalae formally declare that it is time to be terrified.

When the amygdalae are injured or ill, that is bad news. Lesions of the amygdalae can cause panic attacks.[3] Conversely, destruction of parts of the amygdalae can cause unusual calmness or a placid affect. In a research study with mice, destruction of a specific part of the amygdala lowered anxiety and increased social behavior (Wang et al. 2014, 358). Clearly, a lot is riding on two little almonds.

For those of us with social anxiety, those almonds seem to be a bit paranoid and over-the-top sensitive. The amygdalae misinterpret even non-threatening social situations as dangerous, which sets off a chain of physiological events designed to be protective (like an adrenaline rush and quickened breathing). Except there is no danger, and thus the physiological events serve no constructive purpose and are just super annoying.

Several studies have reported that the level of amygdala hyperactivity is directly related to the severity of social anxiety symptoms (for a

---

[2] Wright, Anthony. 2014. "Chapter 6: Limbic System: Amygdala." *Neuroscience Online.* http://neuroscience.uth.tmc.edu/s4/chapter06.html
[3] Ibid.

complete review, see Brühl et al. 2014, 260–280). So the amygdalae bring different levels of hyperactive...touchy, combustible, or nuclear. And social anxiety directly follows suit. Three studies have found that antidepressants help to normalize the activity level of the amygdala.

The amygdalae are not only overactive in social anxiety but may be structurally different as well. Our almonds are not quite the same size as everybody else's. In a recent study, brain imaging revealed that the amygdalae were larger than normal in young SAD patients (Machado-de-Sousa et al. 2014, 4). This is in contrast to an earlier study that found the amygdalae to be smaller in older patients (Irle et al. 2010, 129). Scientists suggest that the amygdalae may initially be enlarged, but atrophy as social anxiety disorder progresses (Machado-de-Sousa et al., 2014, 4).

In other words, those spicy almonds initially swell from overuse but then begin to shrink because they are overworked and stressed out. Additional research has shown that prolonged stress or trauma can cause atrophy in many areas of the brain (Bremner 2006). Unmedicated depression, for example, is also linked to a smaller volume of the amygdalae, possibly due to atrophy (Hamilton, Siemer, and Gotlib 2008, 995).

The next time someone comments on your social awkwardness, just tell them that your spicy almonds are acting up.

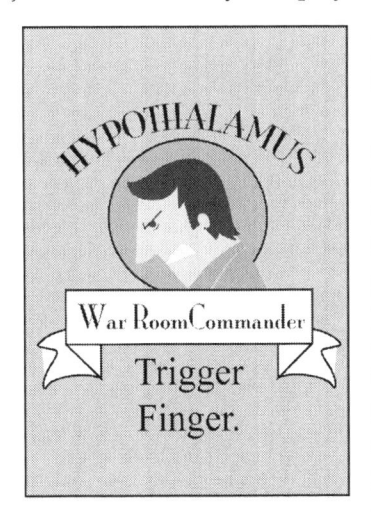

HYPOTHALAMUS: WAR ROOM COMMANDER

The classic "fight or flight" response occurs when the amygdalae receive danger information via the senses.[4] The amygdalae then send a distress signal out to the hypothalamus. The hypothalamus pushes the proverbial red button, activating the sympathetic nervous system, which releases a cascade of adrenaline to prepare the body to flee or engage in combat. That adrenaline rush is responsible for many of the physical symptoms of social anxiety: increased heart rate, altered breathing, trembling, sweating, etc. Needless to say, the hypothalamus tends to be overeager and ready to go at all times.

INSULA: THE MYSTERIOUS ISLAND OF FEELS

Another key brain structure involved in the fear circuit is the insula (also known as the insular cortex). Insula is the Latin word for *island* (think pen*insula*). The insula is the fifth lobe of the brain and the least un-

---

[4] "Understanding the stress response." 2011. *Harvard Health Publications March*. http://www.health.harvard.edu/newsletters/Harvard_Mental_Health_Letter/2011/March/understanding-the-stress-response

derstood (Stephani et al. 2010, 137). The insula (one in each hemisphere) is buried beneath other brain structures. The location of the insula makes it difficult to study with noninvasive techniques. Researchers have been able to establish that the insula is highly connected to the amygdala (several studies cited in Brühl et al. 2014). When the amygdala is activated, the insula is often activated simultaneously.

In one small study, electrodes were placed within the brains of five individuals (Stephani et al. 2010, 141). By stimulating the insula with electricity, researchers were able to generate sensations of warmth, pain, stomach activity, tingling, numbness, pulling, and taste. The insula is pretty important for just feeling stuff. That's why I call it the Mysterious Island of Feels.

One recent study found that the insula in people with SAD was smaller in volume than in people without SAD (Kawaguchi et al. 2016). Once again, we socially anxious people have pieces and parts in the brain that do not quite measure up to normal. Though our Mysterious Island of Feels is smaller than normal, it seems to be hyperactive as well. It is a small island, but a bustling one!

It is likely that an overactive insula results in particularly strong bodily sensations, which would explain the intense physical discomfort socially anxious people experience in triggering situations. Nobody else notices when our breathing rate has changed, but we do. It doesn't feel good—at all.

Thus an overactive insula, paranoid hypothalamus, and oversensitive amygdala combine to create the "perfect storm" for social anxiety. The amygdalae are too spicy, the hypothalamus is too ready for war, the insula is too feely. It all adds up to a very dysfunctional fear circus. But that's not all.

Hippocampus: the Seahorse That Never Forgets

Finally, the hippocampus plays a role in the fear circuitry of the brain. The hippocampus gets its name from the Greek word for *seahorse* (because it is shaped like a seahorse, duh!). It communicates directly with the amygdala (Maren, Phan, and Liberzon 2013, 423). Similar to the amygdala, the hippocampus has consistently been shown to be overactive in social anxiety (Bruhl et al. 2014).

The hippocampus plays a key role in memory formation.[5] It's kind of like the fear circus record-keeper. Every time something bad happens at the circus, the hippocampus dutifully writes it down. In ALL CAPS. And **BOLD TYPE**.

It is possible that negative social experiences are deeply encoded in the memory, creating a lasting post-trauma effect. We go through something bad. We remember. We fear it will happen again.

Prefrontal Cortex: The Strongman

To manage the human brain fear circuit, God designed a highly efficient control center. Some of this control center lies within the prefrontal region of the brain. The prefrontal cortex receives inputs of danger from the fear circuit, evaluates the danger, and then proceeds to either calm or initiate action. The prefrontal cortex can be thought of as the Strongman of the Fear Circus. Prefrontal regions are associated with the ability to regulate and manage emotions (Brühl et al. 2014, 14). The Strongman keeps the circus in check and everything running calmly. The Strongman is all about self-control.

PREFRONTAL CORTEX

The Strongman

Yells a lot.
Ineffective

The prefrontal cortex does not mature until we reach our 20s or 30s (Hofmann and DiBartolo 2010). This is in stark contrast to the development of the amygdala, which matures during adolescence. Sex hormones activate the amygdala during adolescence, while its controller (the prefrontal cortex) remains immature for quite some time after.

This may explain why social anxiety tends to emerge strongly during adolescence. The amygdala is working hard, in a very paranoid sort of way, but the Strongman (prefrontal cortex) is still a baby. And the baby is in charge.

From a brain perspective, adolescence is an extremely vulnerable period for social anxiety. If I could say anything, anything at all to parents of socially anxious children: Draw closer to them during adolescence. You will be tempted to run, run, run away, but **Insert brave, unearned love here**

---

5 see http://psycheducation.org/brain-tours/memory-learning-and-emotion-the-hippocampus/

now is when they need love the most—and earn it the least.

Strangely, research has consistently found that the prefrontal cortex is overactive in social anxiety (Brühl et al. 2014, 14). The Strongman is on the scene, receiving input from all the players in the Fear Circus, and brilliantly advising them all on how to keep calm.

"Keep calm!" He says, calmly and confidently. And because he is so active and on the job, the rest of the circus should really be keeping calm. But his messages are not getting through. So he begins to yell, and all that yelling makes him look hyper. Yet, the more he yells, the less anybody seems to hear him.

Researchers believe the pathway between the prefrontal cortex and the rest of the fear circuit is poorly connected. Somehow, the calming commands cannot reach their destination. Like our Oregon highways, the connections are littered with potholes, rock slides, and road kill. *Ew.*

Socially anxious people can often think rationally and conclude that a social situation is harmless, fear is completely unwarranted. Yet we cannot halt the physiological chain reaction. We would like to regulate our emotions effectively, but our Strongman is just not getting the job done. Personally, I would like to fire him, but I haven't been able to reach him by phone yet.

THE BRAIN NAPKIN: LET'S CONNECT

To test for connection problems, researchers have begun focusing on the pathways between the fear circuitry and emotion regulation brain regions. These connections consist largely of gray and white matter. Gray matter covers the entire surface of the brain. It is responsible for routing sensory and motor stimuli to the proper channels. The gray matter is what connects the circus acts.

The brain's gray matter (also called the cortex) consists of multiple folds and valleys. It is all bumpy and squished and tucked and stuff. Imagine a crumpled up table napkin draped over the entire brain. If the cortex of the brain were unfolded and laid out flat, its surface area would be almost 2.5 square feet (McDowell 2010, 379). A pretty big, wrinkly napkin.

The cortex generally measures approximately 1/8th of an inch in thickness, or the height of two pennies stacked on top of each other (Sisodiya et al. 1996, 425). This measurement is called cortical thickness. So it is also a pretty thick napkin.

Different factors can affect the thickness of the brain napkin (gray matter layer). Thin places in the napkin often occur because of breakdown and decreased use. Some thinning of the napkin is a natural result of aging and is apparent by middle age (Salat 2004, 725). Thinning is also present in certain mental disorders, indicating altered brain function (several studies cited in Kuhn et al. 2014, 2). Schizophrenia (Williams et al. 2012, 35), cluster headaches (Seifert et al. 2012, 1364), and marijuana use (Lopez-Larson et al. 2011) have been associated with decreases in cortical thickness. Yet another good reason not to do dope.

Motor and intellectual exercise can increase thickness. One study found that adolescents who played video games for a little over 12 hours per week had increased cortical thickness on the left side of the brain (Kuhn et al. 2014, 4). This area controls decision-making, working memory, and predicting future outcomes. I bet those teens' game-play brain napkin area looked like…super heavy, triple layered velvet—a high-class napkin suitable for fine dining—while their schoolwork brain napkin area was probably transparent.

Meditation (Lazar et al. 2005) and juggling (Draganski et al. 2004, 311) have also been linked to increases in cortical thickness. It appears that the outer layer of the brain can be "strengthened" (i.e., thickened) somewhat through use.

> **Video games make your brain like velvet**

My brain napkin is probably pretty thin. Maybe you can see sunlight through it. I am older, I don't do crossword puzzles, and I definitely can't juggle. But I bet the part of my brain napkin responsible for surfing the Internet is like a horse blanket.

Researchers have only recently begun investigating cortical thickness, gray matter, and connectivity in social anxiety, and the results are mixed. For a complete review see Brühl et al. (2014). Sometimes researchers find thick areas of brain napkin, sometimes they find thin areas. That must be frustrating for them.

One study found thinning in the area responsible for sensory processing and social anxiety symptoms (the post-central region; Syal et al., 2012, 302). It also found thinning in areas responsible for social and emotional function.

A 2010 study found that 12 weeks of treatment with escitalopram (trade-name Lexapro) reduced napkin thickness, making it look more normal (bilateral superior temporal cortex thickness; Cassimjee et al, 2010, 372). All this to say: The napkin is important, but we don't really understand how or why just yet. People will be staring at the napkin in their little research cubicles for a very long time to come.

Beneath the gray matter layer is white matter, obviously named for its…ahem…white color. White matter is rich in myelin, a fatty substance that provides insulation and speeds nerve impulses. Fiber tracts beneath the gray matter layer consist of white matter and connect different brain regions. The white matter is what lies just beneath the napkin, and it is very important.

AMYGDALA

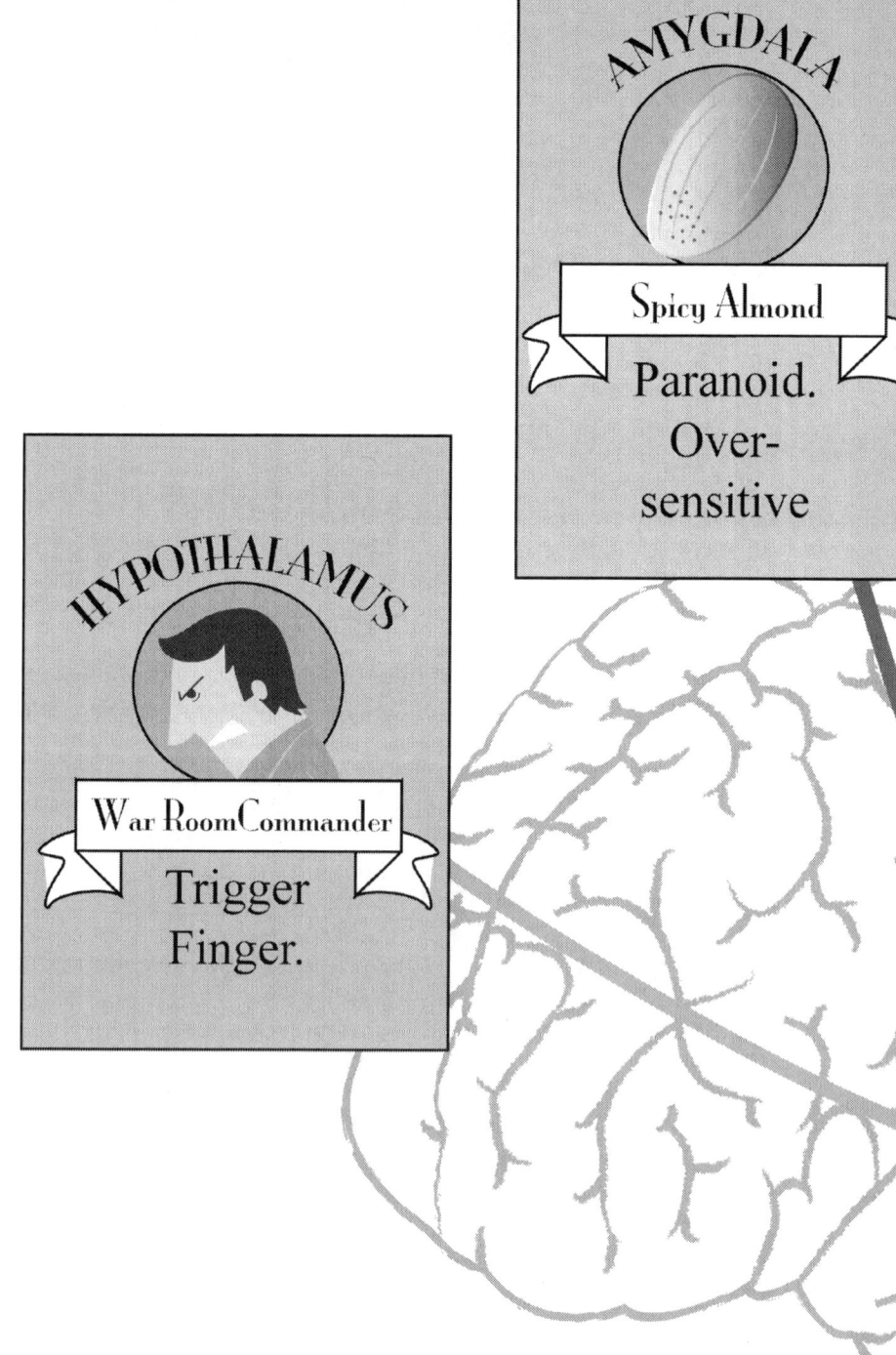

Spicy Almond

Paranoid. Over-sensitive

HYPOTHALAMUS

War RoomCommander

Trigger Finger.

*Brain anatomy placement is approximate.
Neurosurgeons: please don't use this as a template for surgeries.

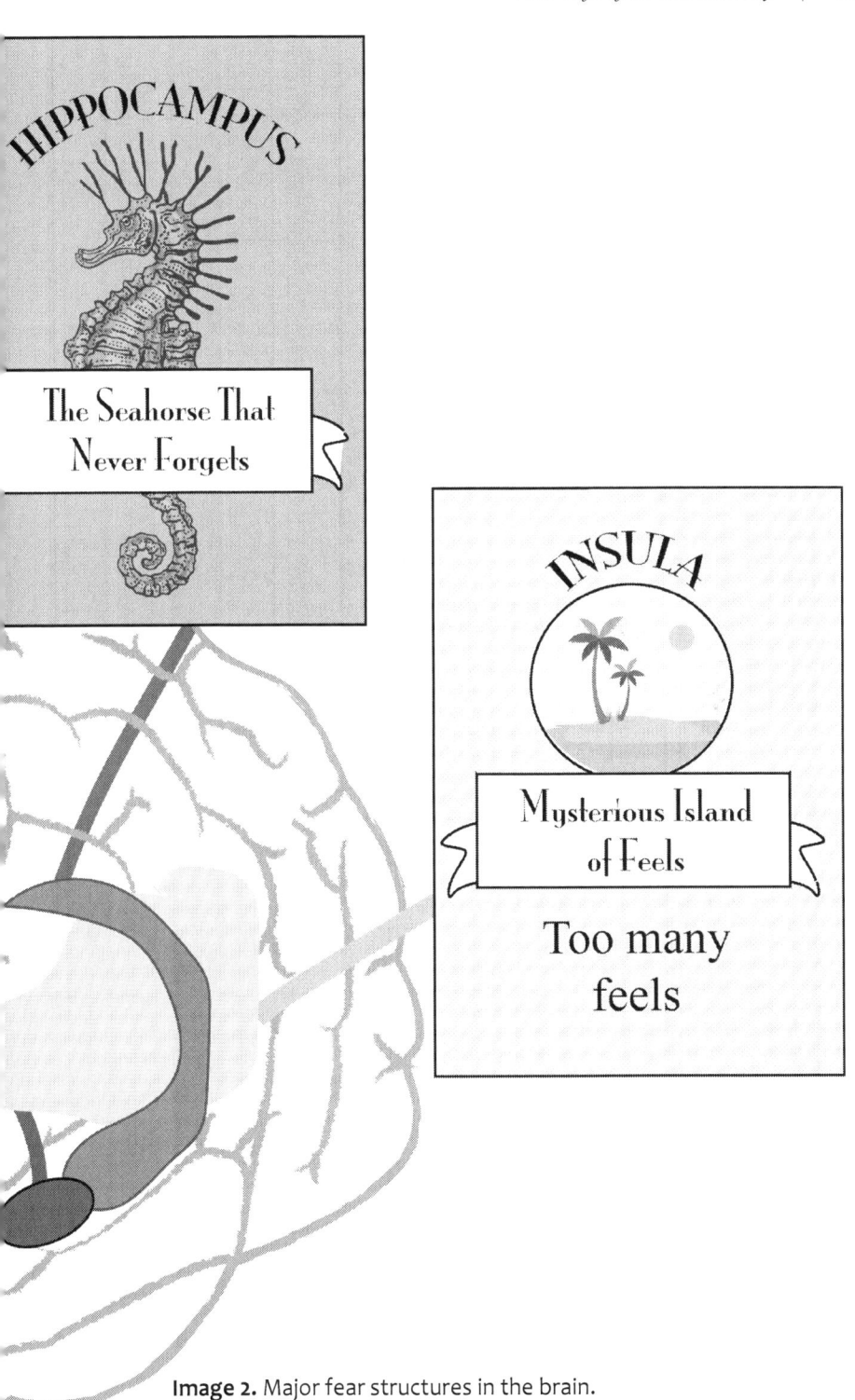

Image 2. Major fear structures in the brain.
All circus characters have been adapted from designs by *Freepik.com*

One special area of white matter is the **uncinate fasciculus**. This is the little connecting path between the parts of the brain that detect fear and then make rational decisions (Dolan 2007, 796). The left uncinate fasciculus appears to be less fluffy (has lower volume) than normal in people with SAD (Baur et al. 2013, 443). This could indicate the brain is not as well connected as usual, or that we are not utilizing the connection enough. In any event, uncinate and fasciculus are two words that you simply must use in conversation sometime before you die.

> "My Uncinate Fasciculus is jacked. Sorry."

Overall, connections are important. Not just in Hollywood, but in our brains as well. The weaker the connections between important brain areas, the worse social anxiety symptoms seem to be (Laeger et al. 2014, E19-21). Some brain areas in SAD are even too connected (Brühl et al. 2014, 10). The study results are not too clear. Certain drugs (oxytocin) normalize connections (Sripada et al. 2012, 257-258; Gorka et al. 2014). It is likely that future medications will be designed specifically to help our brain areas connect better. From an earthy, human perspective, that seems like a good idea.

"I Hate Math" Said My Resting Brain

Interesting tidbit: one facet of the brain was discovered totally by accident (Buckner, Andrews-Hannah, and Schacter 2008, 2). I feel like this is *exactly* the kind of brain discovery I could make. In this case, it happened during the natural course of research.

Most brain imaging research was designed to record the brain during various tasks, such as looking at photos, memorizing words, or solving math problems. Often, a scan of the brain at rest was taken before the research task, to be used as a base comparison. These scans showed what the brain looked like when participants were staring at the ceiling, daydreaming about lunch, or possibly picking their noses.

> Craving solitude may be related to our Default Mode Network

Thirty years of brain imaging built up a large database of these control images featuring the brain at rest. Surprisingly, researchers began to notice unusual features of these images taken during "default mode." The brain seemed to be just as active during default resting mode as it was in working mode (Buckner, Andrews-Hannah, and Schacter 2008, 2).

More specifically, certain areas became highly active when individuals were allowed to passively think (or pick their noses) undisturbed. These brain areas became known as the Default Mode Network (DMN).

The DMN seems to be activated when individuals recall the past, muse about the future, or consider the perspectives of other people (Buckner and Carroll 2007, 55). The DMN is also central to human fantasy life, daydreaming, imagination, and creativity. It is activated during thoughts about morality, self-reflection, and judgments. Contemplation of God, evaluating moral dilemmas, and prayer are seated in the DMN. Introverts who crave solitude may be seeking uninterrupted activation of their DMNs. My DMN and I are totally besties (but I would never, ever pick my nose).

The DMN consists of areas of the prefrontal cortex, hippocampus, posterior cingulate, inferior parietal lobule, and lateral cortex (Buckner, Andrews-Hannah, and Schacter 2008, 5). Got all that? The DMN is a huge gas guzzler, consuming 20% of the entire body's energy requirements.[6] So, if you eat an entire cake, one-fifth of that cake is just for fueling your DMN (that's pure math, right there). I don't know what the rest of the cake is for.

DMN function is disturbed in certain conditions, such as autism (Washington et al. 2013, 1284–1296). A core feature of autism is hyper-focus on environmental stimuli, rather than the internal states of others or oneself. Tommy sees a cluster of pretty marbles. He is utterly fascinated with them. He doesn't even notice the kid who is sitting near them. He is probably just thinking "Marbles. Marbles. I love marbles." That's what I would be thinking.

The default mode seems to be under-functioning in autistic individuals, making empathy, imagination, and social connection difficult. But autistic children can also be gifted in areas that do not involve the DMN, such as attention to details, math, and factual knowledge.

Meanwhile, individuals with schizophrenia have an overactive DMN. Core features of schizophrenia include bizarre delusions, hallucinations, and altered perceptions of reality.[7] It is as if the schizophrenic is unable to distinguish between imagination and real life. Three studies have provided early support to the idea that the DMN is overactive in schizophrenia (Buckner, Andrews-Hanna, and Schacter 2008, 27).

So if autism shows low DMN function (reduced imagination) and schizophrenia shows too much DMN function (too much imagination),

Schizophrenia
=Too much DMN function

that looks like I'm cussing, but I'm not.

---

6 Dougherty, Stephen, 2011. "Inside Your Brain on Holiday," available at http://brainblogger.com/2011/11/23/inside-your-brain-on-holiday/

7 National Institute of Mental Health, accessed February, 2016. http://www.nimh.nih.gov/health/topics/schizophrenia/index.shtml

where does social anxiety fit? SAD is a complicated mix of the two extremes. In social anxiety, areas of the DMN have been found to be overactive but poorly connected to other regulating brain systems (Brühl et al. 2014, 12). In other words, we have a rich, contemplative inner life, but also an inability to shut off that inner life when necessary. The DMN needs to go away when we put our brains to active work, but we find it difficult to do that. We are stuck in internal dialogue overdrive.

Ideally, the DMN will deactivate during difficult brain tasks, such as mathematical problem solving. In SAD, it was found to deactivate less than normal (Maresh, Allen, and Coan 2014). Again, it appears that socially anxious people have difficulty shutting off their inner dialogue when needed. This likely translates into a heightened state of vigilance and internal self-awareness. Perhaps while others are efficiently doing their taxes we are off imagining the bad things that could happen.

The most fascinating part of all this DMN research is that you can tell the difference between a healthy person and a socially anxious person just by looking at DMN imaging (Zhang et al. 2014). Or at least, the scientists can. They were able to diagnose social anxiety based on brain imaging alone with 76.25% accuracy. The images consistently revealed unusual DMN patterns in social anxiety. They also revealed sensory processing abnormalities in the visual, auditory, and bodily movement networks.

The use of the antidepressant citalopram (Lexapro) for 8 weeks deactivated major areas of the DMN for socially anxious individuals (Carey et al. 2004). Perhaps medication enhances our ability to not "overthink" when we simply need to focus?

Neurotransmitters: The Special Sauce

Neurotransmitters are chemicals in the brain that enable information to pass from neuron to neuron.[8] They are the special sauce that keeps everything flowing. Researchers have identified more than 100 neurotransmitters in the human brain, and likely many more remain unidentified. That is a lot of special sauces.

Specific neurotransmitters that have been implicated in SAD include: serotonin, norepinephrine, glutamate, gamma-Aminobutyric acid (GABA), and the neuropeptide oxytocin (Marazziti et al. 2014, 100–111). We will take an in-depth look at neurotransmitters, along with the medications that target them, in Chapter 6.

Our Brains Are Like Silly Putty,[9] Except Brainier

Someone reading this chapter could get really discouraged. Here I am, just wanting to go to church without freaking out. Turns out I have an entire circus, a napkin, an overactive resting brain, and too many special

---

8 Cherry, Kendra. 2015. *About Health.* available at http://psychology.about.com/od/nindex-/g/neurotransmitter.htm
9 Silly Putty is a registered trademark of Crayola LLC

sauces to count. That, by itself, is kind of freaking me out. But not so fast, my friend. The brain actually has the capacity for change. Yes! Even its size, shape, and connections.

Freaking out

In a review of 19 studies exploring brain changes in socially anxious participants after various interventions, Bruhl et al. (2014, 260–280) found measurable changes in brain activity level, connectivity, and size. These magnificent changes were brought about by psychotherapy, antidepressants, cognitive emotional regulation instruction, and/or cognitive behavioral therapy. We see that largely body-based treatments have at least some positive effect on body-based symptoms. The brain can be molded, just not quite as efficiently as Silly Putty.

Researchers now know that some people are just more likely to get better, thanks to their brains. When it comes to cognitive behavioral therapy, individuals with the most brain health related to emotion regulation benefited more (Klumpp, Keutmann, et al. 2014, 1-7). They also did better if they had better brain health related to attention (Klumpp, Fitzgerald, and Angstadt 2014, 3116). I take these studies to mean that for those with the highest performing Fear Circus, CBT is a very viable option. Perhaps less so for the rest of us.

Strength of the flesh

With all this talk of science, studies, brain biology, and other heady stuff...let's not forget that we are talking about strength in the human body (flesh). The corpse. Our dead nature. If we just happen to be born with stronger brains, we will do better socially and with therapy. If we are not, we might not do so well. What does it matter to God? We simply do the best we can with what we have and rest in God's love, no matter what.

Social anxiety is *clearly* influenced by the human flesh. It should come as no surprise that human flesh is very, very weak (in various ways). God illustrated this point in the story of Gethsemane (Matthew 26). Jesus asked His disciples to stay awake and pray for Him. The disciples were extremely tired and fell asleep instead. Their brains were probably flooded with melatonin (the sleeping hormone), and they succumbed. Three times He requested their prayers, and each time they...went back to bed. The tiredness of their physical bodies prevented them from doing what He had passionately requested. The whole circus kind of went on vacay.

Jesus' response was, "The spirit indeed is willing, but the flesh is weak" (Matthew 26:41). Jesus already knew the weakness of the human flesh, as He was God in fleshly form. He was the only human who ever had perfect control over His human flesh. He was able to achieve perfect control only because He was actually God.

Thankfully, our bodily human weaknesses are no longer God's concern because they were put to death with Jesus on the cross. Dead. We cannot control our flesh through willpower or determination or through obeying rules. We will never control our bodies as Jesus was able to. But we get credit for it, anyway.

If your uncinate fasciculus is jacked, that's OK. It's dead anyway.

And here's an interesting tidbit for you to chew on. I believe the power of God's unconditional love produces major brain changes. Though I do not have the studies to prove it, as soon as I get that fMRI machine set up in the house, I'm all over it. It seems perfectly reasonable to assume that the relief of knowing we are loved, accepted, and not judged will release happy chemicals that cause happy thought-patterns, thicken the brain napkin and neutralize our spicy almonds. That's just a really, really reasonable assumption, if I do say so myself.

A 2011 review of more than 1,200 studies and 400 reviews conducted by Drs. Alex Bunn and David Randall[10] of the Christian Medical Fellowship did find various health benefits associated with Christian faith. For example, Christians are less likely to commit suicide or suffer anxiety, display fewer psychotic tendencies, and are less likely to suffer alcohol and drug abuse.

Rest assured that through the eyes of grace, the workings of our physical bodies are not held against us. The whole circus can be as dysfunctional as peanut butter *without* jelly. Or *decaffeinated* coffee. But our standing with God remains always and forever: loved.

* * *

---

10 Bunn, Alex, and David Randall (2011). "Health Benefits of Christian Faith." Available at http://humanjourney.org.uk/articles/health-benefits-of-christian-faith/

REFLECTION

1. Based on the information you just read, what factors do scientists believe is at the physical root of social anxiety?

2. Are changes in the brain possible?

3. Does reading about the brain areas involved in social anxiety make you feel hopeless or hopeful? Why?

4. What does God think of brain-based weaknesses?

5. Do you believe that the human body is dead, its actions irrelevant, according to God?

5

The Autism-Sensory Connection

"We don't have a priest who is out of touch with our reality. He's been through weakness and testing, experienced it all—all but the sin. So let's walk right up to him and get what he is so ready to give. Take the mercy, accept the help."
Hebrews 4:15-16, The Message Bible

I'm going to be transparently honest here…the best day of my life was the day my daughter was born. My wedding, my son's birth, and being baptized are all right up there, too. But the day my first baby entered the world will forever be number one.

My labor lasted eight hours, from first twinge to grand finale. Paige Deveraux arrived remarkably beautiful, loud, and healthy. For the first time, I felt the full depth of what love means. Never before had something been so mine, so dependent on me, so entwined with my soul. Innocence, personified. She had my wispy blonde hair and would grow to inherit her father's ice-blue eyes.

We had a bit of a rough start once we came home from the hospital. Anemic and still recovering from labor, I developed a nasty case of the flu. I became too sick to care for her, and had to hand her off to my energetic and capable mother. But eventually, I recovered and our little family settled into a routine.

It takes some time to adjust to having a stranger in one's home. In this case, it was a demanding, crying stranger. I had to learn her likes and dislikes. When she was happy, she would coo contentedly from her bassinet. When she was unhappy (which was far more frequent), she would fuss, cry, and protest angrily. She was a finicky sleeper, often waking up 10 to 12 times each night.

After the first few weeks, I learned that she did not care to be held or touched. She would allow me to cuddle her for a minute or two but then fuss and cry until I laid her back down in her bassinet. I learned to sneak cuddle time by picking her up as she slept. Then I could hold her as long as I wanted, and she remained blissfully unaware.

Today, as an adolescent, she is still not a big "toucher." I can forcibly wrest a hug from her, but only under duress! Of course, this doesn't sound out of the ordinary for adolescents.

When our son was born a year and half after his sister, he was her complete opposite. He could not get enough touch. His personality was less intense than his sister's; he was laid back and easy and enjoyed sitting on my lap. His arms and legs never stopped twitching and kicking.

He had his own unique sensory quirks as well. He very clearly preferred a low level of certain types of stimulation. While he was nearly always content when left undisturbed, too much audio or visual activity upset him.

His most pronounced sensitivity was to noises. Once, we took him to our local fireworks display. Lying beneath the night sky on a blanket, we expected the light show to delight him. But the loud pops of even the smaller firecrackers were clearly painful to his ears, and he cried for the duration of the show. In other environments, he would cover his ears and cry at any unexpected or piercing noise.

He was also very sensitive to social situations. Too much movement, too many noises, colors, people…and in about an hour he would generally have a meltdown. Attending church became difficult, and leaving him in the church nursery was impossible. He would cry and throw angry fits, disturbing the other children and wearing out the caregivers. Eventually we adjusted by allowing him free access to crawl near our feet (under the church pew) during the service. There, it was quiet, peaceful, and he knew we were close. Bliss!

Another sensory quirk of his involved sticky substances. Basically, anything gooey (lotion, jelly, mayonnaise, etc.) repulses him. I could not get lotion on him after a bath without a miserable struggle. To this day, he does not like to touch shampoo or lotion and will not eat jelly or condiments of any kind. His eccentricities delight me! I don't like the discomfort he experiences, but I do enjoy that he is different from anyone else I know.

My children's sensory quirks during the early years fall within the normal range of childhood behavior. Still, I paid special attention to these things. I recognized discomfort in them that I, too, experience. I feel quickly overwhelmed by many types of stimuli, particularly those present in social settings. Some noises (such as the sound of someone whistling or eating loudly) drill painfully into my brain. If someone touches me, I nearly always flinch with the startle reflex. I detest the feel of water on my face or tight clothing/jewelry. I sometimes find direct eye contact too intense to bear. I smell even the subtlest of scents (which is both a blessing and a curse!). These are all minor idiosyncrasies, but I have often wondered if there is a connection to social anxiety. The answer seems to be: yes.

The Autism Connection

Sensory sensitivity is a central feature in autism, and may play a role in social anxiety as well. In one study, nearly all autistic children (94%) were affected by sensory issues (Leekam et al. 2006, 903). Another study found that people with social anxiety were also prone to sensory overstimulation and sensitivities (Neal, Edelmann, and Glachan 2002, 370). Those with social anxiety and those with autism seem to have a lower threshold for comfortable sensory stimulation.

SAD is the most common condition to co-occur with autism

Autism and social anxiety are also linked in other ways. Individuals with autism and normal intelligence show high rates of SAD (Bejerot, Eriksson, and Mortberg 2014, 706). One large study revealed that 29% of children with an autism spectrum disorder also qualify for a SAD diagnosis (Simonoff et al. 2008, 926). It was the most common condition found to co-occur with an autism spectrum disorder.

Both autism spectrum disorders and social anxiety contribute to unsuccessful social interactions, poor eye contact, and difficulty forming friendships (Taylor 2012, 296-298; Tyson and Cruess 2012, 1485). A lack of enjoyment in (and avoidance of) social interactions, as well as a preference for aloneness, is associated with autism and social anxiety (White, Bray and Ollendick 2011, 880-881). Young people with social anxiety are more likely to have characteristics of autism. It can be difficult to distinguish between high functioning autistic individuals and individuals with SAD.

So autism and social anxiety are linked, but probably in a roundabout way. It is believed that autistic individuals experience an unusually low sense of pleasure across many normal activities, such as social interactions, game playing, and monetary reward (Richey et al. 2012, 367–377). For a person with autism, these things just aren't all that fun. But you know what is fun for someone with an autism spectrum disorder? Repetitive behaviors, such as lining up toys or rocking back and forth. For whatever reason, these kinds of actions provide a deep sense of reward.

Socially anxious individuals also display an unusually low sense of reward, but only in social interactions (Richey et al. 2012, 367–377). For many with SAD, being around people just does not bring a "normal" sense of pleasure. These unusual low reward responses in both autism and social anxiety are related to a part of the brain called the basal ganglia and dopamine activity.

Autism: games, money, and people are no fun

SAD: just people are no fun

Beyond lowered pleasurable responses, individuals with autism and SAD may also experience heightened negative responses. Lots of things don't feel particularly good, and some things feel...very bad. So-called normal sensory experiences, such as certain noise pitches, clothing textures, or temperature fluctuations, actually feel painful.

People who are highly sensitive to sensory input have also been shown more likely to develop social anxiety (Neal, Edelmann, and Glachan 2002, 368-369). But why? What is happening? The theory is that the central nervous system is unable to efficiently process input from the various senses (i.e., touch, smell, sight, taste, movement, etc.). This sensory processing is also referred to as "gating."

Only useful and important stimuli should be allowed through the brain's attention "gate." Faulty sensory gating either permits too much stimuli to be noticed or denies important stimuli a normal level of attention. Growing up on a farm, I know that gates are important. Without them: chaos. Imagine cows eating your tulips and horses on the porch. That's what life feels like for someone who is overly sensitive.

There are seven areas in which individuals may be unusually sensitive to sensory input (James et al., 2010, 715): touch, balance, inner body sensations, visual, auditory, taste, and smell. Individuals can be both oversensitive in some areas and under-sensitive in others.

Welcome to a concept known as **sensory threshold.** This is the amount of sensory input that feels comfortable and is easy to cope with. Some people have a very, very low sensory threshold. The sound of the radio at low volume is just enough to be distracting. Add in the phone ringing or bright sunshine and a meltdown is on its way.

People with a low sensory threshold show higher levels of anxiety and depression (Liss, Mailloux, and Erchull 2008,

Too Much stuff floods through the gate

257-259). Interestingly, individuals who have difficulty identifying and describing their feelings also showed high levels of anxiety/depression. Researchers think that overwhelming sensory experiences, combined with poor emotional understanding, may lead to social withdrawal (258).

> *"Too much! that hurts! please stop!"*
> *-love, your brain*

In her book, *Too Loud, Too Bright, Too Fast, Too Tight,* Sharon Heller, Ph.D., has created a comprehensive list of unusual sensory reactions (reprinted with permission; Heller 2002, 313-317). She uses the term sensory defensiveness for those who are over-reactive to certain sensations.

SYMPTOMS

TOUCH/TACTILE
- Reacts excessively to light, unseen, or sudden touch, especially of strangers, exhibiting anxiety, hostility, or aggression and spontaneously flinching, withdrawing, or lashing out
- Tenses at friendly or affectionate pats and caresses even from loved ones, but at times accepts same
- Dislikes hugs or craves deep pressure of hug, but irritated by light touch of a kiss
- Scratching or rubbing the spot that has been touched
- Irritated and anxious standing in line, taking an elevator, people standing too close, or weaving through a crowd
- As infant, not calmed by cuddling or stroking
- Prefers to touch rather than be touched
- Fussy about clothing, such as stiff new clothes, rough or synthetic textures, shirt collars, tags, turtlenecks, belts, elasticized waists or cuffs, hats, scarves, and panty hose, or clothing tight in certain places
- Frequently adjust clothes, as if uncomfortable
- Irritated by clothes that touch certain places, such as skirts that brush the legs, and to movement of clothes against skin during clothing changes
- Overdresses to minimize skin exposure, regardless of weather
- Wears minimal clothes, regardless of weather
- Avoids touching certain textures or surfaces, like some fabrics, blankets, rugs
- Bothered by footwear, particularly sock seams, and may prefer to go without socks or panty hose and wear shoes loosely tied or untied
- Avoids walking barefoot, especially in sand or grass
- Bothered by touching certain textures or material with hands such as sand, clay, finger paint, paste or food, or getting hands dirty
- Chooses bedding and sleepwear to create pressure against the skin

and minimize light touch and displacement by body movements
- Dislikes touch of certain animals-dogs, horses, cats
- Certain parts of the body especially sensitive to touch
- Excessively ticklish
- Irritated by hair displacement, as when brushing hair, receiving a haircut, shampoo, or pat on the head
- Dislikes nail trims
- Bothered by creams or lotions, make-up, lipstick, chapstick
- Avoids jewelry, even wedding band
- Dislikes baths or showers, and especially being splashed
- Seeks tight spaces, especially during sleep

ORAL/TACTILE
- Picky about food, preferring or avoiding certain textures, like mushy, crunchy or chewy, or taste, such as sharp, bitter, or spicy
- Dislikes objects in mouth, like a toothbrush, dentist's fingers, or drill
- Dislikes taste of toothpaste
- Mouths objects, like pens

TEMPERATURE/TACTILE
- Easily cold
- Easily hot
- Fussy about food temperature
- Fussy about bath or shower temperature
- Irritated by quick change in temperature (hot shower to cold air)

PAIN/TACTILE
- Overreacts to pain
- Underreacts to pain
- Excessive reaction to inoculations

VIBRATION/TACTILE AND AUDITORY
- Dislikes touching vibrating objects
- Annoyed by vibration in vehicles
- Annoyed by vibration in buildings from heating or cooling, elevators, or trucks going by
- Unnerved by loud bass of music, especially in cars

SOUNDS
- Dislikes loud, high-pitched, high-frequency sound
- Vigilant to and easily distracted by ambient noise
- Overreacts to unexpected or loud noises (sirens, fire alarms, landscaping or construction equipment)
- Picks up sounds before anyone else, or sounds others can't hear
- Excessively irritated by and unable to tune out sounds in the environ-

ment, like air conditioners, vacuum cleaners, noisy appliances, toilet flush, running water, alarms, or lots of different kinds of sounds at once
- Unable to tune out ticking clock, dripping waters, etc.
- Irritated by volume and pitch of certain voices
- Difficulty listening against background noise, such as whispering, eating, sneezing, or coughing, in a movie theater or at a concert or large gathering

VISUAL SENSATION
- Irritated by bright light-sunlight, fluorescent lights, car lights
- Annoyed by objects close to face, like car sun visor
- Easily distracted by visual stimulation
- Annoyed by moving visual field
- Overexcited by busy and complex visual field
- Over-stimulated by eye contact
- Fears visual cliffs (i.e. stairs, balconies, inclined theaters)
- Hyper-vigilant of environment

VESTIBULAR/MOVEMENT AND BALANCE
- Feels threatened when tipping head backward, tilted, or upside down as when having hair shampooed in the sink
- Feels uncomfortable surge in stomach, and even panic, on a swing, jumping off a diving board, riding a roller coaster, or on carnival rides that spin
- Fearful or hesitant when climbing or descending stairs and holds tightly to banister or walls
- Uncomfortable in elevators, especially when open, and on escalators
- Experiences motion sickness in car or airplanes
- Fears heights, even slightly raised surfaces, such a stairs or curbs
- Fearful of visual cliffs (i.e. stairs, balconies, inclined theatres)
- Fearful of activities moving through space
- Avoids activities that challenge balance or center of gravity
- Uncomfortable maintaining balance on uneven terrain, like grass
- Fear of falling when no real danger exists-primal terror
- Fears flying

SMELLS
- Dislikes sharp odors that don't seem to bother other people
- Smells odors before others, or faint odors unnoticed by others
- Hypersensitive to body odors such as breath, underarms, skin or hair, scents of soap, perfume, etc.
- Easily light-headed or nauseous from chemical smells: paint, carpet, gasoline, cleaning supplies, dry cleaning, laundry soaps, certain perfumes

- Dislikes certain food smells
- Dislikes certain shampoos, lotions, or perfumes

Sensory Quirkiness

There are three types of abnormal sensory patterns: oversensitive, under-sensitive, and sensory-seeking (Hilton et al., 2010). The person who never remembers to put on his coat even in the dead of winter? Probably under-sensitive. The kid who loves to spin, spin, spin? Probably sensory-seeking. And, finally, the kid (or adult) who is a super picky eater? Oversensitive.

Over-Sensitive
too much too much

According to James et al. (2011, 716), individuals who are sensory over-responsive will react to sensations in a manner that is more intense, faster, and longer lasting than normal. These individuals will also exhibit the fight-or-flight response, which can lead to impulsive, aggressive, or withdrawn reactions. If you become enraged when your spouse wakes you up by bouncing on the bed, you might be a little sensory oversensitive. And your spouse might also need to seriously calm down.

The oversensitive individual is incapable of finding a balance between noticing stimuli and adapting to it (Ben-Sasson, Carter, and Briggs-Gowan 2010, 1193). If you put an oversensitive person in a loud, busy church sanctuary, he will be flooded with stress hormones. He is unlikely to be able to deeply relax—*ever*. This is why, for many of us, true worship happens far more often in a private, quiet atmosphere. And there is *absolutely nothing wrong with that*.

Researchers Aron, Aron, and Jagiellowicz (2012, 277) wrote (warning: highly paraphrased) that sensitive people notice more stuff, take longer to process said stuff, and react stronger than other people to that stuff. They cite research linking the insula (that Mysterious Island of Feels), dopamine, and serotonin as contributing factors to high sensitivity (776). For the highly sensitive person, the world is just a less welcoming place.

The World is hostile

Social interaction requires the processing of multiple sensory stimuli at once (Hilton et al. 2010, 942). It is really a veritable stew of sensory ingredients. We use sight to monitor body language, hearing to interpret tone and inflections, while surveying the environment, temperature, light, background noise, internal processes, etc. Social interaction is likely one of the richest and most complex of all sensory experiences. Socializing is not mere observation or passive experience. It is a complex give-and-take, a dance of dialogue and interpretation. We socially anxious people are the ones with two left feet.

Sensory oversensitivity can lead individuals to become easily overwhelmed, have limited diets, and avoid certain movements, sounds, and textures (Parham and Mailloux 2005, as cited in Reynolds and Lane 2007). Personally, I tend to eat the same thing for lunch and dinner for months at a time. Right now, I am all about ham-and-cheese sandwiches. Give it a few months (or years), and I will probably switch to something else. As long as it has ham and cheese in it.

Highly sensitive people also experience strong emotional reactions or engage in disruptive behaviors when unable to adapt to their sensory environment. I have a musician friend who notices even the tiniest mistake during a musical performance. And when she hears it, it causes a full-body reaction of irritation. It takes all of her self-control not to...well...tackle the person playing the wrong note. She faces the challenge of being an incredible musician while also maintaining "love for her neighbor." This polarity between gift and curse is the challenge written into the DNA of highly sensitive Christians.

Sensory over-responsivity takes a toll. It has been shown to be a cause of both childhood and adult anxiety (Lane, Reynold, and Dumenci 2012, 599; Engel-Yeger and Dunn 2011, 214). It has also been linked to social functioning problems, depression, and low mental health (Ahadi and Basharpoor 2010, 570-574).

It takes a toll.

In normal children, about 10 to 20% have sensory over-responsiveness (Van Hulle, Lemery-Chalfant, and Goldsmith 2015, 17). One study found that approximately 5% of normally developing children display severely maladaptive responses to seemingly harmless stimuli (Ahn et al. 2004, 291). That is the equivalent of 220,000 kindergarten children with severe sensory processing problems in the U.S. Oh, those unique, precious, probably misunderstood kids!

An oversensitivity to inner body sensations has been directly linked to social anxiety (Terasawa at al. 2012, 264). This is called **interoceptive processing.** Inner-body sensations, such as a racing heart, trembling, or other autonomic responses are felt strongly and are impossible to ignore for some of us. It is hard to pay attention to the outside world when our inside world feels like chaos.

Many individuals attempt to cope with oversensitivity to stimuli by limiting sensory input. These individuals actively work to avoid stimuli (Shankar, Smith, and Jalihal 2013, 25-26). At home, they may keep the lights low, avoid music, and wear soft clothing in order to maintain a sense of calm. They may do shopping in the middle of the night (Yes! Or, better yet, online). Sensation avoiders are often thought of as introspective or reclusive. And perhaps they are, or they may just be trying to avoid the physical wear and tear of overstimulation.

Others will employ a passive strategy to cope with their sensory discomfort (Shankar, Smith, and Jalihal 2013, 25). Instead of attempting to control their environment, these individuals simply endure their discomfort. Unfortunately, they live in an ongoing state of physical alertness. They frequently become overwhelmed by sensations and may be chronically fatigued from ongoing physiological stress.

I think many of us use a mix of control and passivity. We control what we can and endure what we must. And really, what else can we do?

One particular form of audio-related oversensitivity is **misophonia**, which literally means "hatred of sound" (Edelstein et al. 2013). It includes an autonomic arousal (an involuntary fight-or-flight response) to specific sounds such as chewing, pen clicking, and lip smacking. Other reported triggers include breathing sounds, sniffing, whistling, scratching sounds, slurping, swallowing, yawning, humming, trickling water, typing, and crinkling paper. The offending sounds may trigger anxiety, panic, irritability, and/or rage.

Misophonia: hatred of sound

I have to confess that the sound of whistling feels like a drill spiraling directly into my brain. My husband and I used to argue about this because he really likes to whistle. And I really like my husband. But I am unable to help my dislike of the two together.

Strangely, individuals with misophonia do not experience discomfort if the sounds originate from themselves. In fact, some individuals find that copying other people's offending sounds is a way to cope. For example, chewing while someone else is chewing tends to cancel out the irritation.

People also report that when babies or animals make the triggering sounds, it is not offensive (because "they don't know any better"; Edelstein et al. 2013). Frequently it is the individual's close friends or family members who trigger misophonia. Similar sounds made by strangers may be tolerable. People with misophonia are aware that their reactions are unreasonable but feel helpless to stop their reaction. We know the rules for reasonable reactions. We just cannot manage to obey them.

There is very little research on misophonia. One case study demonstrated possible effectiveness for cognitive behavioral therapy in coping with misophonia (Bernstein, Angell, and Dehle 2013). In their case study, researchers stated:

> "Effective coping strategies included regular exercise, redirecting her attention towards other ambient or self-made sounds, and focusing on people over their eating sounds. Ineffective behavioural strategies (e.g. sighing, eye rolling, glaring) were extinguished."

Unfortunately, there do not seem to be any promising treatments for actually reducing misophonia itself.

Misophonia shares certain features with social anxiety, such as stress in social interactions and avoidance as a coping mechanism (Schroder, Vulink, and Denys 2013). It has been linked to obsessive-compulsive disorder in children, attention-deficit hyperactivity disorder, autistic spectrum disorder, Tourette syndrome, generalized anxiety disorder, and fragile X syndrome (Cavanna and Seri 2015). To my knowledge, no clinical studies to date concretely link misophonia to social anxiety. Unless you want to count me as one super single case study.

Faulty Senses Are Dead

From a grace-based perspective, we recognize that sensory issues are failings of the human body (the flesh). They are largely out of our control, at least to varying degrees according to the physical strength each person possesses. What we are not able to overcome in the flesh, the spirit overcomes through grace. In other words, the body may repeatedly fail to process stimuli as desired. Meanwhile, our spirit has already received credit for perfect sensory processing, purely by believing in the goodness of God.

Sensory quirks rest squarely in the old, dead body. Thankfully, they neither commend nor disapprove us in God's eyes. Sensory processing is irrelevant to God's love and acceptance towards us. Still, just because the human body is spiritually dead does not mean that we are no longer allowed to care for it. The following methods represent body-based means of caring for sensory issues. Even though our old, human nature is dead it still manages to sneak in a fair amount of pain and suffering. Those are just the cold, hard facts.

> *failings of the human body*

Sensory Integration Therapy

Sensory problems have been referred to by various terms, including **sensory processing disorder** (SPD), **sensory integration disorder,** and **sensory modulation disorder** (Polenick and Flora 2012, 30). Sensory issues have been included in the most recent edition of the American Psychiatric Association's diagnostic manual specific to autism, but SPD as a diagnosis on its own was rejected. There is no doubt that sensory abnormalities exist, but the underlying pathway is poorly understood. For this reason, most treatments do not have a lot of research to back them, and some are even controversial.

The current treatment of choice for sensory issues is known as **sensory integration therapy** (SIT), which is used mainly in children. SIT has been practiced for over 40 years (Polenick and Flora 2012, 33). The premise of SIT is that providing certain sensory experiences will cause brain pathways to adapt and normalize. Hypothetically, this will lead to an improvement in daily functioning.

Sensory therapy equipment is often utilized, including swings, ball pits, pressure vests, body pods, and therapy brushes (Polenick and Flora 2012, 31). So little Johnny shows up for his therapy appointment and gets to play with some super cool, sensation-rich equipment. What could be better than that? Practitioners believe this type of sensory stimulation helps to fulfill the sensory "needs" of a child (also referred to as a **sensory diet**). Ninety percent of occupational therapists who work in school settings use SIT (28).

SIT: Does it work?

Now, the bad news. SIT is an expensive choice, often costing $100 or more per hour (Polenick and Flora 2012, 29). Likewise, there is very little evidence to support its central premise (28) that sensory experiences alter the way sensory information is processed. Thus, many consider SIT a pseudoscience. It is not supported by the American Academy of Pediatrics, and the National Autism Center's National Standards Report has classified SIT as "unestablished" (28).

Though it seems like a good idea, is SIT really rewiring brain connections to change a person's sensory preferences? Probably not. Researchers (Lang et al. 2012, 1004–1018) reviewed 25 studies on the use of sensory integration therapy for autism spectrum disorders. Only three of those 25 studies showed effectiveness for SIT—and all three had serious methodological flaws, while eight of the studies showed mixed results and 14 found no benefit at all.

After 40 years of use, "There is presently no objective, scientific evidence to suggest that SIT is more effective than alternative treatments or even no treatment at all" (Polenick and Flora 2012, 32). Other experts state that the continued practice and promotion of these interventions is a disservice to clients (Rodger, Ashburner, and Hinder 2012, 338). Researchers concluded: "Given the lack of scientific evidence, it would seem alarming how often SIT is reported delivered to individuals with ASD (Autistic Spectrum Disorder) by agencies that are mandated to use evidence-based interventions" (Lang et al. 2012, 1016).

This is not to say that SIT has no benefit for children with sensory issues. Many parents report excellent experiences using SIT. I have no personal experience and thus no dog in the fight. It has occurred to me, however, that it may well be the human-to-human care and investment of energy that provides improvement. Children with unique sensory requirements are likely experiencing grace through their SIT sessions. Their needs are being attended to in a nonjudgmental way. This is a mini-example of grace, and grace is healing. Still, grace does not cost $100 per hour. Extra playtime that includes positive sensory experiences can only enhance a child's life—and can be accomplished for free.

There's (Not Really) a Pill For That

Current medication treatment options for sensory problems are limited. Aripiprazole (trade name **Abilify**) has recently been approved by the United States Food and Drug Administration (FDA) as a treatment for irritability in autistic children (ages 6 to 17; Fung et al. 2012, 245). It works by altering the serotonin and dopamine systems. One study found that it effectively improved sensory abnormalities in autistic children and adolescents (246). It improved attention, distractibility, processing of sounds and visual input, emotional responses, and activity levels (247). Unfortunately, none of these improvements translated into a reduction in disruptive behaviors. This paints a picture of lingering discomfort. Medicine seems to be just missing the target.

Recently, a diuretic named bumetanide was studied for the treatment of sensory issues in autism (Grandgeorge et al. 2014). Here's the summary:

Lingering discomfort

> A ten year old girl with an autism spectrum disorder was given bumetanide for three months. The medication reduced her sensory discomfort significantly. She noted no side effects, and reported her life had improved quite a bit.

Still, it is important to note that this is a single case study of bumetanide. Many more, longer lasting studies are needed. It offers hope that a medication may prove useful for sensory sensitivities in the future. Right now, however, the best approach is probably more organic...read on.

I Love Cats! But Dogs Are Useful Too

Another compelling avenue of sensory modulation is the use of animal-assisted activities (Ostrove, Egan, and Higgins 2012, 343-344). Dogs are particularly suited for therapeutic interventions, as they tend to represent unconditional love (which, ultimately, reflects the nature of God). The use of dogs in therapy has been shown to lower blood pressure, decrease stress, increase social interaction, and provide a sense of wellness. Animal-assisted therapy provides multiple pleasurable sensory opportunities, through touch, sight, sound, and pressure.

It stands to reason that happy sensory experiences might offset some of the emotional and physical costs of uncomfortable sensory experiences. Matching the pet owner's sensory preferences with the pet's characteristics would be paramount. A wise person (me) once said: *Don't get a howler monkey if you don't like howls.* I'm going to make that saying into a t-shirt.

It seems pretty obvious that acquiring a pet is not going to substantially alter sensory problems. It is a drop in the bucket—a nice, fuzzy, sweet drop in the bucket, nonetheless. We low-pleasure people need as many clean, positive experiences as possible.

Why Exposure Might Not Be the Ticket

One therapy technique highly tied to the sensory experience is exposure therapy. Exposure therapy attempts to gradually expose the client to levels of anxiety that can be mastered. So, let's say I'm afraid of spiders. Exposure therapy might have me begin by imagining a spider (eek!). Eventually, we would work up to actually (ee-gads) handling a spider. I would hold it until I felt my body getting used to the sensation, adjusting, and beginning to calm down. Theoretically, this would begin the process of wiring my body to relax around spiders.

Let's play with spiders!

Because individuals with sensory issues have trouble habituating (i.e., physically adjusting) to some stimuli, exposure may not be the best choice of treatment. I might hold onto that spider for an hour and feel terrified the whole dang time. The same can be said about social exposures. Some exposure to feared situations absolutely will create improvement. We all have a certain ability to get used to things. But it is impossible to rewire social discomfort completely out of a person's DNA. I will, most likely, always be running in high gear when in a social situation. No matter how much I face my fears.

Previous research has established that exposure therapy is, indeed, not as effective compared to cognitive behavioral therapy in treating SAD (Ougrin 2011). Exposure to painful stimuli, without the neurological ability to cope effectively, may represent a daunting challenge in SAD. To be worth the extreme discomfort they bring, sensory-based exposures would need to have a high payoff. That payoff (a cure for social anxiety) has not been proven yet.

Engel-Yeger and Dunn (2011, 215) recommend a cognitive approach to working on sensory issues that includes being aware of unique sensory quirks and working around them. It is also extremely helpful to have reasonable self-expectations (explored in the next section).

Unfortunately, cognitive therapies most likely will not alter actual sensory intensity (unless via God's intervention). What we believe about sensory issues can make a difference, however. I personally believe sensory problems are the equivalent to giving out vegetable snacks at Halloween (and I don't even celebrate Halloween). Who wants that? But I also believe my sensory system is dead to God and so how I cope or fail to cope is no longer all that important.

EXPECTATIONS AND CONFESSION: 2 GOLDEN KEYS

Reasonable expectations seem a whole lot more, well, reasonable. If an individual is highly sensitive to strong scents, working in a perfume factory is NOT REASONABLE. You probably already knew that, though. I, on the other hand, just thought God would take away my sensory issues if I had enough faith. I asked. More than three times. He said no. I'm good with that. For now. But when I get to Heaven, I am going to float around in a haze of sensory pleasantness. I cannot wait. Nothing about Heaven will be hostile.

Highly sensitive people should not only have reasonable expectations of themselves but of others as well. When others trigger painful reactions, they nearly always do so innocently. For instance, a child who is chewing loudly does not do so with the malicious intent of irritating others. The temptation for the audio-sensitive person (at least, for me) is to display irritation or dismay. A better coping tactic is confession. In fact, I believe frequent confession is the only genuine way to walk through this life.

When most people think of confession, they imagine a dimly lit cubicle and a priest. But the whole basis of confession is simply an admission of being a flawed human being. Listen to this: "Therefore confess your sins to each other and pray for each other so that you may be healed. The prayer of a righteous person is powerful and effective" (James 5:16, NIV). Confession is saying, one human to another, "I've got a few...shall we say... deficiencies." And there is no shame in that.

Confession is totally counterintuitive. At least, it is for me. My first instinct is to hide the things I struggle with. I am in a constant pursuit of fake normality. Confession is throwing my struggles right out there for others to see. I am both terrified and relieved that nothing is hidden from God. But I control a lot of what I hide from other people. In a strange and beautiful mystery, admitting our struggles to each other makes us *teammates* in this journey of life. And there is healing in that. Healing comes through unity and by pleading with God on each other's behalf.

Confession about sensory issues is really just gentle honesty. Maybe something like this, "Johnny, you are doing absolutely nothing wrong. But, for some reason, your crunching is hurting my brain. Do you think you could try to chew more quietly?" We assign blame accurately and place it on our own flesh (dysfunctional physical response) rather than on the innocent behavior of others. A confessing attitude ensures nobody gets hurt from my problem.

Confession about our weaknesses (whether sensory, social, or other) is so useful and healthy, it is central to peaceful living. But it's not easy! It's wise to choose *assertiveness* about confessing our weaknesses. I don't know about you, but assertiveness does NOT come naturally to me.

Here's an example. Say you are on a big family vacation. You spend a lot of time with your relatives and are feeling pretty burned out.

Everybody will be staying up late tonight to play that eternal game of Monopoly. Everybody wants you to participate, to enjoy bonding and laughter and making memories.

> *"I find that I am unable to help myself. Can you extend me grace anyway?"*

You love these people, but you are just worn out. You need a little time to yourself. You can feel your candle burning down, down, flickering... You can sense what everybody else wants from you. But you can also sense that you are approaching a meltdown. So you say, boldly, "I am just worn-out, guys. I know you'll have lots of fun, but I think I'll retire early tonight. Maybe read my book, surf the 'net. I just need a little alone time to recharge. See you in the morning!"

Some of your family members might think you're weird. Most probably won't think twice. In any event, your assertive confession of weakness was the right and brave thing to do. God knows who you are and doesn't expect you to be anybody else. And after a little alone time, you can resume socializing again. Welcome to the Human Club. No judgments from God. Thank you, Jesus.

SEEKING OUT SHADE

If you leave a human out in the desert sun for seven days straight, that human will get burnt to a crisp (especially a very pasty human like myself). Humans were not designed for that type of harsh physical exposure. We are actually quite fragile beings. We require a "goodness of fit" between ourselves and our environments.

In the same way, some people are not meant to endure a harsh onslaught of sensory input with no "shade." It's just going to cause a lot of wear and tear on the body. With sensory problems, this means modifying school, work, home, and church environments to make them easier for thriving in. The goal is thriving, not just surviving. That's what finding a "goodness of fit" is all about.

Many sensitive people believe they should just be able to get over their quirks. I mean, nobody has ever *died* because the church service was too loud. Isn't sensory sensitivity kind of, well, a first-world problem? Yes it is. And yet, there it is. And since it's there, let's make it go away as much as possible. That's just another extension of God's nonjudgmental, unconditional love, towards ourselves and others.

So just how do we find shade in this overly sunny, sensory world? First, we become aware of our sensory profiles (take one of the sensory tests at the end of this chapter). Once we are clear about what wears us out and what doesn't, we move on to **sensory matchmaking.** We put a little bit of effort into making our work, home, and church environments a good fit for us. For example, for those sensitive to noise and light, a nighttime work shift might be a good fit. Others might find that a quiet, serious church is a better sensory fit than a more charismatic one. If they are both teaching biblical grace, what difference does it make?

Online school options are often an excellent fit for individuals with sensory issues because the learning environment (home!) is more controlled and predictable. God has granted us a tremendous amount of freedom. We are free to choose environments that are less hostile (in a sensory way) than others. We may be leading a life that looks nothing like anyone else's, but that is what freedom is all about! That freedom is a blessing—a gift of God's love and grace.

> **Sensory Matchmaking.**
> *No romance.*
> *Lots of relief.*

One promising technique is the use of a specially designed space known as a "comfort room" (Ostrove, Egan, and Higgins 2012, 337-339). A comfort room contains special lighting, items with varying textures, scented air fresheners, etc., all of which can be adjusted to fit the individual's sensory preferences. The premise is that a highly sensitive person can retreat to the room, adjust the sensory environment, and achieve physical calm. Imagine going to church and sinking into a comfort room with other people just like you, people who need space and quiet. That's the stuff dreams, and teams, are made of.

These rooms could be available in the workplace, at church, or in the home. For believers, a comfort room would be ideal for reminding us of our human need to rest. Even our senses need rest. It kind of makes sense that the Christian church would be a place that offers rest. Ultimately, the genuine source of rest (rest from rules, from works, from human frailty) is found in the grace of God. And the grace of God (Jesus) is what the church is built on.

A Few Notes on Church

Let's not forget even for a moment what church really is. It is *us*. It is believers. It is not an official group or denomination or building. God wants us to continually gather together in order to remind one another of the good news of grace. The exact details of what that gathering looks like can vary tremendously. Any joining of Christian lives, whether amongst family, friends, via the Internet, etc., is a functioning church. When you are a part of a system that displays various spiritual gifts, you are experiencing church. There really are no rules about that.

In a traditional church service, two things will encourage and welcome introverted, shy, or socially anxious people. First, make the meet-and-greet portion of the service *optional*. The announcement from the pulpit could sound like this, "For those of you who love to visit, you have the option to take five minutes now to greet your neighbor! We're one big family here. And if you are on the shyer side, feel free to remain seated.

Everyone is valued and welcome here."

Second, during times of corporate prayer, give attendees the option to *pray alone* or with one another. The goal, after all, is communication with God. By inserting freedom into these traditional church activities, we encourage authentic living and *rest*. And that is so beautiful amongst believers.

Another Good Test for Quirkiness

Do you want to know if you officially belong to my "The World is Hostile" group? One recently developed tool to measure sensory sensitivity is the **Sensory Perception Quotient** (SPQ; Tavassoli, Hoekstra, and Baron-Cohen 2014). The SPQ comes in a short, 35-item version, as well as a longer 92-item version. Both versions have been shown to accurately measure sensory perceptions related to vision, hearing, touch, smell, and taste. This questionnaire can be used for adults with or without autism. Unfortunately, this one is only administered by a professional, so you would have to make an office appointment. However, a free, online, informal assessment for adults is available at http://www.sensory-processing-disorder.com/adult-SPD-checklist.html.

Sensorystreet.com provides a free, downloadable, informal parent assessment for school-aged children at http://www.sensorystreet.com/uploads/StudentSPD.pdf. The Sensory Processing Disorder Foundation provides an informal checklist for infancy through adulthood at http://spdfoundation.net/symptoms.html. Psychcentral.com also has an assessment tool for autistic spectrum disorders in adults, available at http://psychcentral.com/quizzes/autism.htm.

For children younger than two years old, professionals recommend the Infant/Toddler Sensory Profile (Eels et al. 2012, 324). This assessment is designed for parents to complete on behalf of their infants. It is administered by a trained professional, such as a teacher, counselor, etc.

Conclusion

Sensory sensitivities are invisible, unpleasant, and can be quite debilitating. They probably play an important role in social anxiety. God feels tremendous compassion towards those who experience the world in a frequently painful and challenging way. If any human ever suffered via His senses, it was Jesus. His senses of sight, sound, touch, hearing, inner body, and even smell (remember the vinegar?) were assaulted by enemies. He understands completely what it feels like to be human, and to suffer.

For individuals who are over-responsive to sensory stimuli, a regular retreat for the purpose of rest and rejuvenation is a really good idea. Jesus modeled the concept of retreat in Luke 5:15-16: "However, the report went around concerning Him all the more; and great multitudes came together to hear, and to be healed by Him of their infirmities. So He Himself often withdrew into the wilderness and prayed" (NKJV). Notice that even when the demands of ministry were great, Jesus chose to withdraw.

Even more importantly, Jesus is our rest. The perfect human being, with the very nature of God, gives us credit for His own actions. As a result, we no longer have to work to be perfect. Our sensory coping or lack of coping becomes a non-issue in our being loved and accepted by God.

* * *

Reflection

1. Do you identify with any of the sensory sensitivities discussed in this chapter?

2. If so, how have you learned to cope?

3. Which sensory sensitivities seem the most debilitating for Christian life?

4. Does your church cater to low or high sensory thresholds? (i.e., is the sound system loud? Are the songs quick tempo? Are the lights always bright?)

5. For those with sensory issues, did reading this chapter increase your self-focus on sensory input? Did that increase your discomfort?

6. Have you ever attempted to address your sensory needs in a sinful way (e.g., yelling at someone to be quiet, complaining angrily about the loud music)?

7. What are loving, gentle ways to have your sensory needs met?

8. Is it wrong to seek refuge or rest from sensory overload?

6

PILLS, PLANTS, & FOOD

Concerning this thing I pleaded with the Lord three times that it might depart from me. And He said to me, "My grace is sufficient for you, for My strength is made perfect in weakness."
2 Corinthians 12: 8, 9a, NKJV

I will never forget the day I gave in and popped that first pill. Sertraline, trade name: Zoloft. A small, oval, blue tablet. I was crying as I swallowed it, thinking: *I am an utter failure.* Then I crawled into bed, a limp rag of despair, and quickly escaped into sleep.

For months, I had fought the idea that I was depressed. But exhaustion and hopelessness pressed more heavily on me every day. No amount of prayer, begging, pleading, or Bible reading had lightened the burden. I was sinking, sinking, until I was so wretched I was forced to reach out to the one thing I was sure would *not* help: medication. I finally waved the white flag. I gave up.

Fast-forward two weeks. Through the numbing fog, something stirred. Life slowly reawakened in me. I know where life comes from—God—and not from a little blue pill. But I also know that God can use anything for our benefit.

For some reason, God's plan for me did not include a miraculous spiritual healing from depression. Why? Looking back now, I most likely would have become prideful (that wretched corpse of mine!). My attitude would surely have been, "Depressed? Just pray for healing! It worked for me. What are you doing wrong?" And, oh, how much harm I would have done to others with that approach!

No, God wanted me to get well acquainted with the failings of my human flesh. He intended for me to come face to face with my own helplessness. In God's scenario, spiritual failure is actually winning. Giving up, and being broken, was the first step in recognizing that I am not God. Only God is God. Ultimately, that is a tremendous relief.

SOMETHING TO FIGHT ABOUT IN CHURCH

Ten percent of the American population is currently prescribed an antidepressant medication (Rabin 2013). From 1988 to 1994, antidepressant use went up an astonishing 400% (Ross 2012). According to a report from the Centers for Disease Control and Prevention, over 10,000 American toddlers (aged 2 to 3 years) are being medicated for attention disorders (Schwarz 2014).

> **10% of Americans use antidepressant medication**

Let's think about that for just a moment. Ten thousand little toddlers, naughtily exploring their terrible twos. Medicated.

These statistics are alarming. Somehow, our expectations of the behavior and attention span of toddlers has become terribly unrealistic. Medication can clearly be overused, and the meaning of "normal" too rigidly defined.

The tremendous appeal of antidepressant medication is the hope of a lightened burden with little to no self-effort. Depression is a terrible, terrible burden (I know this firsthand, and did I mention that it's pretty terrible?). We are tired. We have come to the place where no amount of self-effort does any good. *We are helpless to fight it.* We desperately need an outside force to rescue us. And when we are in the pit of despair, we welcome just about anything that promises to help us. Medication serves as that gravely needed outside force. It is, in some ways, a mini-example of grace. It promises hope independent from effort. And very often it lives up to its promises.

Deeper beneath that, of course, lurks a longing for an Outside Force—an Outside Force that is even more meaningful and powerful than our physical mood experience. It is a longing for Grace with a capital G—the real thing. The popularity of antidepressant medication represents the worldwide longing for the unconditional love and rescue of Christ. When we come across someone who has been desperate enough to try medication, we very often come face to face with someone aware of his own weakness and humanity. That's a beautiful thing, in my book (and this is my book). It makes for a great jumping-off platform for discovering the grace of God.

Meds= help from an outside source

While the world has become highly medicated, the Christian church has swung in the opposite direction. The church knows that grace is the real answer and often blatantly or subtly discourages medications for mental suffering. We form rigid rules about psychotropic medications. Perhaps we are afraid individuals will find wellness outside of Christ and thus never realize their need for Him?

That is an astonishingly small view of God's love. He draws whom He will, and I doubt He thinks twice about whether medication is in the mix or not. True wellness can be found in no other place than God's grace (I believe I just wrote a song lyric!).

Maybe medication is overused, given too much glory, or even made a substitute for divine help. But it can also be under-used. In an overly rigid, religious worldview, depression and anxiety are considered the result of spiritual failure—personal sin. I cannot really argue with that. I know all about spiritual failure. But I need to know what comes after that—is it condemnation or hope?

Big newsflash: I am totally a sinner. Smaller newsflash: You are, too. Do my sinful thoughts and behaviors contribute to social anxiety? I would have to say yes. Yes, indeed, in ways I will probably never understand or see. When it comes to the blind leading the blind, I may be one of the blindest.

What comes after that realization is *critical*. If my social anxiety is the result of my own sin (embedded in every facet of my body and soul, passed down from the Garden of Eden), then how am I rescued? The religious might say, "By obeying rules. Extended prayers. Bible reading. Fellowship. Confession." Tried that. And I don't mean to shock or offend, but in my experience those things just made everything worse. Yes, the harder I tried to overcome, the poorer state I found myself in.

The real rescue plan is Jesus. What does that mean? Too many things to fit in one paragraph, but here's one big one: Jesus is the proof of just how unconditionally God loves us. Consider that—*loved without conditions*. We cannot provoke His disapproval by taking medication. It's just not all that important. Because we are loved. No matter what. Proof? Jesus. God Himself, on a cross.

Here's a thought: What if taking medication (or a supplement, or whatever) is actually an act of faith? An admission of humility and physical weakness and a surrendering before an almighty God? Giving up on our own willpower and strength and resting in God's righteousness is the same as being righteous!

> But to him who does not work but believes on Him who justifies the ungodly, his faith is accounted for righteousness, just as David also describes the blessedness of the man to whom God imputes righteousness apart from works... (Romans 4:5-6, NKJV).

When it comes to medication, whatever goes into our body (the corpse) is just going to perk up our body (the corpse). And God is no longer concerned with the corpse. It sounds like Paul agrees:

> Therefore, if you died with Christ from the basic principles of the world, why, as though living in the world, do you subject yourselves to regulations— "Do not touch, do not taste, do not handle," which all concern things which perish with the using—according to the commandments and doctrines of men? These things indeed have an appearance of wisdom in self-imposed religion, false humility, and neglect of the body, but are of no value against the indulgence of the flesh (Colossians 2:20-23, NKJV).

In other words, none of it is a big deal. Medication is not a cure-all for all mental and physical suffering. It is not a savior. But neither does it hinder our standing with God. It can be used cautiously, with a realistic view of usefulness and possible side effects. The church is beginning to humbly realize that believers are susceptible to the same physical symptoms of anxiety, depression, etc., as the rest of the world. Realistically, medication just might help us feel better (kind of like having a good meal when we are really hungry or taking an aspirin when we have a headache). It will not save us eternally or produce holiness. The end.

People say: no, no, no!
God says: ♥ ♥ ♥

Let's not forget we are talking about our corpse here. The old us. The *dead* us.

Serotonin Sauce

I alluded earlier to the sauce that keeps everything up in that ol' brain circus running smoothly: **neurotransmitters.** The most popular medications prescribed for social anxiety are based on one particular neurotransmitter: serotonin. Most experts believe that serotonin is the problem in many mood disorders. Either there's not enough available, or too much, or... we don't really know. Most traditional antidepressant medications work by increasing the availability of serotonin. The idea is that more oil in the engine makes for a happier, more efficient engine. Basically, a selective serotonin re-uptake inhibitor (SSRI) blocks the re-absorption of used serotonin. As a result, more serotonin remains floating around, ready to go at a moment's notice.

Serotonin is clearly tied to mood. Chronic use of caffeine (guilty!) or stimulants depletes levels of serotonin. Serotonin levels are also directly tied to carbohydrate cravings (guilty again: sour cream and onion chips!), sleep patterns, pain sensations, sexuality, impulsivity, and digestion (several studies cited in Marazziti et al. 2014).

SEROTONIN:
too much or too little?

Less serotonin is tied to lower mood and attention and memory problems (Jenkins et al. 2016, 8). Research is beginning to show a strong connection between the gut (digestion) and serotonin production. Likewise, serotonin production tends to go up with sunlight, which explains why depression is more prevalent in low-light seasons (Young 2007, 395).

Serotonin is also directly linked to social anxiety. One study manipulated serotonin levels in socially anxious people before a public speaking task (Van Veen et al. 2009, 1590-94). When serotonin availability was lowered, participant's anxiety levels increased. A lot.

Such studies have led researchers to theorize that low serotonin is likely the problem in social anxiety. A more recent study puts a different spin on that serotonin theory (Frick et al. 2015). It found that people with social anxiety displayed *higher* than normal levels of serotonin transporter synthesis and availability. In other words, socially anxious people tend to use up serotonin at a quicker rate than normal. But strangely, they even seem to have more available than normal. If this is true, why would SSRIs (which further increase serotonin availability) successfully treat social anxiety (which they do)?

Researchers believe the explanation is that socially anxious people have a generally overactive serotonin system (Frick et al. 2015). They have lots of serotonin, lots of serotonin being used, and lots of used serotonin floating around. Perhaps SSRIs help normalize the entire serotonin system? Researcher Furmark states, "We may have to rethink how anxiety-reducing drugs, like serotonin reuptake inhibitors (SSRIs), actually exert their beneficial effects in anxiety disordered patients" (Scutti 2015). Time to rethink, indeed.

Although SSRIs help with some of the symptoms of social anxiety, nobody is really sure how or why. For one thing, they may be affecting other neurotransmitters indirectly. Or they may be reorganizing serotonin use so it is more efficient.

I cannot help but think that this hyper-serotonin idea might explain some of my love affair with autumn. Serotonin production goes down during low-sun seasons. I become joyful with relief as summer begins to fade. Surely some of my relief is explained by more moderate temperatures and less sensory stimulation. And some is tied to the rest from physical labor that the end of summer on a farm brings. I think, though, that at the very root of it autumn represents grace to me. I have always said that if Jesus was a season, He would be autumn. Rest from work, an overflowing of God's love apart from effort. That's got to help with the whole serotonin conundrum as well.

Currently six SSRIs are available in the U.S.: paroxetine, fluvoxamine, sertraline, fluoxetine, escitalopram, and citalopram (Stahl et al. 2013, 578). See Table 4 for a summary of benefits and risks when treating SAD. I have also included a serotonin and norepinephrine re-uptake inhibitor (SNRI) in the list. It is the only SNRI approved for use in SAD.

SOCIAL ANXIETY DISORDER MEDICATIONS

Medication (Trade Name)	Dosage (mg/d)	Notes	Evidence	Side Effects/ Info
Citalopram (Celexa and Cipramil) SSRI	20-40	Did not show greater effect than placebo.[1] Rated in top 5 for antidepressant effectiveness, low side effects and cost.[2]	2 studies[1]	Rare but dangerous heart rhythm problems at high doses.[2]
Escitalopram (Lexapro & Cipralex) SSRI	5-20	Good at preventing relapse, reduces SAD symptoms.[3] Rated in top 5 for antidepressant effectiveness, low side effects and cost.[2]	3 studies[3]	Approved for adolescents.[2]
Fluoxetine (Prozac) SSRI	10-60	Appears to be less effective than other SSRIs.[3] Improvements in energy, motivation, and concentration.[4] Rated in top 5 for antidepressant effectiveness, side effects, and cost.[2]	3 studies[1]	Approved for children and adolescents.[2]

Medication (Trade Name)	Dosage (mg/d)	Notes	Evidence	Side Effects/Info
Fluvoxamine (Luvox) extended release SSRI	100-300	"reduction of SAD symptoms, including anxiety, sensitivity to rejection and hostility, and for increase in overall functioning." Approved specifically for SAD.[3]	5 studies[1]	Higher rates of side effects compared to other SSRIs.[2]
Paroxetine (Paxil, Pexeva) SSRI	10-60	Well studied, superior to placebo for SAD symptoms. Approved specifically for SAD.[3]	12 studies[1]	Higher rates of sexual side effects[5], sweating.[2]
Sertraline (Zoloft, Lustral) SSRI	50-200	Approved specifically for SAD. Good at preventing relapse.[3] Improvements in energy, motivation, and concentration.[4] Rated in top five for antidepressant effectiveness, side effects, and cost.[2]	5 studies[3]	Higher rates of diarrhea.[5]
Venlafaxine (Effexor ER) SNRI	75-225	Moderately effective for SAD. The only SNRI approved for treating SAD.[3]	5 studies[3]	May increase heart rate/blood pressure. Higher rates of nausea and vomiting.[2]

Table 4. Sources:
1. Mayo-Wilson et al. 2014, 368–376 (a meta-analysis of medications for social anxiety)
2. Consumer Reports Best Buy Drugs™, 2013 (a consumer guide to using antidepressants for depression)
3. Blanco et al. 2012, 235-249 (a thorough review of studies regarding medications for social anxiety)
4. Stahl et al. 2013, 578-585 (a report on the use of serotonergic drugs for several mood disorders)
5. Gartlehner et al. 2011, 772-785 (a review of antidepressant use in depression only)

A recent meta-analysis found that antidepressant medication was more effective than psychotherapy for SAD (at least during the initial phase of treatment; Blanco et al. 2012, 241). About one half of patients treated with SSRIs or SNRIs for anxiety will experience lasting improvement (Pollack, Otto, et al. 2008, 467–476). Still, this leaves half of us with continued disability, indicating that although targeting serotonin is helpful it is not that ever-elusive magic bullet.

All the major players in the Fear Circus (amygdala, hippocampus, and prefrontal cortex) are dense in serotonin receptors (several studies cited in Bauer 2015, 68). SSRIs have been shown to help down-regulate (calm) the amygdala (Furmark 2009, 10). SSRIs and SRNIs alter serotonin availability, which leads to a cascade of changes in other brain chemicals. So, we are kind of taking a shot in the dark here by targeting serotonin in SAD, and yet it works about half the time.

SSRIs show similar effectiveness to other medications, but they have a very low potential for abuse, are safer, and have fewer side effects. For these reasons, they are the first choice of medications (Farach et al. 2012, 834). More than 20 research trials have shown that SSRIs are moderately effective in treating social anxiety (Davis, Smits and Hofmann 2014, 7). I will take moderately effective over being a couch potato any day of the week.

> *One half will improve with medication*

THE DREADED SIDE EFFECTS

This is how the first few days went as I first started taking sertraline. I slept. I slept some more. And a little bit more. I slept when I should have been awake. But I didn't care. And I slept some more.

As a stay-at-home mom with a husband who works from home, I could do that. Not everybody can. If at all possible, I recommend a time of rest when starting a new mood medication. If not, give yourself a lot of leeway during the early days. This will be an Extra-Grace-Required season. No pressure, no expectations. Eventually, my body adjusted and fatigue was no longer an issue.

Researchers state that there may be an initial increase in anxiety and suicidal thoughts, which fade over time (Bauer 2015, 72). I do remember driving my car and thinking how easy it would be for me to just go off the road. I believe that was on day two of treatment. Somehow I knew, even then, that it was my brain chemicals talking (and the enemy) and not my heart. Have you ever noticed that Satan is emboldened to attack when our physical state is weak? Whatever you do, do not listen to Satan or your brain chemicals in the early days of treatment. With continued treatment, side effects generally fade and improvement occurs.

Somewhere between 30% and 50% of patients will experience side effects, which are usually mild and fade over time (Farach et al. 2012, 834). These may include nausea, diarrhea, headache, insomnia, jitteriness, or restlessness. One-third to one-half of patients will also experience sexual side effects, such as a lowered interest in sex and difficulty achieving orgasm. Drowsiness, fatigue, and discomfort occurred in about 3.6% in one large analysis (Kostev et al. 2014, 4). Drowsiness is the most common reason why people stop taking an SSRI/SNRI in the first 30 days of treatment (5).

With any decisions likely to affect our state of mind, it is always a good idea to weigh benefits and drawbacks. For drawbacks, I found I was frequently thirsty while taking sertraline. Benefits: I was also able to get off the couch and rejoin life. Therefore, I could get as many drinks of water as I wanted, whenever I wanted. And that was good enough for me.

Another con to consider is the difficulty in stopping antidepressant treatment. There is a risk of anxiety-type symptoms if SSRI medication is stopped suddenly, known as **discontinuation syndrome.** It is a real thing, and it's pretty uncomfortable. I have experienced it several times. Hello, irritability! Nice to meet you, weird brain zings! Patients wishing to stop SSRI use should taper off gradually. Really, really gradually. This will be another Extra-Grace-Required season.

> **discontinuatin syndrome:** brain zap city

The decision to start antidepressant treatment must be taken seriously, because it is not always easy to get off. That's the truth. If and when you decide to stop, please enlist the help of your doctor in making it as painless as possible. And tell somebody what you are going through! (Uh, email me?)

How Long Does It Take to Work?

It usually takes approximately 2 to 6 weeks for the patient to feel a "partial" response to SSRI/SNRI treatment (Farach et al. 2012, 834). A partial response indicates at least a 25% improvement in symptoms. It is possible to feel full benefits at 4 to 6 weeks. Dosage amount does not coincide with symptom relief. In other words, taking a higher dose will not necessarily work better.

An optimal trial of medications should continue beyond 8 weeks (Blanco et al. 2012, 243). In one study, nearly 28% of patients who seemed to be non-responders at 8 weeks responded by week 12 (as cited in Blanco et al. 2012, 243). If there is still no response after 12 weeks, a new type of medication (or an add-on medication) can be tried. Current evidence points to a duration of SSRI/SNRI treatment that extends at least 3 to 6 months after a positive response has occurred. Individuals who stopped medication treatment earlier than this ran a higher risk of relapse. Taking medication is kind of a long-term commitment. Maybe not life-long, but often up to 6 months.

> **2 to 6 weeks** to relief

The GABA Theory

Gamma-aminobutyric acid (GABA) is a neurotransmitter vital in controlling anxiety (Luscher, Shen, and Sahir 2011). Its entire job is to regulate all other neurotransmitters. It is the chiller outer of brain chemicals (i.e., it is inhibitory).

Researchers believe that current antidepressant medications may be indirectly targeting GABA (rather than simply serotonin, norepinephrine, or dopamine). This has ushered in an exciting, and possibly life-changing, new GABA theory for mood disorders.

Reduced GABA function has been found in patients who experience panic attacks, generalized anxiety disorder, and post-traumatic stress disorder (as cited in Luscher, Shen, and Sahir 2011). Chronic stress reduces the function of GABA. Lowered levels of GABA have been found specifically in individuals with SAD (Pollack, Jensen and et al. 2008, 741).

Alcohol has been shown to stimulate GABA release in the amygdala and hippocampus (Kelm, Criswell and Breese 2011, 113–123). This may partially explain why nearly one-third of SAD individuals are also dependent on alcohol (Schneier et al. 2009, 979). Self-medication with alcohol may be a desperate attempt to increase GABA activity in the brain. Obviously, the personal, social, and spiritual costs of alcoholism far outweigh any increases in GABA activity. Several drugs currently prescribed to reduce alcohol cravings (naltrexone, prazosin, baclofen, etc.) work by influencing the GABA system (Kelm, Criswell and Breese 2011).

1/3 of people with SAD are alcohol dependent

Electroconvulsive therapy (ECT) has been used for many decades in the treatment of depression. Yes, that stuff you saw in old horror movies, where they hooked the poor patient up and administered jolts of electricity, really happened. Strangely, it often helped, thanks to GABA.

ECT shoots an electric current through the brain, which causes a brief seizure in the patient. Treatment providers have long known that electroconvulsive therapy works (though with substantial side effects), but didn't know exactly how. Research seems to indicate that the electric current is increasing brain levels of GABA (Sanacora et al. 2003, 478).

GABA supplements are sold without a prescription, but there is no evidence these supplements can cross the blood brain barrier in significant amounts. Thus, supplemental forms of GABA available over the counter at drug stores are probably useless.

Picamilon, a supplement that includes both GABA and niacin, is able to cross the blood brain barrier. No clinical studies have been done (to my knowledge) on the effects of Picamilon on anxiety levels. It has been on the market for over 40 years, which leads me to believe it is probably not the magical cure for social anxiety. *Before trying any new supplement, please check with your doctor.*

Fun Fact

While researching this chapter I decided to give a few supplements a trial run. I'm a pretty skeptical customer, as I hate to be parted from my money. But, I did find that Picamilon (which targets GABA) provided the tiniest bit of relief from the physical symptoms of anxiety. It has both a stimulating and relaxing effect. Will it change your life? Um, no. Would I sacrifice buying a coffee from Dutch Bros. in order to purchase Picamilon? No.

BENZODIAZEPINES: THE DEADLY GABA TRAP

When first-line treatments for anxiety do not prove effective (or tolerable), benzodiazepines are sometimes prescribed. Benzodiazepines have been used to treat anxiety disorders for about 50 years (Farb and Ratner 2014, 1003). This class of medication works by targeting GABA receptors.

Clonazepam and bromazepam, in particular, have shown some effectiveness for social anxiety symptoms (Blanco et al. 2012, 238-239). No benzodiazepines will improve comorbid conditions, however, such as major depressive disorder. Even more importantly, benzodiazepines have a high risk for abuse and can have a significant number of side effects (Blanco et al. 2012). These include marked drowsiness, along with speech, movement, and thinking impairments. There is often rebound anxiety upon stopping the medication (Farach et al. 2012, 835). For the elderly, there is an association between benzodiazepine use and falls (Blanco et al. 2012, 239). For these reasons, benzodiazepines are not recommended for long-term management of chronic anxiety disorders.

A tragic number of people have used benzodiazepines to relieve anxiety and then become trapped in a cycle of addiction. It only takes weeks for an addiction to build (Ekern 2013). Benzodiazepines are frequently abused recreationally and precipitate many hospital emergency

Warning: high risk of addiction

room visits.

Future work will likely explore a benzodiazepine-type of medication that targets GABA more directly, while eliminating addictive qualities and negative side effects. Two more selective GABA targeting medications, imidazenil and SL651498, have received some study in animals and have shown promise in reducing anxiety-related vigilance with fewer side effects and a lowered risk of addiction or tolerance (Farb and Ratner 2014, 1019). Time will tell if drug companies can tip the balance towards effectiveness and away from possible addiction. We do not want to trade one problem for another.

BDNF Hypothesis

Brain Derived Neurotrophic Factor (BDNF) is a modulator of the levels of neurotransmitters such as serotonin, norepinephrine, and dopamine (as cited in Turck and Frizzo 2015). It is highly tied to GABA and linked to neurogenesis. **Neurogenesis** is a big word for new cell formation and survival...or a healthy, happy, regenerating brain. Levels of BDNF seem linked to how resilient a person is in response to stressful life events (Duclot and Kabbaj 2015, 21–31). Some people are able to recover quickly, while others run a greater risk of developing depression.

Neurogenesis: growing a new brain

Researchers think that low levels of BDNF are likely tied to depression (Duclot and Kabbaj 2015). Reduced levels of BDNF have been found in the blood of depressed and anxious patients (Suliman, Hemmings, and Seedat 2013). Treatment with an antidepressant normalized BDNF levels (Duclot and Kabbaj 2015).

Testing BDNF levels in the blood can actually predict whether an antidepressant is likely to help or not (Kurita et al. 2012, 5). This kind of testing is not widely available yet, but just imagine the time and suffering it could save.

Some have speculated that the antidepressant effects of exercise are related to the role of BDNF. Even a single session of exercise raises BDNF levels (Szuhany, Bugatti, and Otto 2015, 60). Researchers have concluded that each session of exercise is akin to a "dose" of BDNF, and regular exercise enhances the dosage (61). It is possible, however, that exercise will not enhance mood if BDNF levels are not high enough to start with (Duman et al. 2008, 148–158). Likewise, a recent review of therapeutic measures for social anxiety did not find exercise to be effective (Mayo-Wilson et al. 2014, 372).

I am an official card-carrying member of the Couch Potato Club. I get all their free mailings. Nevertheless, I have, from time to time, taken up jogging. I run slowly, like a fragile old woman. And it helps. Though, admittedly, I would never have the energy for jogging during a state of clinical depression. But when I do have the energy, I notice that my brain is just slightly happier. Not as happy as grace makes it, but every iota counts.

GLUTAMATE GLUE

Glutamate is a neurotransmitter similar to GABA but with opposing actions. While GABA works to chill brain messages, glutamate puts the pedal to the metal. *Let's get going!* it screams.

It appears that a critical balance between GABA and glutamate is needed for well-being. When GABA is too low, and glutamate is too high, there is a tendency towards anxiety disorders. Researcher Roger Lane states, "A growing body of evidence implicates glutamate system dysregulation as a key pathophysiological feature of mood disorders, thereby making the glutamate system a prime target for innovative treatments" (2014).

Here's the English translation of what was just said: "Glutamate is probably important!"

The role of glutamate in anxiety-related disorders is becoming more and more obvious (Riaza Bermudo-Soriano et al. 2012, 753). Higher levels of glutamate have been found in social anxiety disorder (Pollack, Jensen and et al. 2008, 741). This has led to increased interest in the use of glutamate-altering medications as a treatment for mood disorders.

Glutamate: "Let's get this anxiety party started!"

Ketamine is a drug that limits glutamate activity and is used in anesthesia (Lapidus, Soleimani, and Murrough 2013, 1103). It has also shown antidepressant benefits. At the time of this writing, it is being studied specifically for the treatment of social anxiety.

Unfortunately, ketamine (aka "special K") is also a drug commonly abused (Schifano et al. 2015, 17). When misused, ketamine causes a host of serious health problems, including bladder, breathing, and cardiac issues, psychosis, numbness, and muscle weakness.

Other medications that target glutamate are being investigated for mood disorders. It will likely be some time before researchers are able to establish a glutamate-focused drug that is safe, non-addictive or non-abusable, and useful for social anxiety. I will be waiting by the phone.

OXYTOCIN: TRICKED INTO LOVING MY BABIES

When my babies were born, it would have been nice if I had remained cool, competent, and level-headed. Instead, I became an adoring love-obsessed fan. I can (partially) blame oxytocin for that. The rest of the blame is placed squarely on my husband, who makes the most amazingly adorable babies.

Oxytocin is a neuropeptide produced in the hypothalamus (Gorka et al. 2014, 278–286). Oxytocin is frequently referred to as the "trust" hormone because it plays a vital role in relationship formation, bonding, social attachment, stress management, and anxiety. Researchers believe oxytocin reduces anxiety and increases a sense of reward from social interactions (Bethlehem et al. 2014). Pregnancy is a time during which oxytocin levels are high and is often a protective time for some anxiety disorders (Marazziti et al. 2014). Oxytocin is also integral in newborn/mother bonding.

Oxytocin is tied to amygdala activity, and its administration has been shown to normalize amygdala over-reactivity in SAD (Labuschagne et al. 2010, 2408). Another study found that oxytocin helped enhance connections between the amygdala and the area of the brain responsible for social activity and emotional regulation (the rostral medial frontal cortex; Sripada et al. 2012, 257). Remember how I said the brain has connection problems in SAD—that there's a lot of shouting going on and nobody listening? Yeah, oxytocin seems to directly affect that.

A recent study explored brain connections in healthy versus SAD participants (Gorka et al. 2014). After administering oxytocin to SAD participants, connection differences disappeared. Imagine the scientists staring at their little brain images. Suddenly, they could not decide which one is the "normal" brain and which one is the SAD brain. That is a very encouraging finding!

-Which one's normal?
-Uh, I dunno
-Bill, did you label these correctly?

Strangely, oxytocin given to healthy individuals actually creates the opposite effect—a reduced connection between the amygdala and insula. Now who's the normal one, buddy?

A review of oxytocin studies prior to 2014 revealed that oxytocin seems to activate the areas of the human brain responsible for social reward (including the insula; Wigton et al. 2015, E18). This leads researchers to believe it may be an effective treatment for social anxiety. It just might make "people-time" feel a little more fun. Several studies have already established the usefulness of oxytocin, with very few side effects, in the treatment of autism, schizophrenia, depression, and general anxiety (several studies cited in Wigton et al. 2015).

Here is how oxytocin treatment might work. Awkward Julie takes a snort of oxytocin nasal spray just before church coffee hour. (This would happen somewhere private, because I never snort in public.) Within a few minutes it would take effect, reducing fear and increasing a sense of pleasure from social interactions. Oxytocin would be the oil to "grease" social interactions, making them more bearable and successful. I would flit from church lady to church lady, leaving a trail of smiles and laughter in my wake. I would be home napping long before it wore off. #dreamlife.

The most frequently studied dosage has been 24 IU (international unit; Wigton et al. 2015, E4). Oxytocin drops and nasal spray are currently available without a prescription at roughly $2.50 per dose. Researchers warn, however: "OT is not a generic wonder drug that promotes positive feelings, behaviors and relationships independent of context, personality and personal history" (Bakermans-Kranenburg and van Ijzendoorn 2013). Dang...because that's exactly what I was hoping for.

Researchers do not recommend self-medication with oxytocin because the long-term effects are still unknown (Azar 2011). Its possible chronic use may even decrease social behavior or build a tolerance to the hormone. I know you are tempted to go on Amazon.com right now and buy some. But, what if once you started using it you built a tolerance to it and then NEVER wanted to be with people, EVER? That could happen. That is why future studies will attempt to discern concrete benefits, best dosage, and optimum frequency of use. Put down that mouse and step away from Amazon.com.

THE COSMIC FUTURE

Pherin Pharmaceuticals is investigating a neuroactive steroid nasal spray named Aloradine NS (or PH94B) for the treatment of social anxiety.[1] Aloradine NS has completed an initial phase III clinical trial (at the time of this writing). Phase III includes administration of the drug to large groups of people to confirm its safety, side effects, and usefulness. After phase III is completed, if approved the drug goes into marketing and becomes available to the general public. Phase III generally takes about 3 years, with an additional 1 to 2 years for a New Drug Application to be approved. It is possible we could see Aloradine NS become available for use in 2019.

Aloradine NS
Coming Soon
(maybe)

One completed study has already shown that a single dose of Aloradine intranasal spray dropped distress levels in socially anxious women (Liebowitz et al. 2014, 675–682). Out of 34 participants, 75.6% reported an improvement in anxiety after a single dose. The nasal spray was administered just before a public speaking task and was effective within 15 minutes. No side effects were reported. While the sample size (34 participants) was very small, the appeal of a single-dose nasal spray is high. It would only be used when needed, which limits the cost and side effects and enhances convenience.

CHRISTIANS LOVE A NATURAL PRODUCT

When it comes to food, I naturally prefer highly processed chemical bombs. But, hey, I have never been a cool kid. Most cool kids like foods

---

[1] Read more at http://www.pherin.com/programs.html

and supplements to be as au naturel as possible. Christians generally like to put high-quality substances in their bodies, substances as close to God's original creation as possible. This makes alternative medicines a nice fit.

Alternative medicines (including nutritional supplements and herbal treatments) have a wide appeal not just for Christians but just about anybody suffering from SAD. First, no trip to the doctor or prescription is needed (thus avoiding a stressful contact with an authority figure). Also, because natural products are available online and fairly affordable, the consumer has a measure of control over his or her own treatment. Finally, public opinion holds that "natural products" have fewer side effects and are safer than traditional medications. Unfortunately, that's just not always the case.

There are a number of facts to consider before investing time and money into alternative products. There is a large deficit in quality control measures over alternative, plant-based medicine preparations (Gelfuso et al. 2013, 8). In other words, the exact dosage of the active ingredient in a nutrient or herb may vary from company to company, from container to container, and even from pill to pill. Let's say the first dose makes you a social butterfly? But the next time, your dose is accidentally quadrupled, and you become a flying tree made out of social butterflies? Although the phytotherapy (plant-based medicine) industry is working to address this issue, the problem has not yet been fully resolved.

Natural may not mean quality

Another large concern regarding plant-based remedies is a lack of known effectiveness. Many people will rate natural products (particularly in online reviews) as being highly effective in treating their ailment. A certain amount of reported success, however, must be attributed to the placebo effect. I once tricked my husband into thinking that sugar-free ice cream was regular ice cream. He totally loved it until he saw the label. That is not exactly the definition of the placebo effect, but it does illustrate the power of the mind.

An average of 30% of people experience a perceived benefit from a "fake" treatment (such as a "sugar pill").[2] This is why clinical studies are of such importance. Most clinical studies incorporate the placebo effect as a part of their research, isolating the true beneficial action of the treatment being tested. Good scientists know their stuff.

Finally, the largest concern regarding natural products is the possibility of side effects or toxicity (Gelfuso et al. 2013, 12). Many alternative medicines have been used in cultures for centuries, thereby lending a reputation of safety. Certain active plant ingredients, however, can be deadly when mixed with modern-day medications. Likewise, alternative medicines

---

2 Brown, Walter. 2006. " Understanding and Using the Placebo Effect ." Psychiatric Times. Available at http://www.psychiatrictimes.com/articles/understanding-and-using-placebo-effect

do have the potential to cause troubling, and dangerous, side effects. The decision to use a supplement or alternative product must not be taken lightly.

I reviewed nearly 100 different plant and nutritional approaches for the treatment of social anxiety. It nearly fried my brain, albeit in a very natural, organic way. While several treatments had some evidence for effectiveness in treating general anxiety, there is almost no research directly on their use in treating social anxiety. I have included only the most widely studied in the chart below.

The clinical studies seem to show that some of these products may help with very mild anxiety. None will provide a social anxiety cure (unless God miraculously permits it!). In light of the clinical evidence, I would advise you to exercise great caution before purchasing or using any of these products. Again, it is also wise to get a medical doctor's opinion before trying anything new.

PLANT-BASED SUPPLEMENTS FOR ANXIETY

Name	Dose	Use	Effectiveness	Evidence	Possible Side Effects
Kava Kava *Piper methysticum* (plant extract)	Up to 400 mg per day[1]	For general anxiety[1]	Mixed results on effectiveness[2]	11 studies[1]	Interacts with alcohol, anticonvulsants, and antipsychotics.[2] Possible liver toxicity, drowsiness, weight loss, hypertension.[3]
Passionflower *Passiflora incarnata L.* (plant extract)	500-700 mg[4]	For general anxiety and pre-surgery anxiety[1]	As effective as benzodiazepine for general anxiety in one study[1]	2 studies[2]	Drowsiness, sedation, tachycardia, allergies,[3] nausea, vomiting. May interact with sedatives, blood thinners, and antidepressants.[2]

Name	Dose	Use	Effectiveness	Evidence	Possible Side Effects
Lemon Balm *Melissa officinalis* (plant extract) Cyracos®	300-600 mg per day[1]	For mild to moderate anxiety and insomnia[1]	Possible effectiveness[1]	4 studies[1]	Delirium, excitability, hyperactivity, talkativeness[3]
Valerian *Valeriana officinalis* (plant extract)	750 mg per day[1]	Obsessive compulsive disorder, general anxiety,[1] insomnia[2]	No strong, conclusive evidence[1]	4 studies[1]	Skin rashes, difficulty breathing, hepatoxicity.[3] Indigestion, headache, palpitations, dizziness. Interacts with alcohol, sedatives & antihistamines[2]
St. John's Wort *Hipericum perforatum* (plant extract)	600-1800 mg per day[4]	Anxiety, obsessive compulsive disorder[1]	No strong evidence for use in anxiety.[1] Not recommended.	5 studies[1]	Dry mouth, dizziness, sensitivity to sunlight, fatigue, caution in pregnancy[3]
Common Lavender *Lavandula angustifolia* (essential oil)	varies	Anxiety[1]	Some promise shown given orally or as aromatherapy[1]	4 studies[1]	Constipation, dermatitis, respiratory depression, headache, nausea, vomiting[3]

Name	Dose	Use	Effectiveness	Evidence	Possible Side Effects
Rain of Gold *Malphigiaceae Galphimia glauca* (plant extract)	620 mg per day[4]	Generalized anxiety disorder[1]	Some evidence[1]	5 studies[4]	Drowsiness, dizziness[3]
Roseroot *Rhodiola Rosea*	340 mg per day[4]	Fatigue, depression, anxiety[4]	Limited data[4]	1 study[4]	Blood thinning, increased blood pressure[5]

Table 5. Sources

1. Gelfuso et al. 2013
2. Parashar et al. 2012
3. Thakur and Rana 2013
4. Sarris, Mcintyre, and Camfield 2013
5. http://www.herbwisdom.com/herb-rhodiola.html

CANNABIDIOL: LIKE MARY JANE, BUT NOT REALLY

One additional plant based extract, cannabidiol, is receiving a lot of research attention for treating various disorders. Cannibidiol comes from the cannabis sativa plant (i.e., marijuana). Marijuana use is widely known to cause anxiety and other adverse side effects (Crippa et al. 2010, 121–130). This is likely due to the mind-altering constituent in cannabis, tetrahydrocannabinol (THC). Low doses of THC seem to alleviate anxiety, while high doses actually cause anxiety. As marijuana use increases, anxiety worsens.

Cannabidiol is a completely different compound from THC found within the marijuana plant. It has no hallucinogenic effects, so it produces no "high." Cannabidiol has been shown to decrease anxiety in animal and human studies (Crippa et al. 2010). It has been tested directly in relation to social anxiety. Researchers administered gel capsules containing 400 mg pure (99%) cannabidiol dissolved in corn oil. Blood levels of cannabidiol peak 1 to 2 hours after the dose. Using brain-imaging techniques, researchers found decreased anxiety markers. Participants also rated their anxiety as lower after the dose of cannabidiol. (For some reason I imagine participants being all like, "Dude...this stuff's good. Got any Cheetos?")

Guaranteed to not get you high.

Another more recent study found that individuals with SAD who received 600 mg of cannabidiol before a public speaking task had less anxiety and experienced less discomfort (Bergamaschi et al. 2011, 1219–1226). The evidence for cannabidiol is fascinating, considering it only took a single dose to affect anxiety levels. Future research, on larger groups, is needed to firmly establish the effectiveness and safety of this plant extract.

A commercial preparation of cannabidiol, Epidiolex, is currently being tested in childhood epilepsy.[3] Nonprescription preparations (i.e., hemp oil) are available online but at a fraction of the cannabidiol potencies tested in the clinical trials mentioned above. It is likely that nearly all commonly available cannabidiol preparations are far too weak to exert any noticeable effect. They are also incredibly expensive, up to $249 per 1 oz. bottle. I will be waiting until Black Friday (in the year 2025) to place an order.

Foods

Finally, how about using foods to boost brain chemicals? I mean, we are already going to be eating, so we might as well eat stuff that helps the old corpse out.

How do we like our food? Rotten, that's how!

A recent study discovered that individuals with social anxiety who ate more fermented foods tended to have fewer symptoms (Hilimire, DeVylder, and Forestell 2015, 205). Researchers believe it is the probiotic function of fermented foods that is doing the trick.

We all have beneficial living organisms in our digestive system called probiotics. Research is beginning to demonstrate a clear link between the gut (digestive system) and brain chemicals, particularly when it comes to anxiety. Fermented foods just happen to be high in probiotics. See the table below for a list of probiotic-rich fermented foods. Each meal, you will not only be feeding yourself but millions of your own personal creatures as well. When you open the fridge door, you should definitely shout "Time to feed the herd!"

Gut Friendly Foods

Food	Type
Sauerkraut	Fermented cabbage
Yogurt	Fermented milk; look for "live and active cultures" on label
Kefir	Fermented milk drink

---

3 Read more at http://www.gwpharm.com/Epidiolex.aspx

Food	Type
Kombucha	Fermented green or black tea drink, often flavored with herbs or fruit.
Kimchi	Fermented spicy cabbage
Dark Chocolate	Contains catechin and epicatechin, which are gobbled up by good gut bacteria
Pickles	Fermented cucumbers
Raw Cheese (unpasteurized, soft, like Gouda)	Fermented milk
Sourdough Bread	Genuine sourdough bread includes a fermented starter

Table 6. Possible social anxiety symptom reducing foods.[4]

There is no physical substance that will change who we are at a very basic, human level. And who we *really* are is not our old corpse. Let's get right to the best part—the New Us.

* * *

---

4 see https://authoritynutrition.com/11-super-healthy-probiotic-foods/ and http://www.thealternative-daily.com/dark-chocolate-gut-final-verdict/

Reflection

___

1. Would you be willing to experience side effects like increased thirst, diminished libido, etc., in order to improve some social anxiety symptoms?

2. Do you have internal rules about the use of antidepressant medication?

3. Have you ever experienced a dramatic health benefit from a medication or natural product?

4. Have you ever felt as though you wasted money on medication or a natural product because of clever advertising or salesmanship?

Section III
A New Creature

The following section is based upon my best understanding of God's plan revealed throughout the Bible. Full disclosure: I am not a theologian or Bible expert. If you are wise (and I am confident you are), you will fact-check everything I say against the scriptures. After all, God is the only Teacher who can be fully trusted.

7

A Brand New Me (and You)

Therefore, if anyone is in Christ,
he is a new creation;
old things have passed away;
behold, all things have become new.
2 Corinthians 5:17 (NKJV)

I was completely healed of my social anxiety. Oh, did I forget to mention that? That's right... gone. Completely gone. I walked amongst mortals with not even a trace of self-consciousness. I was just like Peter striding across the water with eyes fixed on Jesus. It was SO FUN.

This happened during the couple of weeks that I was drunk on a fresh understanding of grace. For whatever reason, the idea that I was unconditionally loved by God, through Jesus...sank in so deep that it **poof** made all my social awkwardness disappear.

Unfortunately, my healing lasted for only one day.

I was grocery shopping at Walmart. I don't mind Walmart because my social anxiety is at about a 4 when surrounded by complete strangers. The worst, though, is if I run into somebody whom I kind of know. There's the awkward moment of either stopping to chat about nothing or trying to hide. My social anxiety shoots up to an 8 or 9, depending on the type of acquaintance I run into.

On this day, it was my Sunday school teacher from when I was 4 years old (Chris Hankins!). I saw her walking up ahead of me. A rush of love and joy and warmth propelled me to her. It was almost as if there was a wind at my back pushing me in her direction. And, for once, it was not against my will. I caught her attention and we had a brief but warm exchange. Lots of smiles involved.

Whoa, this is fun, I thought to myself. *Who am I?*

I then went on to gush at everyone who crossed my path that day. I scattered love like there was no tomorrow without a trace of anxiety or self-occupation. I did not recognize myself. I am surprised Walmart didn't ask me to leave.

Socially anxious people will get what a big deal that is. Instead of being consumed by feelings of nervousness, awkwardness, inner focus, etc.... I felt only love. Like...*easy* love. This must be maybe what "normal" Christians feel like? You normal people are awesome, and I so admire you.

After that day, my grace "high" gradually leveled out. I returned to my same-old self-centered, sweaty self (I am a big fan of alliteration). But God gave me that gift, that little window of perfect healing, to show me what Heaven will be like. To demonstrate what He can do. To remind me that this earth is temporary. Social anxiety is temporary. And also, He gave me a glimpse of the new me. The real me. My full identity.

> **I gushed at everyone who crossed my path**

I had done nothing to achieve this window of no social anxiety. I didn't master a therapeutic technique. I didn't take a magic pill. I didn't drink Kombucha nonstop for 24 days. It just happened, quite unexpectedly. Quite the gift, really.

And though I was really disappointed when I slid back into my old self, I was also enlightened. Now I know what it feels like. And God could turn me back into that unsocially anxious me at any second. In fact, He has promised that someday He will.

In the previous chapters, I talked about matters of our old dead nature, the corpse. The body, medications, etc. If all that stuff is dead to God anyway, what's left? Only a New Us that is completely unrelated to the corpse. What does this New Us look like? Feel like? Can we see it? Can we spot it in others? What is the New Us capable of? What sort of future lies ahead for the New Us?

Adam and Eve were originally "very good" in God's judgment,

yet still merely human. The child in Mary's womb was the first to ever be wholly human and yet wholly divine. This strange hybrid of mere human and divine nature ushered in a brand-new type of creation. God stated many, many times that He was "well pleased" with this combination of human body and His own divine nature.

So we learn what the New Us looks like by focusing on Jesus. He was God transformed into lowly human form. The Bible calls Jesus the exact image of God (Hebrews 1:3). He was everything all of mankind craved to be. He was the first of His kind, destined to be the "firstborn" over many others (Romans 8:29). Jesus (i.e., God) has always existed. Yet, God in a human body was something brand new. He created all things, then allowed Himself to experience life as one of His own created ones. That's like an artist trying out life as a painting for a day. A painting with the mind and heart of the painter. Trippy.

We, through the gift of God, are now also reborn as a strange hybrid creature of mere human/divine nature. We are not gods (please, do not get this twisted and make the mistake of thinking that we have a divine nature of our own). We are given the gift of God's divine nature living permanently in us, via His Spirit. The new created ones (us!) are far superior to the originals (Adam and Eve). It's like Adam and Eve 2.0, except the upgrade is so mind blowing that it rewrites the software with pixie dust and unicorn hairs.

A hybrid creature, *made of earth and spirit*

The first time this New Us is mentioned is in John 17:20-24. Jesus says that those who believed in Him received His glory. That is past tense. As in, we believe...and there is a flash of invisible spirit lightning, and instant glory. The original Greek word for "glory" means dignity, honor, and praise. God looks at us and sees the exact dignity and praiseworthy attributes that He Himself had in human form as Jesus. He sees Himself echoed in us. Wait, what? Even me? Sweaty, narcissistic, awkward me?

OK, so we need to take a minute to actually let that sink in. We. Are. Now. Perfect. In God's eyes, we are just exactly like Jesus. Just exactly like Him, in a human body.

Imagine walking into a church for the first time. The pastor stands at the pulpit and says, "Hey, look at that girl over there. She's new! What's your name? Welcome! Look, everybody, she looks just like Jesus! She's... well, she's perfect! We love everything about you! We hope you never, ever change in any way, because you are an identical twin to Jesus! Oh, we just love you! Everybody, give her a hand!"

If this happened to me, I would blush and turn bright red from all the attention. Then I would sink into my seat. Then I would mentally argue about all the things they didn't know about me. I would sit there feeling like a fraud. And I would never, ever, ever go back to that crazy church again.

But, this is EXACTLY what God is saying. This is why Jesus is such good news. Unparalleled news. It takes all the pressure off. No need to change. No need to hide. God loves us completely because He is love. Jesus proved it. And there are now no more conditions.

There is still one troubling thing. I have *evidence* that I am not perfect. Today, for instance, my husband refused to ever eat frozen vegetables with dinner again (they *were* cooked frozen vegetables). From now on, he stated, he will only eat fresh broccoli salad. Homemade fresh broccoli salad. That involves about 18 ingredients, an hour of chopping, and the frying of bacon. So, naturally, my corpse envisioned a bag of frozen broccoli hitting him in the head.

I am still stuck with this old dead nature, and it does some really nasty stuff. Way worse than throwing frozen broccoli. What about that? Does God want me to keep on doing nasty stuff? Does that not matter? That brings us to the dreaded S-word (no, not salad).

THE S-WORD

I'm talking about S-I-N here. I hate using the word sin, not because it doesn't exist... but because the word has somehow lost its original meaning. Today, we say sin and think: watching R-rated movies, wearing short skirts, homosexuality, swearing, smoking or drinking. That's the Christianese idea of sin.

sin= imperfect love. It's everywhere.

The original Greek word is *hamartanō,* and it means to "miss the mark." And what is the mark? Perfection. Or, even more accurately, perfect love. God is the embodiment of perfect love (1 John 4:16). Whenever we fall short of God's perfect love, we have sinned.

So, technically, perhaps short skirts and smoking are sin because somebody is not being loved or cared for perfectly. But that also means that church gossip, overeating, under-eating, fast driving, hatred, napping, fear, religiosity...are all cases in which someone is quite possibly not being loved perfectly. Sin is so much bigger, more pervasive, and far-reaching than we humans imagine. Sin is everywhere...because everywhere you look you find evidence of imperfect love.

Historically, Christians (as in me...yesterday) have had a very small view of sin. We pick an area in which we easily come close to meeting perfection. Take, for example, listening to music with explicit lyrics. I refuse to do it! And then I feel good because I have rejected sin. It is *sooooo* easy.

But what would perfect love do? Pray for that artist using explicit lyrics...that he would experience the unconditional love of God from his head to his toes. Or maybe try to hear the truths expressed between the curse words in order to understand the artist's heart. How many of us do that? Ah, we have missed the mark, then, haven't we? And we miss the mark approximately 4,598,689 times per day, give or take… In ways we never even see or understand. We are imperfect lovers, the whole lot of us.

OK, so how does the New Us handle sin? Will we keep on sinning even after we are sealed with God's Spirit and are new creations? Yes. And no.

Imperfect lovers, the whole lot of us

Technically, the New Us is perfect. Just like Jesus. We love what He loves. We value what He values. We want what He wants. We are perfect and sin-free in God's eyes.

And then, there's that nasty old corpse. It still wants to be God. It wants to believe it is capable of perfection apart from God and that love is, maybe, not all that important. It wants to look perfect in the eyes of others. It wants to avoid judgment based on appearance, charm, social graces, etc. It shakes and trembles in the presence of possible judgment. It arranges a system of smoke and mirrors to conceal its lowliness. The corpse is strategically non-loving others, and ourselves, all the time.

My corpse sneaks in a remarkable number of unloving acts per day…hour…minute. Any power that I have to defeat sin (and my corpse) comes from God. I know the rules of love; I just cannot obey them. The harder I try to use willpower or self-effort to grow more loving, the more I fail. Love does not work like that. We do not manufacture it. God does. His loves flows in, and then it flows out. And that is all I know.

After my breathtakingly fun social anxiety-free day, I decided to do a test run on the New Me. Just what did I have the power to accomplish now that I understood grace? What kind of control do I have over sin?

Of course, I made my husband my test subject (without his prior knowledge or consent). The next few paragraphs will be quite revealing, so I need my Dad to quit reading right here. Skip ahead 5 or 6 pages (7 to be safe), Dad…because I will be talking about cupcakes and rainbows for a minute—things that clearly don't interest you.

Secret test: sinning against my husband

This was my experiment: I wanted to be the kind of wife who was ready for "romance" at a moment's notice. And by romance, I mean "wrestling." And by "wrestling" I mean…well, you get the picture. The perfect marriage would include a husband who got to wrestle whenever he wanted to. Right, men? I would no longer ever be tired or have a headache or not be in the mood for wrestling. As a gift of perfect love, I would be ready to rumble whenever he desired.

I told him my plan, and he was—right you are—*very* affirmative. And then… I was tired…and oh my goodness…I'm so tired… I mean, I want to, but I don't want to... Wrestling is such a good idea...I know what perfect love looks like... I can't do it... Let's just sleep, OK? Nighty then.

Fail. What? I thought grace would give me the power to overcome my old nature, but my corpse won. I failed at perfect love. I sinned.

And then what happened? Grace abounded.

> "Moreover the law entered that the offense might abound. But where sin abounded, grace abounded much more..." (Romans 5:20, NKJV).

I may not ever get any better at obeying the rules for perfect love. And yet grace is still there. When I am more imperfect, there is more grace. Whether I sin or not, grace is there. I am perfectly loved. I am perfectly accepted. I am not judged. The rules are not the focus anymore. Grace is.

I decided that my husband would just have to take wrestling when he could get it. No more perfect love from me. I gave up on that little rule. Yet, paradoxically, God provided a lot more wrestling sessions when I dropped the rules and just rested in His grace.

So that is how the New Me handles sin. I rest in grace. I set my mind on how fully loved I am by God (not on sin or the absence of sin). The more we focus on rules, performance, perfection, failures, etc., the less success we have. The more we rely on grace alone, the more love we have to share. It's an upside down Kingdom we are living in. I love it!

Here's one story of the work of grace:

> "I come from a long line of alcoholics. In my fifties, I began treating myself to a glass of wine each evening. I was exhausted and lonely, and one tiny moment of pleasure during the day seemed pretty reasonable.
>
> "By the time I turned 55, it had become 3-4 glasses of wine each night. I was very, very good at hiding it. Not a soul knew. I often struggled with guilt. The fact that I kept my drinking a secret was a clear indicator that I was doing something wrong. Sometimes I thought about the day when God says all secrets would be revealed, and I was filled with shame. The shame and guilt would become so intense, I would resolve to quit.
>
> "And so I would. And I would feel good about myself during these times. I would say, 'Look God, this is how much I love you. I'm willing to give up the one bit of pleasure in my life, because you say drunkenness is wrong. We can be close again, because I am doing the right thing, even though it's hard.'
>
> "And then I would see a commercial on TV that included someone

drinking. And I would want a drink so badly. Or I would have a terrible day, or series of days, and think 'Why am I even trying so hard?' Or maybe it would be my birthday, and I would think, 'I deserve it!' And back to secret drinking I would go.

"Then I was presented with the gospel in a way I had never heard before. For the first time, I understood what Jesus meant when He said, 'It is finished.' It meant that my drinking made not one iota of difference in my relationship with God. He loves me because of Jesus. He loves me because He is love. All that guilt and shame I had felt was due to the fact that I had minimized just how all-encompassing the grace of God is.

"So one day, I decided to quit drinking not because it would improve my relationship with God, but just because I wanted a little better health. It just seemed sensible. I didn't have the sensation that I was improving my relationship with God by abstaining. I was already convinced my relationship was solid (drink or no drink), thanks to Jesus.

"The weirdest thing happened. I expected to be tempted by seeing other people drink, or having a bad day, or wanting to celebrate. But I felt nothing… no desire for alcohol at all.

"I marveled to myself. So, this is what grace does. What the law could not do by making me feel shame and guilt, God's love did. I don't know if it always works like this. I just know that for right now, in this period of my life, the confidence I have in God's love for me has erased the desire to drink. Grace did something I could not do on my own, no matter how hard I tried."

Sometimes grace takes away the power of sin. Sometimes it abounds to cover sin. We can not make laws about it, because grace comes from God. He controls it. We just soak it in.

Dueling Identities

Now we are seeing the dueling nature of our identity. One is the real us, perfect in Christ. Yet, we are stuck with the corpse that clings to us with its long, dead fingers. We have received credit for the New Us, but we have not quite received our entire inheritance. The entire inheritance is a New Body that will match the New Us. That is promised for later. For now, the corpse is the temporary vessel housing the New Us. The corpse is no longer comfortable, now that we have a taste of our true identity. The real me is the girl at Walmart so full of love that she didn't even have an ounce of social anxiety. For just a day, the heaviness of my corpse was gone. It was just me, enmeshed with Jesus.

The fake me is the nasty wife who wants to whack my husband upside the head with some very frozen broccoli. I don't like her. I am looking forward to her permanent departure. I am really glad that, in God's eyes, she is nonexistent. Dead.

This is the reason the Bible says we literally groan with desire for the New Body (2 Corinthians 5:1). We are not entirely fulfilled while the corpse clings to us. We wait with great hope (and a certain amount of patience) for the day when all things are finally made perfect. Until then, we tolerate the presence of the corpse. We use it as a house for the New Us. We hate its bad deeds. And we set our minds on the New Us and our promised future. We do not use the corpse, or its actions, as a measure of our closeness to God. We and God are besties, as close as two people can get. Thank you, Jesus.

For now, it is a matter of choosing our identity. But in the future, we will not have to do anything because we will be gifted with a new body that matches our new identity.

Will the REAL ME please stand up?

One of the first questions the new believers in Corinth asked the Apostle Paul was exactly what type of body we could look forward to since the old one is spiritually dead and a new one is coming. Paul described the New Us, when we are complete, as a "spiritual body" (1 Corinthians 15:44). No longer a body like Adam's, formed from dirt, our new body will be created in the image of the resurrected Jesus.

> For our citizenship is in heaven, from which we also eagerly wait for the Savior, the Lord Jesus Christ, who will transform our lowly body that it may be conformed to His glorious body, according to the working by which He is able even to subdue all things to Himself (Philippians 3:20-21, NKJV).

I do not exaggerate when I say I hate my body. It hurts. It disobeys and betrays. It's getting old and wrinkled. It refuses to fit right into clothing, especially jeans. It is very self-absorbed. It lets me down when I need it most. And the more ill-at-ease it is, the more likely I am to behave rottenly. Have you ever noticed that? Lack of sleep, hunger, a pulled muscle—these things turn me into Cruella De Vil. My body really drags me down. Not for long, though.

At a future time, the corpse will be shed. In fact, I think it's going to get cremated (2 Peter 3:10-13). Every iota of my old self will be burned away, and only my new, perfect Jesus nature will remain. Our true selves will finally be fully revealed, recreated in the image of Jesus. "For the earnest expectation of the creation eagerly waits for the revealing of the sons of God" (Romans 8:19, NKJV).

Not only will our true identity be fully revealed, the entire world will also be transformed into something new and spiritual. The mountains, clouds, animals, cities, rivers… All will be recreated in a new and breathtaking way (Revelation 21). We set our hope on this future day. This is our end game.

For now, we live an unusual human/divine nature hybrid type of existence. So we need not become concerned when the sinful desires of the corpse rise up into our awareness once more. This is a good reminder that we are not yet at the finish line, where the corpse will be exchanged with our New Body. We are not the first humans to struggle with this strange hybrid nature. Listen to Paul describe it perfectly:

> For what I am doing, I do not understand. For what I will to do, that I do not practice; but what I hate, that I do. If, then, I do what I will not to do, I agree with the law that it is good. But now, it is no longer I who do it, but sin that dwells in me. For I know that in me (that is, **in my flesh**) nothing good dwells; for to will is present with me, but how to perform what is good I do not find. For the good that I will to do, I do not do; but the evil I will not to do, that I practice. Now if I do what I will not to do, it is no longer I who do it, but sin that dwells in me.
>
> I find then a law, that evil is present with me, the one who wills to do good. For I delight in the law of God according to the inward man. But I see another law in my members, warring against the law of my mind, and bringing me into captivity to the law of sin which is in my members. O wretched man that I am! Who will deliver me from **this body of death**? I thank God — through Jesus Christ our Lord!
>
> So then, with the mind I myself serve the law of God, but with **the flesh** the law of sin (Romans 7:15-25, NKJV, emphasis mine).

We see clearly that our minds and wills are fully committed to the values of God. The New Us is good—*very good*, my friends. But our human flesh, that old corpse, tries to convince us that it is still alive. It is a constant reminder of what our mere human nature possessed (nothing good!). Still, it is simply a charade. The corpse is not alive anymore… Jesus Christ has delivered us from it (Romans 6).

Thankfully, the Apostle Paul has given us instructions on how to handle the phantom corpse that attempts to trip us up. Romans 6:11 says to "reckon yourselves to be dead indeed to sin, but alive to God in Christ Jesus our Lord" (NKJV). The Greek word "reckon" means to conclude, compute, or calculate. Like mathematics, the Christian life is very black and white. In spite of the sins that the old nature manages to sneak in, it is still dead. Dead.

Image 3. 1942 theater poster for the horror movie, "The Corpse Vanishes" (courtesy wikipedia.org, public domain)

We will not receive any punishment from God based on what the old nature does. *What!?!!?* For a girl like me, always afraid of punishment and judgment, that is absolutely astounding! The computation, or mathematical equation, regarding our old nature is this: corpse + Jesus = Jesus. This is the amazing nature of grace.

> # No punishment

So the mathematical equation every Christian must work out is one of identity. This is one math problem I love with all my heart. Are we newly alive and perfect in Christ, or are we just an old dead corpse? Which one is the real us? Choosing our identity is referred to in the New Testament as how we "walk." The Greek word *peripateō* means to tread around or be occupied with. Listen to this verse: "There is therefore now no condemnation to those who are in Christ Jesus, who do not walk according to the flesh, but according to the Spirit" (Romans 8:1, NKJV). As we tread around in our new identity (rejecting the identity of the corpse), we face no condemnation. Get this: When we believe that Jesus is our only claim to perfection, condemnation is *impossible*.

The Bible goes even further so that we might clearly understand our new identity. It blatantly explains who qualifies as walking "in the flesh" (i.e., the old corpse) and who qualifies as walking "in the Spirit." "But you are not in the flesh but in the Spirit, if indeed the Spirit of God dwells in you. Now if anyone does not have the Spirit of Christ, he is not His. And if Christ is in you, the body is dead because of sin, but the Spirit is life because of righteousness" (Romans 8:9-10, NKJV).

Virtually everyone who believes the truth of Jesus is now walking in the Spirit. We must simply make the calculations about our true identity as challenges arise.

> # Walking in the Spirit: *a question of identity.*

I often misunderstood "walking in the Spirit" as performing good deeds and "walking in the flesh" as doing bad things. I read these phrases while still under the heavy burden of performance. From my law-based perspective, I was very rarely walking in the Spirit. Here are just a few of the actions/behaviors the Bible identifies as coming from the old corpse (the human flesh): hatred, jealousy, selfishness, and envy (Galatians 5:19). I can clearly declare myself guilty. A lot. A lot of guilty. When blindsided by these sins, I would wonder in astonishment: "Where did that come from?" Now I know! Those are the works of my old corpse whom I now reject as being the real me. My current response is: "Nice play, corpse, but God has already defeated you."

The New Us has a mind set on the things of perfect love. The corpse rejects the things of love and desires to be a god. Only one is really and truly us. Which shall we choose? Do we really trust that God has killed our old selves? "For you died, and your life is hidden with Christ in God. When Christ who is our life appears, then you also will appear with Him in glory" (Colossians 3:3, NKJV).

What Is On Our To-Do List?

If I don't have the power to make my corpse more loving, more faithful, or more righteous, how am I supposed to live my life? I really cannot go around throwing things at my husband's head. How do I navigate wanting to love others and yet being largely incapable of doing it perfectly?

I have spent the last 10 years of my life homeschooling two amazing kids. And I just totally sucked at it. I LOVED organizing their curriculum, buying their books, making calendars, etc. But when it came time to actually teach...I hated it. And when it came time to teach math...

OK, I have to stop now. I feel rage building up inside me. Math. Again. My lifelong nemesis. So, you get the picture. My children deserved an exciting, engaged, warm, knowledgeable, loving teacher. They got a reluctant, excuse-making, feet-dragging, whining Mrs. Mom instead.

"Math again? Didn't we just do math a couple of years ago? Argh." This was me (not my kids) whining.

Our work: To believe

And yet, in spite of my low humanness, my lack of perfect love... I (in a wishy-washy way) believed God had a plan for our homeschooling. I *kind of* thought it was *possible* He could make up for my failings. And He did because He is awesome like that! My tiny drop of faith was enough. Grace covered my weaknesses.

Believe.

Our work here on earth is to believe in God. To believe in His love for us. To believe that the message of Jesus is enough to truly make me perfect in His eyes. And the more I believe, the more God's power flows through me and out of me. Believing = love.

Believe.

When I am in a scary situation, I have to stop and think: What do I know about my Heavenly Father? I know He is paying attention, holds all power, and loves me fervently. So He sees that I am afraid, and He will handle my circumstances. The more I believe that, the less power fear has over me. Knowing the rule "Thou shalt not fear" does not help me to not be afraid. It just makes me feel guilty for being afraid. But knowing who God is and who I am to Him, now *that* makes all the difference.

Believe.

So when I go into an uncomfortable social situation, I remember this: God loves me. He does not mind one bit if I sweat, stumble, or embarrass myself. He does not rate me based on social awkwardness. He finds me unbearably precious no matter what I do. No matter what my corpse does.

And somehow, mysteriously, that belief takes the edge off of social anxiety.
Believe.
All my efforts go into believing that God is God, He is perfect love, and I am perfectly loved, through Jesus. That is our main work. Our work is not rule-fulfillment. Our work is not work (i.e., doing good works/not doing bad works). Our work is not even perfect love (although that is good stuff). Our work is to believe in the one Perfect Lover of all time.

I could choose to lie around eating Cheetos all day every day. And I might, every now and then. I will still be loved, through Jesus. I will be laying in my bed, licking orange dust off my fingers, believing in how magnificent it is that God loves a slob like me. *Believing* is my work. And I will be hard at work.

BELIEVING SPELLS L-O-V-E

As a lifelong commitment—a life-plan, Cheetos and bed don't sound very fulfilling. The New Me wants more. I would like to *try* loving people. While I am marveling at how loved I am, I become too excited to contain all that love. I want to share. What I believe about God inevitably translates into action (both good and bad).

This is where the corpse comes in quite handy. The Bible describes the human body as a tent for the New Us. Our human body has a tiny amount of strength to do good, urged on by the New Us.

I am a small-boned woman. My weight is in the low 100s. I can almost tie a gum wrapper around my wrist. If you lined me up next to Arnold Schwarzenegger (in his heyday—1980s), you would get a visual of how much strength we have *in our flesh* for loving others. I represent human love; Arnold, Jesus' love. (Totally just made that deep spiritual connection of both Arnold and Jesus saying "I'll be back").

"I'll be back"

The letters to the seven churches in the book of Revelation are a critical commentary on human-love. A lot of so-called "good works" did not receive praise from God. In fact, He may have mentioned something about wanting to vomit...

God had high words, however, for the church of Philadelphia: "I know your works. See, I have set before you an open door, and no one can shut it; for you have a little strength, have kept My word, and have not denied My name" (Revelation 3:8). The open door is grace, and the little strength is what little amount of love we share in the name of Jesus (grace).

We should never overestimate the strength of our flesh to do good deeds. It can exhibit a tiny, tiny amount of love compared to God's love. But something is better than nothing. A little strength, put to good use, is pretty darn precious.

There is another story in the New Testament that underscores the idea that a little is precious in God's eyes. It is Jesus' parable of the Widow's Mite:

And He looked up and saw the rich putting their gifts into the treasury, and He saw also a certain poor widow putting in two mites. So He said, "Truly I say to you that this poor widow has put in more than all; for all these out of their abundance have put in offerings for God, but she out of her poverty put in all the livelihood that she had" (Luke 21:1-4, NKJV).

I've got 50 cents worth of love. Who wants it?

In this parable, a mite refers to a small brass coin worth about 25 cents by today's standards.[1] It was a very, very minuscule amount of money in biblical times. Imagine the collection plate being passed around during church today. The person on the right throws in a $20 bill. The person on the left puts in a check for $50. But you drop in some loose change—a couple of quarters. And it is all you have.

I believe all people have a certain amount of energy (both physical and emotional) to invest in love. Some have a lot. Some have a little. Who am I to judge how much energy another has? Who am I to judge how much God-love spills into and out of another? Nobody, that's who.

TEENY TINY SOCIAL STRENGTH

The concept of "a little is a lot" applies to social interactions as well. Extroverts seem to have a surplus of social energy. Extroverts also replenish social energy via social interactions. God gifted me with a delightful, extroverted husband. He loves golfing with friends, playing card games, and talking on the phone. Not only does he love these activities, he needs them to stay refreshed. These social interactions rejuvenate and re-energize him.

Introverts, on the other hand, have a much lower amount of social energy. Many introverts can happily spend large amounts of time alone. Solitude is a requirement in order for the introvert to thrive. It is rejuvenating and re-energizing. Social interaction is depleting. For the introvert with an already low amount of social energy, social interaction further drains it. Social interaction is quite costly to the introvert and socially anxious.

If social energy is low in introverts, it is quite likely remarkably low for the socially anxious. In fact, social energy may be so low (and social interactions so exhausting) that many individuals with social anxiety will avoid nearly all social interactions. They have nearly no—nil, nada—social energy to spare. Simply going to the post office or answering the phone may drain the last drop for the day.

How does this relate to the widow who gave two mites? She had very little to give, but she gave it all to God. Compared to everyone else, her

---

1 http://www.coinlink.com/News/ancients/the-widows-mite-coin/

Comparison is deadly

gift was pitifully small, almost worthless. Yet Jesus commended her for her gift. In fact, she became our eternal example for biblical giving, giving that God loves. It's not the amount that matters (God doesn't need anything!). It is simply the heart-beauty of the gift. When the socially anxious person gives a tiny drop of social energy away for the purpose of loving God or humans, it is remarkably precious. Thus, one trip to the post office to mail a care package becomes an exceedingly precious gift in God's economy.

Jesus never compared one saint or sinner to another in order to cast judgment. In fact, we are specifically warned not to use comparison. Galatians 6:4 says, "But let each one examine his own work, and then he will have rejoicing in himself alone, and not in another" (NKJV). We need not even pay attention to what someone else can or cannot do. We only do the little we can. Grace covers the rest.

The temptation towards comparison is something that is personally entwined with my own social anxiety. I detest talking on the phone. I will avoid it at nearly all costs. There is something about not being able to see the other person's body language (facial expression, eye movement, etc.) that troubles me. I literally have to save up all my energy for making a phone call. Telephone call avoidance is a common symptom of social anxiety.

I realize concretely that telephone avoidance is my social anxiety in action (the corpse!). It remains unchanged today. It often takes me a day or two to work up the courage to respond to a phone message. Sometimes I fail to respond at all (how rude!). If at all possible, I will utilize an email, text, or social media as a means of response.

Here is the inner conflict (self-judgment) that frequently raged inside of me. Why can't I just answer the darn phone? Everyone else answers the phone. It is self-centered, neurotic, and ridiculous to have to save up all my energy for just a single, rare phone call. It is so stupid!

I weigh the scales (according to the rules) and compare myself to others without social anxiety. In this scenario, I will always come up lacking. And, frankly, I *am* lacking. Compared to the perfect goodness of God, I fall short. But that is no longer my measuring stick.

I frequently know the perfect loving thing to do. Maybe to stop by and drop off a meal for a friend in need. But I don't have the gumption to do it. I would rather send an encouraging email. But that doesn't seem good enough, compared to the perfect thing. So I do nothing. And no love gets moved around.

What if the widow with two mites had spoken to herself like this? What if she had said, "I don't have much to give. Nothing compared to everyone else. Putting in 50 cents is ridiculous!" What if she had shaken her head and refused to drop in the coins, convinced it wasn't enough to do any good anyway?

Sometimes, when I read this parable, I think of it as "the widow's might" instead of mite. For socially anxious individuals, it often takes all of our might to do what others can do without a second thought. Yet, God knows exactly how much strength I have. He designed me, He understands me. He will give me extra strength for the good works He has planned to do through me. And nothing else matters. Again, the pressure is off. (P.S. Forget the meal...send the email! Love is love!)

What God longs to whisper to the socially anxious individual is this: *I made you. I understand you. I gave you a very little amount of strength. But it is plenty for My purposes. I no longer judge you based on what you can and cannot do. When you use that little bit of strength in love, it is precious to Me. I know how costly your giving is. I accept it with joy.*

Expectations... They're Quite Low

We find, then, that God's expectations regarding our behavior are no longer the bar of perfection. He is not comparing us to Himself. That comparison was taken care of through Christ. He expects us to live life as humans, with heavenly values and a weak, rotting corpse in which to pursue them. We are free to live very simple lives, enjoying all manner of things. Some of those things will prove profitable on the Day of Judgment (we will get to that later). The Bible says, "All things are lawful for me, but not all things are helpful; all things are lawful for me, but not all things edify. Let no one seek his own, but each one the other's wellbeing" (1 Corinthians 10:23, NKJV). Some actions are eternally valuable. Most will prove to have been wasted time.

The more we understand how loved we are, the more love we will have to share. Rules cannot regulate love. Only love begets love. And it all originated from Him. "We love Him because He first loved us" (1 John 4:19, NKJV).

This unconditional love is not just for me but for every person on earth. God values every single human being with the same passionate, inexplicable love. Think about the most annoying, rotten person you know (not me! Somebody else!). God loves that person with all of His heart.

This is why sin grieves Him so deeply. It harms His precious ones. For parents, this scenario is simple to understand. No parents want to see their children fight. It is absolutely excruciating when siblings hate, wound, and damage one another. It is particularly heartbreaking when adult siblings do this, tearing the entire family system apart. Long-standing feuds cause bitterness, stress, depression, and permanent injury. God feels pain when we, His children, hurt one another. It breaks His heart. He simply wants us to be joyful, unharmed, together.

God: kids, don't fight!

So we find that God's expectations towards us are extremely low...and what a relief! Sometimes my effort to love someone is so minuscule that it consists of a simple refusal to cause harm. "Love does no harm to a neighbor; therefore love is the fulfillment of the law" (Romans 13:10, NKJV). And that is enough! Imagine a world where we used what little strength we have to not harm one another, no matter what.

Most of us will not be doing "great works" for God. We may not be performing miracles, writing best-selling books, creating ministries, or founding the latest and greatest worship band. Our offerings of love will be so simple, so small. Yet, God will use our micro-love to display His abounding love. His love is a tidal wave, and we are all just tiny breaches in the wall.

So I will rely on His strength alone to give me some physical ability to think and behave according to His values. He values people. He values love. And when I fall short in reflecting His values (which is all the time) I remember my utter acceptance in Christ. This allows me to joyfully move forward, always reminded again, by His Spirit, of His unchanging values.

It is a simple, quiet, restful life. It is described beautifully in 1 Thessalonians 4:10b-12 (NKJV):

> But we urge you, brethren, that you increase more and more (in loving one another); that you also aspire to lead a quiet life, to mind your own business, and to work with your own hands, as we commanded you, that you may walk properly toward those who are outside, and that you may lack nothing.

The expectations are very low, and we are fully equipped to meet the challenge.

Why Judging No Longer Makes Sense

For anyone like me (with a long history of unreasonable self-expectations), judgment is a pretty common problem. If we use harsh judgments against ourselves, we might find ourselves doing the same towards others. We are constantly failing at some of the rules but abiding by others. I vacillate between calling myself a hopeless idiot and a dazzling genius. The rules I do manage to abide by are the ones I am tempted to judge others on.

When we judge others, we are really using the law against them. We are seeing them as a corpse (bound by the law) rather than a new creation (perfected by grace). It is often a whole lot harder to see the Jesus-identity in people. Sometimes I have to squint and stand on one foot while rubbing my tummy—and even then I still only see their nasty corpse.

Only one Judge (but Judge Judy is really good)

But when we judge we are falling back into the law. We are not allowed to use just part of the law. It's all in, or all out. So if I judge someone because he is frequently angry, then I need to judge myself if I am frequently fearful. My corpse vs. your corpse. The ultimate ruling, no matter how I look at it, is this: Everyone is a giant, monstrous, flaming lawbreaker.

"Judge not, that you be not judged. For with what judgment you judge, you will be judged; and with the measure you use, it will be measured back to you" (Matthew 7:1-2, NKJV). I don't know about you, but I am done with the law! Jesus has already fulfilled the law for me and for everyone else who trusts in Him as well. If I am no longer under the law, then I will not put you under the law either.

God says over and over again not to judge the world or other believers. To do so usurps the role of the only true and righteous Judge, God. I believe this is the biggest threat to our churches today. Not sin, but rather using the law to judge one another. Seeing only the corpses, and not the new creations.

Some religious communities have mistakenly taught that we should judge one another righteously, out of "love." Sometimes this judgment is hidden under the "accountability" umbrella. We must always be helping each other to grow more righteous. The bad news is that we are incapable of judging righteously or producing fruit in others. Only God can do that.

Often, we judge others or get angry with them because we want them to change. We see where someone else is weak, and we don't like it. It hurts us. Unfortunately, the anger and judgment of man never produces the result we want. What do we want from them? We want them to love us better. Our judgment certainly does not produce that. "So then, my beloved brethren, let every man be swift to hear, slow to speak, slow to wrath; for the wrath of man does not produce the righteousness of God" (James 1:19, 20, NKJV).

Refusing to judge is not the same as ignoring or relabeling evil. This is what the secular world often attempts to do. The world would like to remove the law altogether. But the law is good because it defines good and evil and reveals our need for Christ. When the world says, "Do not judge" what it really means is "Agree with me that nothing is evil." I cannot do that.

After the law has brought us to Christ, we still recognize evil as evil. Many of the letters in the New Testament teach the proper discernment between good and evil. This discernment is used to protect and love one another, encouraging growth in grace—*not* to qualify or disqualify others or ourselves.

As fully accepted people, we are free to see others as they really are. We will always see both strengths and weaknesses in others, a hybrid of corpse and new creation. When we see both the good and the evil in others we can then choose to extend genuine, unconditional love (grace). We choose to focus on the New Them (what God sees) rather than their corpse (what we usually see).

Still, some heinous acts of evil are so blatant and obvious that even unbelievers could judge them: sexual immorality, greed, worship of a false god, abuse, and blackmail (1 Corinthians 9:5-13). These are the only things we are ever commanded to judge: blatant acts of harm. Far too often, we judge others' motives, heart secrets, or weaknesses. We are surprised (!) when others turn out to be human, flawed. We expect others to be gods.

1 Corinthians 5:9-13 (NKJV) is often used to justify the judging of other believers:

> I wrote to you in my epistle not to keep company with sexually immoral people. Yet I certainly did not mean with the sexually immoral people of this world, or with the covetous, or extortioners, or idolaters, since then you would need to go out of the world. But now I have written to you not to keep company with anyone named a brother, who is sexually immoral, or covetous, or an idolater, or a reviler, or a drunkard, or an extortioner—not even to eat with such a person.
>
> For what have I to do with judging those also who are outside? Do you not judge those who are inside? But those who are outside God judges. Therefore "put away from yourselves the evil person."

Yet, in Paul's very next letter, he urges the church to forgive one of these same sinning believers! He says,

> ...you ought rather to forgive and comfort him, lest perhaps such a one be swallowed up with too much sorrow. Therefore I urge you to reaffirm your love to him. For to this end I also wrote, that I might put you to the test, whether you are obedient in all things. Now whom you forgive anything, I also forgive (2 Corinthians 2:7-10a, NKJV).

The biblical pattern of judging is this: Identify blatant evil (so obvious the world can judge it). Humbly, carefully, call blatant evil what it is—*evil*. Expel blatant evil in order to protect. Once the potential for harm is neutralized, forgive, comfort, reaffirm love, and welcome the believer back into fellowship. The offensiveness of grace is that God continues to love even the most blatantly sinning believers.

Clearly, we humans are quick on the trigger when it comes to using the law against each other. Yet, we do not want the law to

If we judge judgmental people we might be judgmental people

apply to us (at least, not the difficult parts of the law!). Every one of us is guilty of this human streak of narcissism. Ironically, we cannot even judge each other about being too judgmental because we all are judgmental! At least, the old corpse is. Jesus could judge judgmental people (remember the people who were about to stone the adulteress?). We? ... not so much.

After reading the Bible verses about not judging others I often felt guilty for judging others. But I just couldn't help it! *Did you see the way so-n-so was bragging about her cherry pie? If anybody ever deserved to get struck by God-lightning, it's Miss Boasty Pants!* It's all well and good to tell me not to judge (a rule), but it did not help me not to judge! It was only when I stopped expecting God's judgment that I was suddenly set free (mostly) from judging others. We see again that this is how God's Kingdom works. The rule teaches me where I don't measure up. But it does not help me to do better. God's unconditional love (which allowed me to stop judging myself) was what I needed to flourish.

Brant Hansen has written a wonderful book entitled *Unoffendable: How Just One Change Can Make All of Life Better* (2015). In it, he points out the root of many of our conflicts. And (surprise!) it can be traced back to a desire to be like God. Hansen writes,

> God is allowed "anger," yes. And other things, too, that we're not, like, say – for starters – vengeance. That's His, and it makes sense, too, that we're not allowed vengeance. Here's one reason why: We stand as guilty as whoever is the target of our anger. But God? He doesn't.
>
> For that matter, God is allowed to judge too. You're not. We can trust Him with judgment, because He is very different from us. He is perfect. We can trust Him with anger. His character allows this. Ours doesn't.
>
> God loves you and thinks you're special, but no... you're not God (Hansen 2015).

We humans will never know the depths of sorrow, pain, and woundedness in another's heart. We will never be able to accurately quantify the strength someone has or does not have for extending love or doing good. We will never be able to judge the secrets or motives of others because—get this!—*we are not God*. Our discernment of good and evil is commendable but largely shallow and human.

MONEY-BACK GUARANTEE

To strengthen us for this weird hybrid journey, God knew we would need some proof that the New Us is real and not some fairy tale, hopeful myth, or psychological crutch. It's kind of a money-back guarantee. So He supplied proof, and that proof appeared the moment we affirmed that all God has revealed is true. The proof is this: His very own Spirit came to dwell within us.

> In Him you also trusted, after you heard the word of truth, the gospel of your salvation; in whom also, having believed, you were sealed with the Holy Spirit of promise, who is the guarantee of our inheritance until the redemption of the purchased possession, to the praise of His glory (Ephesians 1:13-14, NKJV).

This seal of His promise, the Holy Spirit, can certainly be felt. People describe it as an overwhelming sense of joy, tingling, peace, euphoria. I have compared it to the "high" of being drunk (and so does the Bible in Ephesians 5:18). Yet, the presence of the Holy Spirit goes far beyond whether it is felt or not. God is always present (whether experienced through our senses or not). And God's Spirit is constantly doing things within us, in and out of our awareness. A Bible study on the Holy Spirit will reveal a number of delightful benefits, including comfort, love, direction, teaching, power, hope, prayer, spiritual gifts, and much, much more. Everything good about our new identity is centered in the Holy Spirit, which is always inside us. We cannot accidentally lose it, and it never abandons us. Do you believe the whole Jesus thing is real? If so, then you have the Holy Spirit living in you. The Creator of the Grand Canyon, peacocks, and lightning is forever entwined with your soul. Right now.

You want to know what I got from the Holy Spirit? A sense of humor. Not kidding. Kidding. Not kidding. I became so filled with joy that I became a joke-maker. I have only had a sense of humor for a few months now. It has been a new, and delightful, result of the Holy Spirit inside me. My too-serious self was not expecting that.

One thing that is pretty important to remember is that none of the benefits from the Holy Spirit are ours to control. They are the actions of an outside force (God) graciously existing and working within us. Every good thing flows from God...from love to belief to strength to power. We cannot make ourselves more loving, more fruitful, more free. God's Spirit does this. That is why we do not have to work at changing ourselves. He is shaping us lovingly, using virtually everything in our life (circumstances, joys, sorrows, challenges, successes). We can trust Him to transform us, bringing greater freedom, more joy, and deeper love. And we self-will none of it.

Everything good comes from God

Through grace we all possess these initial benefits of the Holy Spirit. Yet there are even more benefits just around the corner. Romans 8:23 states, "Not only that, but we also who have the first fruits of the Spirit, even we ourselves groan within ourselves, eagerly waiting for the adoption, the redemption of our body." We have the beginning blessings from God's Spirit, and soon we will possess the whole enchilada!

Here is another benefit of the Holy Spirit—He is stronger than social anxiety. I know that is pretty obvious, but here's what I mean: I have the spiritual gift of mercy (I am not boasting...at least I hope not, all credit should go to God's Spirit). Because of that, when an emergency arises and someone is suffering, my desire to love and comfort is so supernaturally strong it cancels out my social anxiety. Because God wants to send His encouragement to another human so strongly, He (temporarily) brushes away my limitations to accomplish His desires. That is fun! Out of my control, but still, fun! I cannot manufacture mercy or brush away my social anxiety. But God can. And He does. So I just go with it.

> Our spiritual gifts often cancel out social anxiety

The Ultimate End Goal: Scared Poopless

I used to have this weird recurring nightmare when I was a child. In it, I was looking up into the sky when, suddenly, a cardboard box came hurtling towards me. I covered my face and head with my arms. *Bam!* Then another box. And another. And soon there were hundreds of cardboard boxes pummeling me. I was a very slender child, and the boxes were literally going to kill me. This is kind of what I have always imagined Judgment Day would be like.

Except, the boxes would be on fire. And they would contain my secrets.

A Day of Judgment should reasonably strike fear deep in the heart of every socially anxious person. It is our worst nightmare. We will be truly known, good and bad. Our secrets will be exposed. Trying to hide will be useless. It is a day when we are judged by the most powerful, accurate Judger around. It is a real day (it's in the Bible) and is guaranteed to happen.

On Judgment Day, we will stand before God with no defenses, utterly naked. I cannot even try to crack any jokes here because Judgment Day has always terrified me. It is the end game for all of us. I always just tried not to think about it too much.

Thankfully, I had made a critical error in my Judgment Day theology. Turns out, this day is not bad news. There is no bad news to follow the good news of grace. If there were, it would not really be that great of news. We need fear no anger from God. We do not know the exact day when judgment will happen. But we do know that our destinies are not to face wrath on that day, but salvation instead (1 Thessalonians 5:1-11).

> No bad news after the good news

On this day God will judge the heart purposes behind every action (1 Corinthians 4:5). Each one's works will be tried by fire, purifying and burning away the unworthy bits (1 Corinthians 3:11-15). Basically, any actions not driven by perfect love will be turned to ashes. Smote.

It seems reasonable to conclude that a lot of our actions will be burned away. The time we spend snacking, watching TV, online shopping…playing Candy Crush. A lot of stuff we do is simply irrelevant to eternal life. Smote. Poof. Ash.

And then there are bad things. I do bad things. You don't need to know about them. You could not pay me enough to tell you. God already knows. Those very, very bad things will also be smote.

But maybe there will be a few good things, right? I will have a few redeeming bits so that I am not a waist-high pile of cigarette ash. Right? Er...even the good things I can think of most likely had some hidden motives. I rarely notice the motives until it's too late. I am pretty sure I never even fully comprehend the selfish motives (unless someone points them out to me). In which case, I mentally do a bad, bad thing to that person. Uh-oh. Smote.

The point is, we will never fully understand the dirtiness of our human nature, at least not until it's revealed on the Day of Judgment. I sometimes think people with depression might actually be seeing their own flawed nature with clearer vision than most. Maybe depression is synonymous with highly accurate self-insight. Those who think they bring anything good to the table of judgment are highly overestimating their human capacity for goodness.

In his book, *One Way Love: Inexhaustible Grace for an Exhausted World,* Tullian Tchividjian describes our good works this way:

> There's a great story of a Lutheran pastor who, on his deathbed, voiced his confidence that he would be received in heaven, because he could not remember having done one truly good work. He meant that he wasn't trusting in any of his works, but rather in Christ alone. That was a man at peace! (2013, p. 134).

All people who accept God's unconditional offer of love through Jesus have their name written inside something called the Book of Life (Revelation 20:12). Got a tiny bit of faith in Jesus, even though you don't understand it all? You're in! My name is written in that book, too. We are kind of famous, in a needy, humbled sort of way. Those in the Book of Life are declared innocent, no matter what! The Book of Life is to Heaven what the Golden Ticket was to Charlie for the Chocolate Factory. Guaranteed admittance. No hidden fees.

Everybody is offered the Golden Ticket of unconditional love through Jesus. *Everybody.* Some

Golden Tickets for everyone!

will reject it. Rejecting the ticket means going toe to toe with God on Judgment Day. It is a game of comparison. If my good deeds are as perfect as God's deeds, I am in. If I fall short, I am out. Oh my goodness, I see cardboard boxes. No, no, no. I want the Golden Ticket. I want Jesus.

The Day of Judgment will be a terrible tragedy for those whose names are not written in the Book of Life. And it is for this reason that God delays the Day of Judgment. "The Lord is not slack concerning His promise, as some count slackness, but is long suffering toward us, not willing that any should perish but that all should come to repentance" (2 Peter 3:9, NKJV). He longs for all of His creation to accept their new identity in Christ. To be declared perfect. And have nothing to fear.

Rewards: More Gifts!

Jesus said a few other things I somehow missed about Judgment Day. "And behold, I am coming quickly, and **My reward is with Me**, to give to every one according to his work. I am the Alpha and the Omega, the Beginning and the End, the First and the Last" (Revelation 22:12, 13, NKJV). And what is our work? "Jesus answered and said to them, 'This is the work of God, that you believe in Him whom He sent'" (John 6:29, NKJV).

I am going to be judged not based on my deeds but on what I believe about Jesus? But He is awesome... He is perfect... He is full of love... He is God's unconditional love act towards me.

Wait... This is easy.

So instead of a fear of punishment on the Day of Judgment, we look forward to rewards for believing in Him! Works driven from the belief that God's approval is complete, through grace, will reap eternal benefits. What we do while in our corpse only serves to reveal what we believe about God.

> So whether we are here in this body or away from this body, our goal is to please him. For we must all stand before Christ to be judged. We will each receive whatever we deserve for the good or evil we have done in this earthly body (2 Corinthians 5:9-10, New Living Translation).

Even *resting* is an act of faith that will be rewarded someday. I have quoted this verse before, but it is just so amazingly wonderful:

> But to him who does not work but believes on Him who justifies the ungodly, his faith is accounted for righteousness.... (Romans 4:5, NKJV).

We have nothing to fear on the Day of Judgment. No fear, only boldness. He is returning not to punish believers for their sins but to rescue those who wait so eagerly for Him (Hebrews 9:28). In fact, we are told to have confidence for this Day of Judgment. We can expect perfect love, not punishment.

> Love has been perfected among us in this: that we may have boldness in the day of judgment; because as He is, so are we in this world. There is no fear in love; but perfect love casts out fear, because fear involves torment. But he who fears has not been made perfect in love. We love Him because He first loved us (1 John 4:17-19, NKJV).

The exact rewards that await us are a mystery to me. The Bible references stuff such as fruit from the Tree of Life, a crown of life, hidden manna, a new name, a position of power/leadership over the nations, a position as pillar in the New City of God, a position sitting with Christ on His throne, etc. Sometimes I imagine Bob Barker saying, ".... and a brand-newwwwww caaaaaarrrrrrr!" I am more than confident that the eternal rewards of God will be more than we deserve or can imagine. I am also quite confident that I will not have accumulated very many rewards. But I have nothing to fear.

That may be the biggest reward imaginable.

* * *

Reflection

1. Do you believe you are perfect in Jesus?

2. Can you identify when your corpse is acting up? Give an example.

3. In what areas do you struggle to believe God's "got your back"? Are you trying to assume more power or control over life than you actually possess?

4. Make a list of unrealistic self-expectations. How does God view each one?

5. Recall a time when you judged someone. What "rule" were you using to judge them by?

6. Do you judge yourself harshly? In what areas?

7. Just for fun, what cool features do you hope your new spiritual body has?

8

THE TOP TWELVE RULES

I am a phony, yes it's true,
I am not good, neither are you.
And so I boast and sing this song,
When I am weak, then I am strong.
                    — *Kathleen J. Miles*

The journey of life tends to progress something like this…

First, we learn what the rules of life are. We begin with no sense of right or wrong. As tiny babies, we are self-centered, angry, loud, messy… But no one holds us accountable for these things. Babies have no rules. Imagine Aunt Jane stating, "Your baby seems to only be concerned with himself. Poor dear: Looks like you got a bad one." Everyone knows that a baby is just a baby, and so the rules are not applied.

The introduction to the rules of life begins the moment a parent first tells the toddler, "No!" As toddlers, we are astonished, angry, and petulant to find that there are limits to our freedom. *We want that stinkin' toy. That toy is ours and ours alone. Sharing is for losers!* Good parents begin training their children not to be self-centered, angry, loud, messy people. Rules are necessary to show what is good. They are not there just to frustrate the child and make his life miserable—but to make it better, to make *us* better.

Most of us mature slowly, getting a better understanding of the rules as we grow. Our families, communities, schools, churches, the justice system, TV, etc., are all places where we incubate in our rule-pods. The kind of rules that go into our rule-pods depend largely on these environments. Family may teach us that fathers are rejecting. School may teach us that blending in is vital. TV may teach us that sexuality is power. Church may teach us that loving each other is ideal...or that faking it is making it. There are good rules and bad rules. Often, we cannot tell the difference. That is what the Bible is for.

When it comes to good rules, we will (without exception) fail at obeying them. *I shouldn't eat that scrumptious parfait because it's not good for me? Pass me two more!* Eventually, most of us will likely break a rule big enough to cause major consequences. We offend someone and sever an important relationship. We become lost in self-pity and slide helplessly into depression. We cheat on our spouse and lose the love of our life. We fail at our job. We become addicted. We are poor parents. Check, check, check. We slide into the Failure Stage of life.

For some, failure leads to blame-shifting. *It's my husband's fault I am so depressed. If my boss wasn't such a #$@@%, I'd still have my job. If my parents had known how to parent, I wouldn't be so messed up.* There is no doubt that other people's rule breaking has a powerful effect on us. Still, we grow up to break rules too. And reap the consequences. Blame-shifting for our rule-breaking only leaves us stalled.

For others, the Failure Stage leads to self-condemnation. *I cannot do anything right. I will never amount to anything. I hate myself, and anything self-destructive is appealing.* Again, we become stuck at Failure.

Neither response—blame-shifting or self-condemnation—is necessary because failure has always been guaranteed. Every single human on the planet will find himself parked squarely in the Failure section eventually (though some of us are really good at hiding it). In fact, God designed the rules for that very reason—to be broken. And when the rules get broken, we tend to break, too.

Failure has always been guaranteed

But, the Failure Stage is when we have the opportunity to truly come alive. We recognize that we want to be rule-followers. We want to be perfect, or at least good, like God. But we are unable to obtain this. We are face to face with the reality that we are not like God. We can either stay stuck in Failure or we can allow God to welcome us into uncharted territory—unconditional love.

The entire lesson of the Garden of Eden is this: We are not like God.

Even after we eat the magic fruit that gives us the ability to see right/wrong as God does, we only become aware of how unlike God we are. And we are ashamed. We need Him. We need Him to love us. Without conditions. Without requirements. Without our own goodness being part of the equation.

Image 4. The circle of life.

To my dear, sweet, fellow failed people, I say: We *need* failure. It is a blessing to become aware of how far from God's nature we are. *That* is what rules do. "Therefore the law was our tutor to bring us to Christ, that we might be justified by faith. But after faith has come, we are no longer under a tutor" (Galatians 3:24-25, NKJV).

So the gift of failure creates a longing for unconditional love. We often look for this highest form of true love from others—spouses, parents, children, friends. We might find moments of grace (unearned love) from these sources, but Grace with a capital G only comes directly from God. Throughout all of history, failure to obey the rules has been the driving force towards God's generous love.

Failure moves right into love. And God's unconditional love actually restores our innocence. Like babies, we still fuss and cry and demand, but babies are babies. Humans are humans. Corpses are corpses. The rules no longer apply. We have overcome the rules through God's gift of grace alone. They were there to teach us that we need grace. And once we have grace, we are innocent once more.

The New Us is free from rules. Any rule-obeying comes only through the power of God living in us. So the New Us agrees that the God-rules are good but no longer measures our worth by them. Instead, we rest in Jesus' obedience.

In social anxiety, the journey begins with an understanding of what rules are at play. Some rules are good rules because they display God's values. They teach us what is wonderful and good. They point to the goodness of Christ and drive us to rest in Him. Other rules are man-made or cultural and often only oppress. Identifying the rules makes grace all the more clear.

THE TOP RULES OF SOCIAL ANXIETY

Rule	Origin
1. Fear of judgment	God/man-made
2. Control the body perfectly	Mostly man-made
3. Love others perfectly	God
4. Hide all flaws	man-made
5. Face all fears	God/man-made
6. Quiet is bad	man-made
7. Shyness is bad	man-made
8. Introversion is bad	man-made
9. Boring is bad	man-made
10. Please God and man	God/man-made
11. Others must come first	God
12. Isolation is bad	Mostly man-made

Table 7. The rules of social anxiety.

The following is one young man's list of judgments regarding his social anxiety. Multiple "mini-rules" branch out from the central rules of SAD, like blood vessels from the heart. This is how insidious social anxiety is. A few rules are not enough. God-rules are not enough. The rules grow and multiply like yeast in dough, creating judgments for even the most innocuous of behaviors.

- I hate being scared to drive my friend home from a get together

because I don't know what to talk about in the car.
- I hate having awkward body movements.
- I hate sounding weird when I talk.
- I hate the dead silence after I kill a conversation.
- I hate my personality.
- I hate that I'm the only one that sucks in my family.
- I hate that I'm too scared to call my friends.
- I hate that all my conversations on the phone are awkward and I never know what to say.
- I hate that my siblings can talk to relatives on the phone and I can't.
- I hate when people call me weird just because I'm quiet.
- I hate that I haven't enjoyed one moment of my life since I was 12 years old.
- I hate that I will never be normal.
- I hate that my whole life is forced.
- I hate that having fun with friends is work for me.
- I hate going to work because I don't know how to joke around with the other guys.
- I hate not being able to talk to girls.
- I hate being boring.
- I hate being scared to say hi to my friend's parents.
- I hate having a blank mind.
- I hate that you have no choice.
- I hate that there is nothing I can do, I will always be this way until I die.
- I hate that my kind of personality is just thrown into the world just to make it different; not to make it better.
- I hate the feeling that I am worthless to my parents and to the world.
- I hate that no one gets it that some things are freaking genetic, and you can't change that crap.
- I hate that everyone has something to say after a movie and I don't.
- I hate when I just absolutely don't feel like talking and it's more painful than nails in my skull just to utter one word.
- I hate that I've lost so many friends because I can't talk to them.
- I hate that I don't know how to handle myself and end up just looking like a dork.
- I hate that I suck at being social.
- I hate that most everything you do requires socializing.
- I hate feeling so awkward being alone with one of my parents or siblings because I don't know what to say.
- I hate being a social outcast, loser, suck-at-life bum, who just fails

at everything.[1]

This young man is dissatisfied with everything from his personality to the way he moves and speaks. He longs to be a completely different person. His rules mean that awkward body movements make him bad, sounding weird makes him bad, being scared to make a phone call makes him bad. Yet, he clearly feels helpless to change these things. He knows the rules. He just doesn't know how to fulfill the rules of being good. It is the age-old dilemma for all of mankind.

THE RULES OF NORMAL

Mental health diagnoses have shot through the roof in modern times. We live in a culture that tends to over-pathologize unusual traits or behaviors. Quirks that were once labeled as odd or eccentric are now identified as disease. People from all eras and cultures have been noticed due to their extreme shyness or unusual withdrawal from society. Historical terms for the socially anxious include: hermits, recluses, shut-ins, and loners. Social anxiety has never been considered ideal, but today it is distinctly *against* the rules of society.

History has a long list of famous people who fit this prototype, as either intensely reclusive, introverted, or shy. Famously shy writers include: Agatha Christie, C. S. Lewis, Emily Bronte, Emily Dickinson, and Harriet Beecher Stowe (Cuncic 2012). Today, famous actors with social anxiety include Donny Osmond, Barbara Streisand, Kim Basinger, and Ricky Williams (Cuncic 2014a). Well-known shy musicians include: Adele, Bob Dylan, Britney Spears, Carly Simon, Carrie Underwood, Cher, David Bowie, and Ella Fitzgerald (Cuncic 2014b). Somehow, these individuals were able to achieve cultural success in spite of being socially different. They managed to skirt the rules of normal by being really good at something. What if you are not really good at something (like me?).

God's rules for normal are completely topsy-turvy. Biblical culture reveals a pattern of...well, let's be frank, freaks...achieving God's purposes. Take, for example, John the Baptist. This guy wore a gnarly (and surely itchy) outfit made of camel's hair. He lived in the wild. He ate only grasshoppers and honey. He could clearly be a contestant on the reality show *Naked and Afraid* (except he was neither naked nor afraid). And yet, God gave him the honor of announcing Jesus' presence on earth.

You know what would happen if John showed up at my church on Sunday? I would sit on the *wayyyyy* other side. I would not make direct eye contact. I would

I'm not normal. Neither are you, freakazoid

---

1 Failguy. 2009. "I hate..." Social Anxiety Support Forum (online post). Accessed October 29, 2014. http://www.socialanxietysupport.com/forum/f35/i-hate-69823/

make sure I was between him and my children. And I might have my husband slip him a $20 to get some new clothes at Ross' Dress for Less.

It could be argued that in God's Kingdom, there really is no normal anymore. Personally, the craziest people have uttered words that God embedded in my soul. I spent a little time counseling prisoners in the local jail. These people were, for the most part, *not* normal. But sometimes they could speak truth, gritty unpleasant genuine truth, in a way no appropriate or normal person ever could. Fitting in or being similar to the majority have *nothing* to do with your usefulness as a child of God.

Now, back to us abnormally socially anxious people. Do these adjectives sound familiar: quiet, shy, introverted, boring, people-pleasing, self-centered, isolated? Some of these adjectives are meant to be insults, while others are neutral. None are considered compliments. But, what do the rules say? Let's examine all the rules. I have already touched briefly on a few, while others are new. None of these rules define us anymore. Especially this first one. The Grand Daddy of all rules.

The first rule, a fear of judgment, is absolutely central to the experience of social anxiety. Most of us think it is a fear of judgment from people. Dig a little deeper, though, and you will expose the real fear: We fear our standing with God. We believe we are fundamentally not good enough. Flawed beyond repair.

> **Rule #1**
>
> THOU SHALT
> FEAR JUDGMENT

Unlovable. Unacceptable, in the deepest, most hidden parts of ourselves. Even as Christians, we are never growing fast enough, spiritually fruitful enough, or loving others perfectly enough. Our bodies, minds, and spirits expect judgment...because it is only fair.

As I have already said, **judgment has been declared eternally through Jesus: Innocent.** Psalm 103:12 says, "As far as the east is from the west, so far has He removed our transgressions from us" (NKJV). We can be real, flawed, slinky slinkers...because He loves us. Just as we are. At this second. If no other truth from these pages sticks, let it be this one. This is it. The Big Kahuna.

If you never prevented, defeated, or squashed another sin in your life...guess what? You are innocent. If you don't grow spiritually one millimeter? Innocent. If you do not manage to love another human being in your entire life? Innocent. If you live the rest of your life without socializing *EVER?* Innocent. A perfect example of this is the thief on the cross (read Luke 23:32-43). He did nothing good. Except believe. And was declared innocent.

This rule is so utterly destroyed, it now lies in a million pieces beneath your feet. Go ahead, give them a kick. Stomp on them. Dance on them. And be forever done with them!

Human judgment, on the other hand, is not so settled. No human is declaring me innocent continually. Humans are far more likely to declare me guilty and, often, rightfully so. *Did I just snub that guy I sort of know from church?* Guilty. *Did I neglect to call my mother again?* Guilty. *Did I just lie to get out of a social event?* Guilty.

Human judgments of guilty are GUARANTEED. Sometimes they are fair and just (according to the laws of good). Sometimes they are not fair at all. In all cases, they are meaningless. The core of all judgment is a comparison of the flawed human to a perfect God. Weighing and measuring me by the law. We do not play that game anymore. I bet this is really starting to sink in now.

I love to watch the *Real Housewives* television series (don't judge me, judgers). I will watch all branches, from the O.C. to Atlanta to Miami to Beverly Hills. It would be hilarious if they would do one for us housewives in Malin, Oregon. And by hilarious, I mean boring and stupid.

The most riveting show of the season is always the reunion show. This is where everyone airs offenses and judgments, and it usually gets ugly. There is invariably a moment when one woman says to another woman, "I would never do that!" What is really being communicated is "That is one rule I would never break!" The human tendency is to claim God-like perfection in one tiny area of life and use it to condemn someone else's lack of God-like perfection. This is what we all do! Yet, none of us can claim personal God-like perfection in all areas of life. So what's the point in illuminating someone else's humanness?

Frankly, we all suffer from a severe case of Human Personality Disorder (HPD). Some of the obvious symptoms of HPD include: overestimation of personal goodness, selfishness, self-righteousness, judgment, etc. If we all have HPD, why be shocked and dismayed when someone's HPD symptoms flare up? It is much more shocking when HPD symptoms disappear for a moment or two.

The cure for HPD is obvious. Grace. Unconditional, unearned love… in spite of our humanness. There is safety in grace because all judgment is neutralized. Judgment of every form, size, flavor…inactivated. Amazing. Grace.

And when someone's judgment hits you square in the face, it hurts. Not gonna lie. But, still, grace wins.

> **Rule #2**
>
> THOU SHALT CONTROL THY BODY

The second rule is the need for perfect control over bodily processes. Uncomfortable trembling, nervousness, blushing, palpitations, and adrenaline flow play a large role in the maintenance of social anxiety. Inexplicably, we humans have formed rules about bodily control. Blushing is bad. Trembling is bad. Sweating is bad. These rules do not even exist from God's perspective. I'm not sure who invented them, but I'd like to kick that guy. (So much for the rule about perfect control over our impulses, too...)

Perfect control of our bodies would indicate God-like abilities. Imagine having the power to prevent the release of adrenaline or cortisol! Nobody can do that! Unfortunately, we have limited control over our bodily functions, and that is perfectly acceptable. I hereby give you permission to blush, sweat, shake, and stutter. In fact, I will probably like you more if you do these things.

Thus, I am making a new rule that all of mankind must follow—a rule that is binding and eternal: Be awkward at all times, in all ways possible.

> **Rule #3**
>
> THOU SHALT LOVE PERFECTLY

The third rule, love others perfectly, is a wonderful rule. It reflects the deeply held values (and the abilities) of our Father. He dreamed it up. He can do it, and do it well. The rest of us...not so much. It is impossible to keep this rule apart from moments of His supernatural intervention. Thus, we will use what little strength we have to honor this value and rest in the grace of God when we fail. Which we will. Over and over again. There is grace for that.

The miracle is that we manage to love anyone, even a little. These moments are moments of the real us, the New Us. I thank God for these.

> **Rule #4**
>
> THOU SHALT HIDE ALL FLAWS

The fourth rule of social anxiety is the importance of hiding our flaws. This is a very, very bad rule (and does *not* come from God). It can be traced all the way back to Adam and Eve, and it would be funny if it was not so tragic.

Remember the first thing Adam and Eve did when they received the ability to judge good and evil? They covered their naughty bits. And hid. In shame. They were, for the first time, able to see how they differed from God. (Apparently, God does not have naughty bits.) And it made them feel pretty rotten.

We have been hiding, and ashamed, ever since.

Our fear is that if our true self is exposed, it will be judged and rejected. The ironic truth is that our lowly human nature is already quite well known by the One who created us. And, better yet, for those who have faith in Christ, it has been replaced by His own lovely nature. It's like a crime scene where the cop keeps waving people on. "Nothing to see here! It's just Jesus! Keep it moving!" Did you already forget that you are perfect, through Jesus, deep in your core?

Also, on Judgment Day all our corpse-y stuff is coming out anyway. Not for purposes of punishment...but for purification and praise. There really is no need to hide. Of course, that may be easier said than done (say I, hiding in my bedroom right now).

Hiding is so integral to social anxiety that the professionals actually have a name for it: safety behaviors (see Chapter 9: Safety Behaviors and PEP). These are all the things we do to conceal real or perceived flaws. Ironically, the more we reveal our humanness to one another, the more deeply we experience well-being. "Therefore confess your sins to each other and pray for each other so that you may be healed" (James 5:16a, NIV).

Transparency is risky, bold, and rewarding. The rule about hiding is a sneaky trickster... Don't fall for it! A complete lie. You can throw this rule right out the window. If you find yourself clinging to it, know that you are loved anyway, by the One who sees all.

Rule #5

THOU SHALT FACE FEARS

We all know that the Bible says over and over again to not fear. Yet, anxiety is fear. Social anxiety is fear. And it is crippling, foul, and exasperating. We know not to fear, so we fear even being afraid.

One major side effect of fear is that it alters our plans. We want to attend a birthday party. Fear persuades us to stay home. Fear leads to avoidance. Most professional counseling strategies work at reducing avoidance behaviors. Avoidance is common for the socially anxious and might include skipping school, becoming house-bound, or refusing opportunities to form relationships. Avoidance can create a vicious cycle in which the person greatly desires relationships but refuses relationships due to fear.

So we feel bad about avoiding the things we know we should face. We feel like failures for acting out of fear. We know the rule: Face your fears and overcome. But we break the rule over and over.

Grace says this rule is no more. When we are certain we are approved of, no matter what we do, we are released from condemnation. We are free to choose which events to engage in and which to avoid. Even if we feel afraid and avoid something, we know that we are still perfectly loved and accepted.

I can assure you that if God has something in mind for you to do... you will be doing it. One week, He may empower me to attend a Bible study. The next four weeks, He may not. *There is no more keeping score because Jesus already won the entire war.*

Are you starting to glimpse the freedom involved in resting in God's goodness? The freedom to stay home when you want…or venture out when you want. God can use *all of it*, and will, for His purposes. Yes, even avoidance.

I am here to tell you that if you spend the weekend trembling in your bed, paralyzed with fear (which I have done), you are still perfect. Beloved. Innocent. If you remain the Cowardly Lion in a world full of Dorothys, you are still treasured. Let's not forget that it is when we are weak that we are strong. And grace abounds all the more.

Can't muster up the courage to face your fears? Well, be loved instead.

The next few rules are perhaps subtler and even more insidious. For this reason, I will address each one in depth.

Rule #6

THOU SHALT NOT BE QUIET

Not all socially anxious people are quiet by nature, but many are, at least in social settings. This quietness is sometimes rooted in an inability to relax and let conversation flow naturally. *I cannot just be myself.* So instead, I stay quiet. I listen. I observe.

But other times, quietness really is just how I am. I have always hated this quality in myself because it comes across as cold, aloof, uninterested. But that perception is not true. I am a watcher rather than a talker. I am even quiet at home where I am comfortable.

Of all the adjectives used to describe us, quiet is by far the most noble and positive one. Throughout the Bible, quiet is regularly associated with peacefulness. When cultures were experiencing the absence of war, the Bible labeled this as dwelling in safety, quietness, security, and peace (Judges 18:7, 18:27, 1 Chronicles 4:40, 22:9, 2 Chronicles 14:11, and many more). Quietness and peace are frequently intertwined in the Bible.

Quietness is so cherished in the scriptures that it is considered the opposite of strife. Proverbs 17:1 states, "Better is a dry morsel with quietness, than a house full of feasting with strife" (NKJV). I know a married couple in which both spouses are intensely quiet. I have never heard either one speak more than two words. Sometimes I wonder what their fights are like. Maybe they never fight. Or maybe they fight but neither one knows it. Does that count as a fight? Ah, it's the old *If a Tree Falls in a Forest* conundrum.

Many different Bible verses praise quietness and warn about long-windedness (Proverbs 10:19, 17:8, 27; 1 Peter 3:3,4; 1 Thessalonians 14:11-12). God even describes Himself as having a still, quiet voice (1 Kings 19:12, GWT).

If quietness is so clearly considered a virtue, why does American society seem to hate it? One woman with social anxiety writes about a childhood experience in which her quietness irritated her grade school principal. "My quietness bothered him so much he and two other teachers went to my home to speak with my parents to find out why I was so quiet" (Richards 2014a). This type of curiosity and attention inadvertently (or sometimes intentionally) communicates that quietness is a problem rather than an asset.

The cultural view of quietness has not always been so negative. In 17th-century Europe, it was considered appropriate for children to be initially shy and quiet with strangers (Hofmann and DiBartolo 2010). Two hundred years later, the old saying, "children should be seen and not heard" was a widely held belief in Victorian society (Briggs 1975, 13). The social rules have changed remarkably since then.

Image 5. "Quiet" free stock image courtesy www.morguefile.com

In her book, *Quiet, the Power of Introverts in a World That Can't Stop Talking*, Susan Cain writes that it was during the 1920s that shy and quiet children were first conceptualized as "maladjusted," at least in American culture (2012). Parenting experts began emphasizing social skills and personality while warning of the dangers supposedly associated with shyness (i.e., alcoholism and suicide, 27). Quietness lost favor, and an outgoing nature became the ideal for children, synonymous with a healthy personality. The new rule was: Healthy children should not be overly quiet.

Today, American culture still places great value on outgoing, talkative, and charming personalities. Americans make major voting decisions often based largely on televised presidential debates. If the presidential candidates cannot hold their own in a fierce public argument, they receive a beating in the press. This puts the quieter, more reticent individual at a clear disadvantage in the election process, regardless of other valuable qualities such as character, experience, or wisdom, which our society and world sorely need.

The rules are different for different cultures. East Asian culture promotes and highly values submissive, quiet behavior (Schreier et al. 2010, 1132). From a biblical viewpoint, quietness is not a characteristic that requires change. Instead of breaking the rules, quietness actually fulfills the rules. Did you hear that? The rule that you thought you were breaking is no rule at all. Be as quiet as you want. Quiet, I said! When God wants you to speak up, He will empower you.

Rule #7

Thou Shalt Not Be Shy

Shyness is defined as "hesitation or discomfort in response to social situations, particularly novel ones" (Yang et al. 2013). Shyness is not considered a disorder but rather a common trait within the continuum of normal human personality (Stein and Stein 2008, 1117). Did you hear that? Shyness is actually considered normal by the rule makers! In spite of what you may have been lead to believe.

Nearly half of America's population claims to be shy (Carducci and Zimbardo 1995). It usually starts quite early in life. Researchers have established that a predisposition towards shyness and social withdrawal begins at conception and is the result of both "genetic and environmental factors" (Miller and Coll 2007, 87). In other words, shyness can be blamed on both nurture (environment, parenting, etc.) and nature (a genetic predisposition).

Shy children tend to be timid when meeting new people. This is referred to as being "slow to warm up" (behaviorally inhibited). It generally takes much longer for the shy child to adjust to a new social situation before engaging and exploring. Take my son, for instance. As a toddler, he would hide behind my legs for about an hour. Then he would creep out, like a mole rat, for seconds at a time. Creep...retreat. Creep...retreat. As long as we stayed somewhere for what felt like 144 hours, he would eventually crawl out, blinking in the sunlight.

This is in contrast to the child with an uninhibited temperament, who is quite comfortable spontaneously embracing new and exciting settings. I once approached Walmart while holding my toddler cousin. As we got closer to the people, movements, sounds, and lights, she began to kick with delight. Oh, she wanted down *soooo* bad! So many new things to touch and people to interact with! She is un-shy to the tenth degree. What a delightful variety God has built into children!

Professionals continue to debate whether shyness is a mild form of social anxiety or something totally different (Yang et al. 2013). Ultimately, few shy children will have extreme shyness persist and become social anxiety during adulthood (Stein and Stein, 2008, 1117). Likewise, about 50% of adults with SAD do not report experiencing extreme shyness during childhood (Cox, MacPherson, and Enns 2005, 1024). The relationship between shyness and social anxiety is complex.

Shyness can best be conceptualized as an innate, cautious, and vigilant approach to life. This built-in vigilance breaks none of God's rules. Shy, sensitive people tend to notice more details in their environment, take longer to process stimuli, and proceed more cautiously than others (Jagiellowicz et al. 2010). Scripture points out the need for vigilance against spiritual danger in 1 Peter 5:8: "Be sober, be vigilant; because your adversary the devil walks about like a roaring lion, seeking whom he may devour" (NKJV). For many species, a built-in high level of vigilance is a God-given aid for survival.

Unfortunately, some Christians believe that shyness is rooted in a sinful form of fear, pride, or lack of love. David Berg states: "Shyness is a form of pride! It's a combination of two things—fear and pride" (Berg 2016).[2] Another pastor (Clarke 2009) says, "It seems to me that perfect people – which is what we are called to be – won't be shy or boring. So I said it's a sin to be shy or boring." He concludes with, "Being shy is therefore, in one sense, unloving." This is a rather extreme view of shyness, a rigid rule *not* found in the Bible.

This rule is not a God-rule. In fact, it is not even a *good* rule. Be shy, people! Let your kids be shy! Be cautious, be slow, be tentative. And when God strengthens you to be bold, watch out! You will really shock people, which might be just exactly what God had in mind.

Rule #8

THOU SHALT NOT BE INTROVERTED

The personality concepts introversion and extroversion are familiar to just about everybody. Secular psychiatrist Carl G. Jung created these terms in 1921.[3] Jung described introverts as inward looking, whereas extroverts tend to seek sensation and satisfaction in the outer world. The population in America is split approximately 50/50 between these two types (Hammer and Martin 2003). Individuals with social anxiety are far more likely to be introverted than the general population (Janowsky, Morter, and Tancer 2000, 123). I find it incredible that some socially anxious people are extroverts. Needless to say, extroverted persons with social anxiety face extraordinary challenges in getting their social needs met.

Extroverts are innately outgoing, sociable, gregarious, congenial and fun-loving. As I said before, this description fits my husband to a tee. He is a delightful, life-of-the-party kind of guy. Meanwhile, introverts (such as myself) tend to be more reserved, reflective, creative, and serious. Individuals can fall anywhere on the continuum between extroversion and introversion. Jesus probably fell somewhere in the middle of the spectrum. He frequently sought solitude, but He also spent a vast amount of time ministering to and interacting with people. And, of course, He was perfect.

Although we find no explicit references to extroversion or introversion in the Bible, certain individuals in scripture fit the labels. Among Jesus' disciples, Peter was reckless, enthusiastic, and clearly extroverted. John

---

2 http://deeptruths.com/daily-bread/shyness_timidity.html.

3 Diamond, Stephen. 2012. "Essential Secrets of Psychotherapy: Jung's Typology, Eudaemonology, and the Elusive Art of Happiness." *Psychology Today*. Read more at http://www.psychologytoday.com/blog/evil-deeds/201205/essential-secrets-psychotherapy-jungs-typology-eudaemonology-and-the-elusive-

was more thoughtful and completed a major God-ordained mission (the writing of Revelation) in isolation. Both personality types comprised God's dream team of disciples.

Favoritism towards extroversion has permeated both American culture and the Christian church. Author and ordained minister Adam S. McHugh has written a wonderful book entitled *Introverts in the Church: Finding our Place in an Extroverted Culture* (2009). McHugh writes about his own struggle to fit in as a highly introverted pastor. He describes an underlying sense of guilt for a deep need for solitude in order to recharge. He also found many traditional pastoral activities, such as greeting and counseling, quite physically draining.

Many introverted Christians feel intense pressure to live up to extroverted social expectations of ministry. Guilt seems to go hand in hand with introversion in the church. We perceive the rules of ministry (i.e., be available for person-to-person love at all times!), but are unable to achieve them.

Extroverted versions of Christianity place a high value on social gatherings, conversational evangelism, small groups, coffee hours, meet-n-greets, etc. (the very things that drain the life out of us introverts). Many churches emphasize the importance of these activities as inherent to spiritual growth and maturity.

Unfortunately, many of these activities fill introverts with a sense of dread, given their intensely draining nature. We all know and fear the worst element of any church service: the meet and greet. *Yes, please force me to shake hands and make meaningless small talk,* said no introvert or socially anxious person ever. I have skipped church numerous times just because this portion of the service is sometimes more than I can bear.

Introverted Christians often lean towards quieter practices, such as personal prayer, private Bible study, contemplation, worship, and behind-the-scenes ministry. These activities refresh and empower us spiritually. Even the word "worship" has become synonymous with extroverted corporate singing rather than private adoration. Worship encompasses both activities or either one. American culture has deemphasized many of the quiet and private activities of the believer.

Thank goodness God does not have a favorite personality style. If God was an American, I would be toast. According to James R. Beck, author of *Jesus & Personality Theory: Exploring the Five-Factor Model*, our personality style is not important to God (1999, 36). We are invited to use our personality style, infused with love from Him, flowing out to others. This love can be filtered through both an extroverted and introverted personality style. As Beck states clearly, both personality styles can serve God well (132).

The introverted need not feel guilty about carving out time for solitude and rest. God actually made a rule for that (one of the Top 10 rules in fact)…honor the Sabbath. The rule was given for our benefit, that we would not be overwhelmed. Today, Jesus is our Sabbath rest. Grace says we do not have to work in order to earn God's love. Every single day is a day of rest.

The introverted Christian can spend as much time alone, resting in Jesus, as desired. Jesus once commended Mary for choosing to rest with Him instead of rushing around working with Martha (Luke 10:42). Rest is designed to empower greater and greater love, spilling out to others. True, sincere good works will happen, but not by any human effort. God invites us to have a part in His work while resting from our own. Jesus makes this rule completely null and void.

Rule #9

THOU SHALT NOT BE BORING

Nearly everyone agrees with this rule. A boring personality is really not what anybody's working hard to achieve. Interestingly, only humans have the capacity to be bored with other humans. Never in Scripture will you find an instance of God's boredom. Scripture describes God's emotions towards us as loving, angry, jealous, compassionate, merciful, and grieved...but never bored.

Image 6. Background image is in the public domain: https://commons.wikimedia.org/wiki/File:Tablets_of_the_Ten_Commandments_(Bible_Card).jpg

Imagine reading this line in the Bible: "God looked down at Moses...and was bored." Thankfully, mankind was not created with the responsibility of entertaining or titillating the Creator. Instead, humans were created for His enjoyment, and enjoy us He does.

To God, humanity is infinitely interesting, never dull. To humans, an unusually quiet or socially awkward person might be perceived as boring. But we are incapable of boring our Creator.

This rule is just plain stupid. Tear it up and throw it away. And try your best to bore every single person you come into contact with, today and always.

There are elements of social anxiety that are, quite frankly, not good. As in...bad. The tenth rule is one of those rules that really cuts like a knife—*if* we were still under the rules, that is.

> **Rule #10**
>
> Thou Shalt Please God and Men

For the socially anxious, our corpse is really, really into people-pleasing, self-centeredness, and isolation. Colossians 3:23-24 says, "And whatever you do, do it heartily, as to the Lord and not to men, knowing that from the Lord you will receive the reward of the inheritance; for you serve the Lord Christ" (NKJV). This verse clearly addresses two sources of approval: God and fellow humans. Approval from God, well, that came easily. For us, anyway. It was not so easy for Jesus to accomplish it. In any event, we have it. Lots of approval. Lots of love.

Approval from fellow humans, on the other hand, is a bit more hit-or-miss. It can be lost as quickly as it is gained. Just when I think I have captured your heart...bam! You see a bit of my corpse and peace out. *But wait,* I yell, *there's more to me than that!*

Or, even worse, let's say I successfully earn your approval. Now I am on a pedestal. And from there, the only place I am going is down. It's like a game I can't win! (Like playing Monopoly and having to be the hat piece. The hat never wins).

Human approval is distributed unfairly and is nearly always based on faulty assumptions or premises. Approval from others provides no genuine, lasting rewards. It feels good, at first. But then we find we need more. And more. And soon, we are enslaved. We are just trying to make everyone happy. Trying to be approved of. We expend great amounts of energy in reputation maintenance: within our families, churches, or communities. And we will never achieve perfect acceptance from other people. It is impossible.

The worst thing people-pleasing does is create an unstable sense-of-self. We start to believe we are who we see reflected in others' eyes. This is like relying on a carnival mirror to show you how you really look. It will either be too good or too bad. Compared to God's goodness, we are dirt. Through the eyes of grace, we are beyond precious. Humans rarely have a balanced perspective of our own dirtiness compared to God as well as our own loveliness as God's own children. Thus, the pleasure or displeasure those around us display will frequently be off the mark and rarely reflect our true status. If we come to rely on others for our identity, it will be impossible to find stability, peace, and rest. We are high. We are low.

Who I am reflected in God's eyeballs is the only thing that matters. If God has eyeballs, that is. He probably does, but they would be spirit eyeballs and maybe there are more than two. In any case, my identity never changes because it is rooted in His unconditional love. This is our anchor. Being anchored in grace accepts ownership of our lowness, marvels at God's highness, and gladly receives unearned credit for God's highness. Every single minute of every single day.

Sensitive individuals quickly discern the rules that others use to define goodness (from friends, family, church, society, etc.). Values are contagious. These rules may include: get a college degree, get married, earn money, stay out of jail, attend Bible studies, have a successful career, be extroverted, have children, look pretty, volunteer at church, don't do drugs, etc. When we become aware of others' rules, we are tempted to work diligently to fulfill these man-made rules.

You want to know who refused to people-please? Jesus. His values aligned with the Father's...24/7. Nobody else's. He bucked religion. He hung out with bad people. He slammed the know-it-alls. Frankly, it was His lack of people-pleasing that got Him murdered. Well, that, and True Love.

Jesus did it all just right. We will not quite live up to that. Unfair judgments or disapproval from others feels like a knife to the heart. We are humans, after all. This is reality. When unfair judgments come, just know that God understands our fragile hearts completely and feels deep compassion. He absolutely will provide comfort.

Bottom line: We are already pleasing God (through Jesus), continually. Pleasing men is impossible. No need to try.

Rule #11

THOU SHALT PUT OTHERS FIRST

It is probably no surprise that social anxiety is a disorder that is largely concerned with self. *How am I doing? What do they think of me? I feel afraid, uncomfortable, awkward, embarrassed, and so on.* Me, me, me. This is my theme song.

These self-oriented concerns form the basis for social anxiety. Social anxiety may mask itself partially as a concern for/about others, but the bitter truth hidden beneath is a self-focused orientation.

The first time I was confronted with this truth, I found it devastating. It shook the very core of who I believed myself to be. About 10 years ago, I was in a bitter conflict with an extended family member. Her words had cut so deeply I couldn't imagine being in the same room with her. She had criticized my children, which is the perfect way to make me hurt. Just the thought of her caused me to tremble and feel sick to my stomach. When Thanksgiving approached, I decided to skip our family's traditional gathering. I just didn't have the social energy or strength to pretend all was fine and endure debilitating physical symptoms in her presence.

After the missed holiday, I received a scathing email from her. Didn't I know how hurtful it was to the rest of the family that I wasn't there? Didn't

I understand that I was creating an even bigger issue with my absence? Didn't I understand how self-centered my decision to not attend was?

I was incredibly hurt by these accusations... But the more I pondered them, the more I could see the truth hidden beneath the hostility. I had avoided my family as a means of self-preservation. My actions took no account of how anyone else would feel, or the well-being of my extended family as a whole. For the first time ever, I began to recognize that a wide streak of selfishness runs through my soul. The recognition of my own lowly nature led to a sense of self-condemnation (though it would not have if I had understood the nature of grace at that time).

I very rarely enter a crowded room and think, who can I care for today? Far more often, I am thinking, where is the safest place for me to sit? Who am I comfortable with? Where is it the most quiet? How can I avoid embarrassment? My thoughts are firmly planted in fulfilling my own needs. The Bible has very clear prescriptions about selfishness. Philippians 2:3 states, "Let nothing be done through selfish ambition or conceit, but in lowliness of mind let each esteem others better than himself" (NKJV). Romans 10:12 says, "Be kindly affectionate to one another with brotherly love, in honor giving preference to one another." I rarely have time for that because I am too busy looking out for Numero Uno.

After recognizing my self-centeredness, I tried very hard to obey the very good rule of not being selfish. Yet my selfishness cropped up again and again. Try as I might, I just could not consistently satisfy this rule. It was a terrible, self-defeating cycle of trying harder...and always failing. Knowing the rules about self-centeredness did not take away my self-centeredness. In fact, I only discovered deeper and deeper layers of self-centeredness! *Pshaw!*

Then God opened my eyes to His own selflessness. He was so not selfish that He allowed Himself to be murdered for rule-breaking that He Himself did not even commit. And through grace, I get credit for that unselfishness. God looks at me, through Jesus, and gives me credit for being the most unselfish Person who ever walked the earth.

Still, my old corpse continues to entice me to selfish acts. I would be lying if I claimed anything different. I am a mere human being. None of us is truly good in our ratty human flesh. I long to be unselfish, yet I am often selfish. Thankfully, God will deliver me from this conundrum someday. Until then, I will celebrate the unselfishness of God's gift of grace. That's what we do with this good rule. We give it to Jesus for fulfillment. Ding! Order up!

Rule #12

THOU SHALT HAVE FRIENDS

Isolation is a concerted effort to withdraw from others. Sometimes withdrawal is directed towards society at large (consider history's hermits).

Sometimes it is directed at loved ones, family members, and friends. A desire for isolation can be a symptom of depression, the result of addiction, an attempt to hide sin, an act of self-protection, or it may simply indicate a need for less sensory stimulation.

Individuals with social anxiety may not choose isolation purposely. Perhaps we feel trapped by fears and physical symptoms. Some of us would like to get out, meet people, and engage in a full, rich life. Unfortunately, social anxiety symptoms become a jail cell, and there does not seem to be a key in sight.

Proverbs 18:1 says, "A man who isolates himself seeks his own desire; He rages against all wise judgment" (NKJV). I used to read this verse and feel quite guilty. First, I made it a law for earning God's approval. Then I went a little further by adding a few sub-rules to it as well.

It goes something like this. First, I have *very few* close friends. I prefer a quiet, solitary type of life. In order to make the rule completely legal, I added in the sub-clause that my husband, parents, children, etc., do not count as friends. Therefore, I am clearly one who has foolishly rebelled against wise judgment. I am living an isolated life and am a doomed rule-breaker.

What actually qualifies as isolation? Extroverts would define isolation far differently from introverts. Some might see having only one or two good friends as being too isolated. Some might see having only online friends as being isolated. Some might view pen-pals as surface relationships versus genuine relationships. Perhaps family members do not count as real friendships. Because the Bible does not give a clear definition of what isolation is, it is difficult to establish a good, precise rule. If nobody agrees on the rule, how can we agree if it has been satisfied to the letter? Thankfully, we do not need to.

Interestingly, the original King James Version (KJV) of Proverbs 18:1 seems to communicate an entirely different message: "Through desire a man, having separated himself, seeketh and intermeddleth with all wisdom." The KJV translation is advocating *for* isolation, when the purpose is to seek wisdom. Theologians continue to debate which translation is more accurate because they are directly opposed to each other. I think the lesson is this: This proverb was not intended to be a rule after all.

We all understand that at least some intimate sharing and self-disclosure with another human creates a precious opportunity to know and be known. Whether a relationship is nurtured via email, phone, letters, text, social media, or other creative, nontraditional ways is unimportant. Friendships do not have to fit any preconceived idea. I believe grace gives value to virtually every human transaction of caring (including Facebook, Twitter, pen-pals, phone calls, etc.) And if/when we fall short of having intimate connection with others, God credits us with His own friendships. And He is our constant Companion, our faithful Friend. He wants to bless us with His love through human relationships, not dictate our worthiness.

My guess is that most people reading this section are not as isolated as they might think. But even if they are, there is no condemnation. God is right there. And for a little humanly expressed love, reach out in whatever creative way you feel capable of. There is an entire community of grace-based wanderers on Twitter…search #gospelposse. There are innumerable blogs and websites centered on grace, including www.dropping-keys.com and www.ExchangedLife.com. There are so many forgiven sinners out there waiting to welcome you with open arms.

We socially anxious can all be isolated together.

At the end of this list of rules we discover two things. First, if it was a good rule, Jesus fulfilled it. Second, if it was a bad rule, we booted it out with Wednesday's trash. So what is left for rules? Nothing, my friends. Do you hear that? That is the sound of the bars swinging open. We are free. The New Us is not bound by rules but rather covered by love. Grace.

> For Christ is the end of the law
> for righteousness to everyone
> who believes (Romans 10:4, NKJV).

* * *

Reflection

1. Do you consider yourself someone on the fringes of society? Why or why not? What rules have you broken?

2. What do you think is God's idea of "normal"?

3. List a few of your own pet rules.

4. Can you identify the unspoken rules of your family, friends, church, and community?

5. Which rules have led to the most disappointment in your life?

6. What would your life look like without any more rules?

7. Which of the social anxiety characteristics (quiet, shy, introverted, boring, people-pleasing, self-centered, and isolated) apply to you the most?

8. What would happen if you never changed, and remained *exactly as you are* this minute?

9. Which rules will you disregard today after reading this chapter?

9

Safety Behaviors & PEP

A ship is safe in the harbor,
But that's not what
ships are built for.
~Poem by Gaal Attal

So, now we are living under grace and not under the law (rules). And yet our New Us keeps on behaving like the Old Us. We know we are fully loved and accepted, just as we are, in Christ. But we may continue to be haunted by our social anxiety symptoms. We are New Creatures, but we act like our old selves.

There are two particular behaviors that the Old Us invented. Before we explore these behaviors, let me first say: THEY HAVE ALREADY BEEN FORGIVEN. (I apologize for shouting, but this is *really* important). When you catch yourself doing these, give a little chuckle and say, "That's not the real me. Thank you, Jesus, for that fact!"

1. Safety Behaviors

The first nasty old habit is called **safety behaviors.** Safety behaviors are an attempt to hide and/or avoid embarrassment. They make perfect sense for someone with social anxiety. We fear judgment, so we work hard to protect ourselves from judgment. On our grace journey, we will learn more and more how to embrace life without fear of judgment. But in the beginning, we will face a steep learning curve. We have spent most of our lives relying on our own protective habits.

Common safety behaviors include the avoidance of eye contact, sitting in the back of the room, doing a project during a social event (like taking photos), wearing neutral clothing, no personal sharing, and over-rehearsal before a task.[1] I can remember the first time I got my prescription for eyeglasses. I was in my 30s and delighted to begin wearing glasses. Eye contact has always seemed...too...much? Unbearably intense. I felt like glasses would give me one tiny extra barrier against potent eye contact. Is that weird? Probably.

We may also lower our heads to conceal an anxious expression. We may mentally rehearse repeatedly before speaking and then rush through our words. We may speak in a soft voice out of fear of saying something stupid or uninteresting.

One theory is that socially anxious people feel inadequate within four dimensions of ourselves: "social skills, personality, signs of anxiety, and physical appearance" (Moscovitch et al. 2013, 477). When I read this, I thought...wait, just four?

We socially anxious believe we are deeply and irretrievably flawed in one or more of these areas. Therefore, we put on a "social mask" to hide ourselves. My social mask also involves a lot of powder and mascara.

The temptation to hide has been around since the moment that fruit hit Eve's lips. The following are thoughts that frequently undergird the use of safety behaviors (hiding) in the four domains.

Social Skills
- I will come across as stupid (better to say nothing at all)
- Others will think I'm unfriendly (might as well withdraw)
- I leave awkward pauses in conversations (better to say nothing at all)
- I will probably say something inappropriate or hurt someone's feelings (better to say nothing at all)

Personality
- They will think I'm too quiet (I can't be myself)
- They will think I'm boring (I think I'm boring, why wouldn't they?)
- They will think I'm uptight or snobbish (so I will restrict my interactions)

---

[1] Marker, Craig D. 2013. Safety Behaviors in Social Anxiety. https://www.psychologytoday.com/blog/face-your-fear/201303/safety-behaviors-in-social-anxiety

Hiding Signs of Anxiety
- They will notice me sweating (wear cool clothes, keep hair off neck)
- They will notice me blushing (wear make-up to cover)
- They will notice my hands shaking (hold hands together tightly)
- They will notice my voice sounds strange (don't speak or speak barely audibly)

Physical Appearance
- I hope I don't spill something on myself (refuse to eat in public)
- I hope they don't notice a blemish or something embarrassing on my face (retreat and check a mirror frequently)
- They will probably think my eyes look red (keep eyes averted)
- If I walk across the room, they might notice that my pants don't fit right (don't move)
- I hope they don't notice the wrinkles on my shirt (groom self intensely before event)
- I would be mortified if someone noticed dandruff or a runny nose (self-groom intensely before event, cover all blemishes)
- They probably think I'm unattractive/ugly (avoid eye contact, hope not to be noticed)

Lookin' Good: Impression Management

Safety behaviors tend to fit into two categories: impression management or subtle avoidance (Plasencia, Alden, and Taylor 2011, 668). **Impression management** is an attempt to create a positive persona. The individual wishes to appear at ease, regardless of inner discomfort. It is, at its core, acting. For example, we may notice our clenched fists and purposely relax them during a conversation. The goal is to appear different from how we feel inwardly.

Look good or die tryin'

Impression management creates "a socially acceptable, albeit somewhat artificial, self" (Plasencia, Alden, and Taylor 2011, 668). Two examples of impression management are wearing make-up to conceal potential blushing or clothing that will disguise sweating. Feigning interest and excessive nodding and smiling are also a part of impression management. We tend to highly monitor our own behavior, carefully censoring words and actions, in order to appear favorably (to make a good impression!). We *act* because we are afraid of judgment.

Impression management is really an unintentional form of lying. All humans engage in some form of impression management. Except children. Have you ever noticed that children are remarkably honest? Often embarrassingly so. For instance, some young socially anxious children wear an angry expression when in an overwhelming social situation. This is an honest communication because these children are expressing their dislike of social pressure. Over time, most children learn to adopt (or fake) a more neutral facial expression to ease social connections (i.e., the social mask). To blend into normal society, the social mask becomes necessary.

It would be much more honest for me to walk around Walmart with a scowl on my face. I am afraid that kind of honesty would not help me achieve my goals, however. (I need good customer service and opportunities to share love.) So the social mask serves some purpose.

Unfortunately, wearing a "social mask" is a double-edged sword. If a social interaction goes well, the individual believes it was the false self that created the success. *They love the act, not me.* The individual is never truly at ease or accepted as his genuine self. Thus, he can never achieve authentic connections.

Extensive rehearsal before a social task is also a part of impression management (Plasencia, Alden, and Taylor 2011, 668). An example is when an individual writes out what he or she will say before making a phone call. I have literally written down what I will say, and possible responses, with possible responses to possible responses. Because I am a fly-by-the-seat-of-my-pants kind of gal.

Life (unlike reality TV) is not scripted

Individuals who engage in impression management may also take extraordinary care with their appearance (clothing, make-up, household, etc.) before a social interaction. I never lower myself to this type of strategy (and my nose just grew three inches...reaching for more make-up!). Nothing is left to chance in order to avoid the feared judgment. It was not all that long ago that I deserved judgment (from God). I am still getting used to the New Me.

Some of us believe that we must make a good impression to all people, at all times. Unfortunately, this is impossible, unrealistic, and unnecessary. Not to mention, exhausting!

You know what's ironic about all this? My very favorite people are the complete opposite when it comes to impression management. I love when someone is comfortable not wearing make-up! I adore it when I go to a friend's house and it is a delightful mess. I want to dance when I get into somebody's car and see a month's worth of old French fries in the back seat. This all screams AUTHENTIC to me. If I admire this in other people, why do I still work so hard at impression management? Because I am a complicated work-in-progress, my dears.

Excessive self-monitoring is also a really big part of impression management. This self-focus, ironically, tends to magnify observable signs of nervousness. An example is the person who grips his glass tightly so that the shaking of his hands will not be evident (Kim 2005, 70). The tight grip itself, however, is more likely to produce a hand tremor. The fear of displaying physical symptoms of nervousness heightens nervousness leading to more observable symptoms of nervousness! It is a farcical cycle.

One study found that individuals with SAD who use impression management neither increased nor decreased others' perception of them (Plasencia, Alden, and Taylor 2011, 673). But, it did not help to lower anxiety levels either. So impression management may not harm relationships but it does not help them either. And it drains a lot of energy.

The next safety behavior tactic, subtle avoidance, does cause some harm. Read on.

I'm Outta Here: Subtle Avoidance

Subtle avoidance is an attempt to "hide" oneself during communication (Plasencia, Alden, and Taylor 2011, 668). This category of safety behaviors includes less eye contact, reduced speech, and low levels of self-disclosure. Self-disclosure is transparent sharing of one's genuine inner state or experience. For a successful deep human-to-human connection to occur, both individuals must have matching and fairly elevated levels of self-disclosure. If I tell you how I am really feeling, you will often respond by sharing how you are really feeling. And *Voila!* Genuine bonding has just occurred.

> **Self-disclosure = honest sharing about self**

In *Bridges Not Walls,* communication professor Dr. John Stewart writes, "Healthy relationships are built on self-disclosure" (2012, 212). Self-disclosure includes being open about one's feelings, values, goals, like/dislikes, interests, etc. Indeed, authenticity (versus trying to please or conform to others) has been linked to "higher self-esteem, stronger emotional well-being and more positive relationship functioning" (Plasencia, Alden, and Taylor 2011, 668). Inauthenticity is the opposite of genuine self-disclosure and tends to erode others' desire for future contact, effectively halting relationship building.

For the socially anxious, self-disclosure is risky business. We are letting it all hang out there, positively *inviting* judgment. Which happens to be our worst fear. The New Us knows better because of grace, but that is becoming more and more real to us slowly (as we grow in grace).

Frankly, we absolutely will be unfairly and harshly judged by humans from time to time. Nevertheless, the benefits of being *real and genuine* far outweigh the risks.

Self-disclosure, at its core, is confession. It is permission for self, and others, to simply be human. James 5:16 (NKJV) states, "Confess your trespasses to one another, and pray for one another, that you may be healed...." When we share our good, bad, and ugly features, we create a safe space for others to do the same. And sharing the human experience together is part of why the Christian church exists.

Differing levels of self-disclosure are appropriate for different relationships. It is not necessary to share intimate details about your past with the grocery store clerk. Emotional intimacy is not always the desired result of a relationship, so self-disclosure must be purposeful and considered. When genuine fellowship is the goal, however, self-disclosure is absolutely key.

> **My soul is closed for business**

Along with using low self-disclosure, we often engage in subtle avoidance by avoiding eye contact (Plasencia, Alden, and Taylor 2011, 668). There seems to be a fear that the other person will "see into my soul." Thus, I keep my eyes on my phone/book/shoes at all times. And hide behind my glasses. When my kids were little, I used them as little eye targets to avoid too much eye contact with others.

Unfortunately, these behaviors usually do not have the positive effect we hope for. (And what, exactly, are we hoping for?) Subtle avoidance actually helps to maintain social anxiety (Morrison and Heimberg 2013, 268). Research has shown that low levels of eye contact and self-disclosure tend to draw out a negative response from others (Plasencia, Alden, and Taylor, 2011, 673). Wait, do you get that? Our efforts to avoid human judgment can actually elicit human judgment!

We give others an impression of disinterest, which is off-putting. Our lack of self-disclosure signals to others that a wall is up. Keep out! In fact, research shows that avoidance-based safety behaviors increase the likelihood of social rejection, the exact thing we are trying to avoid (Plasencia, Alden, and Taylor 2011, 673).

A 2014 study examined the role of safety behaviors in a public speaking task (Rowa et al., 304-315). A total of 146 participants had to give a 5-minute impromptu speech. They were also given The Subtle Avoidance Frequency Examination (SAFE), a self-report inventory used to measure safety behaviors. Scores on the SAFE can range from 32 to 160.

Not surprisingly, participants with SAD received poorer ratings on their speeches (Rowa et al. 2014, 311). The worst performing individuals reported the highest use of safety behaviors. The more participants used safety behaviors, the poorer they did on their speeches. So safety behaviors

---

How Often Do You Use Safety Behaviors?

In the Rowa et al. 2014 study, individuals with social anxiety scored about **73 or higher** on the SAFE. Check your scores-download the SAFE assessment here:
www.centreforemotionalhealth.com.au/files/documents/questionnaires/Safety%20Behaviours%20-%20SAFE.pdf

definitely affect performance in a BAD way.

Rowa et al. assert that poor speaking performance by people with SAD is not due to a lack of social skills (2014, 312). Instead, our safety behaviors undermine or mask our social skills. Researchers highly recommend targeting safety behaviors to help ease social anxiety.

When individuals work to reduce their safety behaviors, their anxiety goes down (Kim 2005, 80). In several studies, participants were instructed to reduce safety behaviors while engaging in a feared social interaction (Taylor and Alden 2010, 226-237). As a result, participants felt like their feared outcomes had not occurred.

> *Safety Behaviors increase the likelihood of rejection*

Self-protection efforts seem to maintain, rather than alleviate, fears.

If it comes down to making a rule that safety behaviors are harmful, and then trying to stick to the rule, that is going to be a heavy burden. But what if we simply tested the hypothesis that we are flawed and loved at the same time? We can test this in little ways, such as increasing self-disclosure or boldly making eye contact. Give people permission to like or dislike the real us. And then see where we stand with God, which *never* changes.

From a sensory perspective, true relationships (with meaningful self-disclosures) require more energy than surface-level exchanges. So we have to be intentional about the conversations and relationships we invest energy into. Not every conversation can/should include relationship building and self-disclosure. Sometimes we just want to order a pizza!

> *Can I be both flawed and loved? Test it.*

We have permission to ride the rhythms of grace. On the days when we have more social energy, we increase our levels of self-disclosure and relationship investing. On the days when we are worn out, exhausted, and frankly, just want to be left alone, we can rest in Christ. Transparency (confession) about where we are will prevent hurt feelings in others. Saying something like "I am just worn out. I'll try to catch up with you later" is a genuine, humble, and acceptable statement.

2. A Time to Worry: Post Event Processing

Safety behaviors happen during a social event. But once the event is over, we are still not in the clear. Here is Bad Behavior #2: Post Event Processing (PEP). PEP is the tendency to repetitively review our performance after a social exchange (Chen, Rapee, and Abbott 2013, 1). The party is over. We are driving home. And we are reviewing all the stupid and ridiculous things we did while at the party. That makes for a jolly good time, right? No.

PEP is considered a major factor in maintaining social anxiety. Researchers believe PEP actually helps to cement safety behaviors into place (Mitchell and Schmidt 2014, 229–233). We think we did well as long as we were carefully hiding or acting. It is those few moments of being real (as in... *real* stupid, or *real* embarrassing) that we regret.

As the socially anxious person reviews his performance, he judges himself harshly with distorted or exaggerated negative perceptions (Zou and Abbott 2012, 250). PEP reinforces our overly negative self-beliefs. We are basically looking for confirmation for all the ways in which we are worthy of judgment. PEP also maintains anxiety for the next social interaction. If I have failed every time, future failure is surely guaranteed.

PEP is also called post-event **rumination**. The word ruminate is defined as thinking carefully and deeply about something.[2] It also refers to a unique digestive strategy for certain animals (cows!). Right now, I need you to imagine a cow. No, a black one. With a white face. There you go.

Now imagine that cow chewing a big tasty mouthful of grass, swallowing it, and then regurgitating it back into her mouth. Then re-chewing it and re-swallowing it. My fellow farm friends know this is called "chewing the cud." Cud chewing helps to thoroughly break down food so it can be digested efficiently. Every iota of nutrition is extracted.

The parallels between post event processing and cud chewing are obvious: we all just want to digest. Food. Information. Unfortunately, when we socially anxious people "chew the cud" (i.e., engage in PEP) we always do so with a negative bias. We only regurgitate and re-swallow the bad stuff. We have an image of ourselves blushing, stumbling over our words, being criticized, or doing something stupid. We relive it over and over and over again. All that re-chewing eventually turns the information into poison. The moral: Don't be a cow!

Don't be a COW

Certain people are more prone to unhealthy PEP. The more severe someone's social anxiety is, or the more negative his self-image, the more likely it is he will engage in PEP (several studies cited in Chen, Rapee, and Abbott 2013, 2). Other traits related to PEP are: higher attention directed towards self, negative assumptions about others/world, a perceived probability of criticism, and a high cost of negative evaluation. It seems the more accurately we see our corpse, and other corpses, the more likely we are to use PEP. Here's the good news: We no longer even need to concern ourselves with the ugliness

---

[2] Merriam-Webster.com. Retrieved March 4, 2014 from http://www.merriam-webster.com/dictionary/ruminate

of the Old Us.

So how do we break the habit of PEP? I have found myself engaging in negative PEP obsessively. It is not an easy habit to break. Let's go back to that cow. All that chewing of the cud is productive. Healthy, actually. Because what Bessie is chewing on is fortifying and nutrient-rich. Remember when I said don't be a cow? Scratch that. Just be a healthy cow.

When we relive events after the fact, we can do so from a compassionate, grace-based point of view. That means looking for God's fingerprints rather than smudges of our own Old Nature. This does not come naturally, but with a little practice, we will grow. Here is my (pathetic) example:

> **Be a healthy cow**

I had the honor of attending my sister-in-law's graduate school commencement ceremony (5 hours away from home). When I arrived at the restaurant for the celebration dinner, my social anxiety kicked in. I was without my husband, in a new environment, and interacting with people I don't know well. That adds up to physical nervousness, which often causes me to babble whatever comes to mind.

Upon first seeing my sister-in-law, we both commented on being nervous and sweaty. She offered me the use of her deodorant, but I proudly replied that I never use deodorant. As soon as this statement left my lips, I realized that I was boasting in the fact that I don't need to use deodorant. I cringed internally, mumbled something, and we moved the conversation on.

While driving home a day later, I dwelled on this interaction. I felt ashamed for being proud of not using deodorant. I felt guilty about turning a tiny moment of my sister-in-law's day into self-glory. I wondered if my sister-in-law had noticed how into myself I am. Even though it was such a tiny misstep, it rattled around in my brain for far too long. These are the tiny, ridiculous things that make up PEP.

> **let's dwell on something ridiculous, like deodorant**

I should note that my sister-in-law has a nature far too gracious to judge me as harshly as I was judging myself. But what if she was a different sort of person, and *had* been offended by something I had done? Would I then be guilty of a misstep? No. Even an action of the flesh that is judged correctly by the law has no consequence. We are no longer under the law. This is how incoming judgment from others is utterly neutralized. Even when they are perfectly accurate in their judgment, via the law, I am still approved by God—and so are you! Guilty in the flesh, innocent in the spirit.

Negative PEP points out all of our mistakes, from a harsh, overly judgmental point of view. It is an after-school judging session. In the story above, had I been a healthy cow, I would have been reliving the sacred honor of sharing in a celebration. I would have been thankful for the opportunity to express genuine love. I would have given myself an imaginary pat on the back for not letting social anxiety get in the way of any of those things. I showed up; I shared her big day! I would chew and re-chew this, sharing the cud with God, all the way home. Now that is positive PEP. And it puts negative PEP in its rightful place.

With all that said, we socially anxious people have a brain predisposition towards noticing the negative and ignoring the positive (Klumpp, Fitzgerald, and Phan 2013, 87). That's why healthy PEP does not come naturally to us. PEP scans for actions of the corpse while ignoring any glimmer of the New Us.

Perfectionism is embedded deeply in PEP. Our after-school judging session is about comparing ourselves to perfection, which is to say: to God. A 2012 study required people with SAD to give a speech (Zou and Abbott, 250-257). They were then rated on their speeches...but just randomly rated. Ratings were not actually related to how their speeches went. The ones who received only moderate ratings did *a lot* of negative PEP. They beat themselves up. These socially anxious people should have just been happy to have completed a very difficult task. There is cause for celebration and self-congratulation. Instead, it drove them crazy that they had not been judged as "very good." PEP in SAD always includes unrealistically high standards of behavior.

I cannot really say this too often: Perfection has only ever been attainable by Christ. He gives us credit for His perfection in spite of our low human condition and universal imperfection. Any false striving for perfection now takes away from the perfect offering of grace. We cannot do it. He already did.

Jesusectionism
rejecting human perfectionism, resting in Jesus

JUDGING MYSELF... BY GRACE

Reappraisal (a cognitive behavioral therapy technique we will discuss briefly in chapter 10) has been investigated as a treatment for PEP. The goal of reappraisal is to reinterpret stimuli in such a way as to change the emotional response. Instead of finding themes of failure, judgment, and rejection, individuals are encouraged to look for more positive themes, such as authenticity and commitment to values. New meaning is assigned.

Unfortunately, several studies (as cited in Brozovich et al. 2014, 208–218) have shown that individuals with SAD have greater difficulty implementing reappraisal. Far more natural (in our old nature) is the tendency to worry and suppress feelings (neither of which is healthy). One study found that socially anxious individuals who had high levels of worry had the highest levels of social anxiety (Brozovich et al. 2014). Worry is our kryptonite. Reappraisal does not always put out the fire.

Strangely, these individuals who worried a lot also had the highest levels of reappraisal (Brozovich et al. 2014). Researchers hypothesized that these participants may use reappraisal more often, but less effectively, than most people. They also considered that increased worry led to a necessary increase in reappraisal (a self-treatment of sorts).

If we find that trying to be more positive in our PEP is not helpful, we might want to let go of the process altogether. Maybe each time we start to relive an event, we "let go and let God" instead? No research, to my knowledge, has examined the effects of an active refusal to PEP.

PEP always focuses on the actions of the corpse. Under the letter of the law, I will always be able to see my failures. Even my best offerings of love are tainted by my humanness. Yet, the letter of the law is no longer the judge. We are judged through the lens of grace. You can chew on that day and night!

* * *

Reflection

1. Do you sometimes resort to safety behaviors? If so, which ones?

2. Are safety behaviors likely to hinder or help the situation?

3. Is there one safety behavior you would like to try eliminating?

4. Have you ever experienced rejection? What did it feel like on a physical/emotional/spiritual level?

5. Do you find yourself engaging in post-event-processing? Give an example.

6. Is perfectionism a problem for you? How does the gospel address perfectionism?

7. Is obsessive worry a problem for you?

8. Do you try to adjust your thinking to have more biblical meaning (cognitive reappraisal)? Does it help with your emotions?

Section IV
Counseling:
The Good, Bad, & Ugly

Some counseling methods naturally lend themselves to a grace-based perspective while others do not. The next three chapters will investigate the top treatments for social anxiety. Find out which are your friends and which are your frenemies. There is a vast selection of good, bad, and ugly methods to choose from. Though I do not believe counseling is the miracle cure for social anxiety, it can be a way to dig deeper into the grace of God. And that, my friends, is the miracle cure.

10

My Strange Thoughts and Behavior

"So I told him, told him everything, about my disgust with my own motives and my thoughts of walking away from it all.
In that moment he said a powerful thing, a life-changing thing: 'You are on the threshold of receiving the greatest grace of your life.'"
~Brennan Manning, *All Is Grace: A Ragamuffin Memoir*

The mind is a magical place. A kingdom of sorts, where battles are raged, territories seized, princes and princesses crowned. The mind is where our dueling identities (the New Us and the corpse) fight for supremacy. The mind is the bridge between the two.

It is in the mind that we either **put on** or **put off**:

...that you **put off,** concerning your former conduct, the old man which grows corrupt according to the deceitful lusts, and be renewed in the spirit of your mind, and that you **put on** the new man which was created according to God, in true righteousness and holiness (Ephesians 4:22-24, NKJV, emphasis mine).

The power of the human mind has inspired the modern counseling movement. The counseling method that has been used most frequently to treat social anxiety is Cognitive Behavioral Therapy (CBT).

The chief focus of CBT is, obviously, thoughts and behavior. CBT "focuses on how problem thinking and problem behavior create problem feelings like depression, anxiety, and anger" (Benner and Hill 1999, 215). Nearly all social anxiety treatment approaches flow from a CBT foundation, including exposure therapy, dialectical behavior therapy, schema therapy, cognitive bias modification, mindfulness and acceptance-based CBT, and acceptance and commitment therapy. Those are all big terms for what is basically *trying to change our minds.*

CBT is considered the gold standard treatment for social anxiety (Klumpp, Fitzgerald, and Phan 2013, 83). It is nearly always the first treatment tried. For the most part, CBT has remained unchanged for the last 20 years (Schmidt 2012, 465). CBT for social anxiety is aimed at identifying the specific faulty thought-patterns, beliefs, and behavior that lead to social dysfunction. In other words, just what kind of nonsense do we have going on up there in our minds? Why do we act so darn weird?

In one study, approximately 60% of socially anxious individuals found some relief from symptoms through CBT (Leichsenring et al. 2013, 763). CBT has the ability to change brain function, increasing and decreasing activity in significant areas related to social interaction (Goldin, Ziv, and et al. 2014, 97–106). CBT provides longer lasting improvements compared to medication alone. Of all the treatments available, individual CBT seems to be the most effective (Mayo-Wilson et al. 2013, 373).

CBT helps about 60% of us

Still, in spite of some success, that leaves 40% of socially anxious individuals unimproved after trying CBT (Leichsenring et al. 2013, 765).

How It All Goes Down

A typical course of treatment for in-office CBT is 12–16 weeks of hour-long weekly sessions (Asghari, Mashhadi, and Seperhri 2015, 38-45). Specific methods of challenging faulty thoughts include: thought monitoring, behavioral experiments, video feedback, and surveys of opinion (Ougrin, 2011). Most of these methods target the socially anxious person's harsh self-judgments. Sometimes viewing oneself on video creates a new, less negative self-image. (I imagine the opposite would happen for me, but whatever.) Most people are often surprised to see that their flaws are not nearly as apparent to others as they had imagined.

CBT is offered in an individual setting, a group setting, and also as a self-help program (i.e., a written manual or online course). The current body of research indicates that individual CBT has a slight edge over group CBT (Mayo-Wilson et al. 2013, 368). That kind of makes sense because how many of us thrive in a group setting?

Internet-based therapy has been shown to be roughly as effective as group therapy for social anxiety (Hedman et al. 2011). There are several free or low-cost smart phone apps available for social anxiety based on a cognitive behavioral model (i.e., "AntiAnxiety" for Android and "Self-help for Anxiety Management" for iPhone). The effectiveness of these phone apps has not yet been well studied. I cannot help but be a little skeptical that a phone app would make a major difference in SAD, but I suppose anything is possible.

Internet-based therapy is a good choice because it is easily available, low cost, and flexible. And, duh, *it is so much easier* than seeing a therapist in person. Many if not most of us would consider seeking treatment if it did not involve changing our clothes or leaving the house. And when it comes to effectiveness, it seems to be about the same as other approaches.

Several countries, including Great Britain, Sweden, and the Netherlands, have incorporated Internet-based therapy into regular healthcare based on studies that show its effectiveness (Schulz, Stolz, and Berger 2014, 6). Online CBT is available in individual or group formats. In an online group format, therapeutic community forums enable peer feedback, mutual support, motivation, learning, and social interaction. Humans interacting, withholding judgment, and extending grace (in any format) can be powerful.

IT WORKS, FOR SOME PEOPLE

A group of researchers from John Hopkins University conducted a meta-analysis of the various treatments for SAD (Mayo-Wilson 2014). They reviewed 101 research trials, which included 13,164 patients (371). Individual CBT seems to be the most effective form of treatment. Still, we cannot forget that around 40% of individuals will not experience a benefit from CBT (Leichsenring et al. 2013, 765). The motto seems to be, "It's pretty good, but...."

CBT is the most researched and most effective counseling strategy currently available for social anxiety. Cognitive behavioral therapy is the best professional tool available, and at least half of those who utilize it will see improvements. Unfortunately, the large number of non-responders has researchers looking for new and better strategies. To date, researchers are not completely sure if negative thoughts cause social anxiety or are symptoms of it. As Dr. Norman B. Schmidt, research professor at Florida State University, states, "A substantial percentage of patients are classified as non-responders...and these rates do not appear to be improving over time" (Schmidt 2012, 466).

When It Does Work...

The exact means by which CBT eases social anxiety symptoms is still a bit of a mystery. One study found that CBT increased the ability of socially anxious people to master their thought-patterns, leading to lowered symptoms (Goldin, Lee, et al. 2014, 11). Somehow, someway, CBT has the potential to increase the amount of strength we have. Sometimes a little. Sometimes a lot.

A 2012 study examined which characteristics cognitive behavioral practitioners believed made the biggest difference for success in their clients (Frei and Peters 2012, 230–237). The top factors in success or failure were: degree of motivation for treatment, intelligence/reasoning ability, and co-morbid conditions (such as depression or personality disorder). Apparently if you are motivated and smart, CBT has a fighting chance. If you are weak and thick-headed (like me), you might be in the 40% whom it does not help. Comorbid conditions also make treatment more complicated and recovery even more challenging.

Sample Studies of Top Treatments

Treatment	Percentage of significant responders	Research Study
Cognitive Behavioral Therapy	60%	Leichsenring et al. 2013, 763
Selective Serotonin Re-uptake Inhibitors	40-66%	Nathan and Gorman 2015, 480
Psychodynamic Therapy	52%	Leichsenring et al. 2013, 763
Cognitive-Behavioral Group Therapy	40-50%	McCarthy et al. 2013
Interpersonal Therapy	42%	Stangier et al. 2011, 692
Pill Placebo	40%	Furmark et al. 2008, 13068

| Waitlist (no treatment) | 15% | Leichsenring et al. 2013, 763 |
| Non-responders to any treatment | 40-48% | Leichsenring et al. 2013, 765 |

Table 8. Top Treatments

    Other positive factors in treatment were: a willingness to experiment with new ways of thinking/behaving, acceptance of the cognitive behavioral model, ability to take responsibility for change, motivation for seeking change, and the ability to form a healthy relationship with the therapist (Frei and Peters 2012, 235).

    A majority of research shows that the relationship between therapist and client is at least as important as any techniques used (Norcross and Wampold 2011, 98–102). It is a caring relationship (face to face or online) that provides the platform for growth. I believe this is a big part of CBT's secret ingredient: love and care shared from human to human. Or more specifically, a mirror of God's love flowing between us.

    Many counselors, Christian or not, model God's grace by simply caring for their clients without judgment. The counseling office is a safe place for an individual to express failures and humbly seek help. It is a place of confession. Repentance. A determination to try a new way, follow a new path. In counseling, clients are fairly assured that they will not be rejected due to their "humanness."

The corpse specializes in bad thoughts and behaviors

The emphasis on healthy thoughts and behavior in CBT parallels the biblical call to "take every thought captive to Christ" (2 Corinthians 10:5) and to behave in accordance with one's faith (Philippians 1:27). Christian therapists have developed uniquely Bible-based cognitive behavioral methods, which appear helpful for many Christian clients (Benner and Hill 1999, 217). Christian-oriented CBT has been shown to be more effective (in 3 studies) for treating depression than no treatment (Hook et al. 2009, 49). Purposely turning one's thoughts towards God (meditation and scripture contemplation) has also been used effectively to treat anxiety (Hook et al. 2009, 62).

    The source of unhealthy thoughts is, of course, our corpse. It still desires to be like a god. Our old nature longs to be perfect, worshiped, wise, and powerful (apart from any help from God). The New Us has been gifted with God's attributes, apart from our own efforts. Our thinking and behavior will waver between the two extremes, and how thankful I am that Jesus has rescued us from the eternal consequences!

Uniquely "Christian" CBT

Licensed psychologist and ordained minister Dr. William Backus wrote a biblically based CBT guide entitled *Learning to Tell Myself the Truth* (1994). His manual provides a 6-week course in what the author calls Truth Therapy. Truth Therapy includes challenging thoughts with truthful, biblical ideas that result in healthier emotions and behavior.

Dr. Backus states that Truth Therapy is very simple but not easy (1994, 17). It takes time and effort to rewire habitual internal dialogs and rebut lies. *Learning to Tell Myself the Truth* encourages a reliance on divine power to make success possible. Backus states: "A relationship with Jesus Christ supplies daily power for making needed changes" (20).

It would seem that Bible-based CBT would be the ultimate in treatment for a socially anxious Christian. First, it is based on absolute truth. Second, it invites God into the counseling process. Third, the counselor and client generally share the same values and likely have similar goals. This should translate into superior results. Unfortunately, that is not always the case.

When we learn the truth of God's unconditional love, it is life-changing. But many of us (yes, me!) first learn the truth embedded with rules, without the context of grace. Many, many individuals report a poor experience with pastoral or Christian counseling. Could this be why? Perhaps, even within a Christian context, rules might be emphasized over unconditional love. It is only God's unconditional love, as expressed in His putting Himself on the cross, that holds real power. Power to change. Power to love. Power to rest.

A New Set of Rules?

Cognitive strategies aim to correct overly negative thinking. Behavioral strategies aim to reduce avoidance. Unfortunately, if we could change our thoughts and behaviors with a snap of our fingers, I am pretty sure we all would. It's just not that easy.

DO NOT think or behave that way!

Part of CBT is learning to discern healthy thoughts/behavior from unhealthy thoughts/behavior. We go to a therapist because we want to learn a new and better way. We are suffering and we want to change. CBT begins the process of teaching us which of our thoughts and behaviors are helping us and which are hurting us. The rules of good and bad, healthy and unhealthy, are necessary!

Unfortunately, greater knowledge about good/bad does not produce the power to perform it. I believe this explains the 40% for whom CBT does not provide improvement. We learn a better way. The rules for better health are more clear. But we cannot do better.

For some of us, traditional CBT will inadvertently create a new set of rules. We may internalize rules such as "Don't think negatively" and then we think quite negatively of ourselves as we catch ourselves thinking negatively. Just reading that sentence is giving me negative thoughts.

We naturally focus on rules. We inherited that lovely talent when Adam and Eve asked for it via the forbidden fruit, which remember was from the Tree of the Knowledge of Good and Evil (a tree of rules). Unfortunately, rules will only make our burden heavier. Rules do not provide freedom. Jesus does. Jesus created a way for us to embrace a new identity even in the face of failure.

Bible-oriented CBT with an emphasis on grace is very, very useful for sorting out our old and new identities. The corpse is frequently shouting lies and acting out. Frankly, it manages to be quite terrifying. We need to be well-armed to embrace who we are in Christ in the face of such bad behavior! Let's examine a few of the truths CBT can teach us.

THAT OLD JURY

Much of our social anxiety begins with the idea of an audience. For whatever reason, we go into a social situation believing that everyone is watching us (Morrison and Heimberg 2013, 251). We suspect that some imaginary audience with high, often unattainable social standards is judging our every move, word, and thought. Social interactions, in our confused minds, are similar to standing before a harsh jury.

A jury *of our peers (but only the* **perfect** *ones)*

Interestingly, the idea of living life before an audience is a natural part of human development. Adolescents go through this stage (called adolescent egocentrism), but most will grow out of it (Henderson and Thompson 2011). Those with social anxiety might be somewhat stuck in the egocentrism stage. *I knew I was still a teenager at heart.*

We not only live life before an imaginary judgmental audience but have a negative skew regarding our own behavior. I might be acting perfectly normal, but my mind rages: *Why do I behave so stupidly? Did you see how my hand shook when I put down my cup of tea? What kind of idiot gets uptight about tea?* Meanwhile, my so-called audience is enjoying her crumpets and has not even noticed I am panicking.

My own high standards, combined with my imaginary audience's high standards, give me no wiggle room for success. And so here we are face to face with the rules again. Their rules, my rules…rules rules rules.

The New Me understands that through Christ judgment will never be turned in my direction again. The New Me knows that I am worthy of examination because I am perfect (thank you, Jesus). My corpse may fall for the rules trick but not the real me. Not the real you. We are living life for an audience of One, and He has granted us unconditional, irrevocable approval. Now that is fun, isn't it? If we can just manage to stay grounded... in Christ.

I think of this journey of life as riding a surf board. Sometimes the waves toss me, and I get scared. I forget I am wearing a fool-proof Jesus life vest. Other times, I am laser-focused, free as a bird, soaring over and through killer waves, totally confident that my life vest is invincible. No matter where I am in my grace adventure, up or down, the vest is always, always there. Even when I forget it.

WHEN A THREAT REALLY ISN'T A THREAT

We also tend to do a lot of mind-reading. We interpret innocent comments or actions as threats when in fact no threat is involved. One goal of CBT is to change the meaning and importance of a threatening cue. For example, when my family member does not call me back for several days, I may go into panic mode. *Well, then,* I think, *apparently so-n-so is mad at me. Somehow, she figured out that I am a phony. A fraud. A fake-Christian who is really just a narcissistic mess! And she is finally giving me the judgment I deserve. Well, I am not standing for it! Now I am the one who is mad! Now I am going to...*wait. The phone is ringing. *Oh, Hi! You were out of town! Of course you were....*

Our negative assumptions tend to create moments, days, and weeks of unnecessary worry. CBT tries to teach us to not instantly jump to bad conclusions. I have gotten better about this...except when my mother-in-law calls and says she wants to come over and talk. I always assume the worst. And you know what happens every time? She brings me a surprise gift (a book, a candle, a painting, etc.). When will I learn?

A POKER FACE LOWERS THE ODDS OF WINNING

CBT also helps individuals lower attempts to hide their emotions from others (Goldin, Lee, and et al. 2014, 11). Emotional hiding is known technically as **expressive suppression.** In expressive suppression, the individual attempts to shut off any body, facial, or verbal communication in order to conceal emotions. It is as if we feel we must always be a blank canvas or a robot, if you will. As if humans do not experience emotions! Where did we get that idea?

Increasing genuine expression is considered important to the success of CBT. In some ways, letting it all hang out there for others to see has a way of releasing the grip of social anxiety. Our ability to *feel* is a gift of God's creativity. And even when the emotions are negative, or not based in truth, they are always honest. They reveal our heart. And there is no need to hide the heart.

Must. Be. A. ROBOT

I have this weird (somewhat pathological) thing where I sometimes start crying and cannot stop. It doesn't happen often, but it is the most embarrassing thing ever. Generally, what happens is that I am already physically primed: overtired, in physical pain, or hormonal. Then, something happens that hurts my feelings (in public, always in public). I find myself fighting back tears, wanting badly to hide my (often irrational) pain. The more I fight it, the harder the tears are to hold back.

I have had to order food from a restaurant menu with tears streaming down my cheeks. I have sniffled and wiped my nose while playing video games with friends. I have been shopping at the mall with beet-red eyes from crying. Other people become intensely uncomfortable. Alarmed. I am an attention magnet. And I cannot seem to control it.

It is particularly mortifying because most of the time I am really, really good at hiding my inner experience from others. I would do just about anything to avoid conflict, attention, or curiosity. This is classic emotional suppression. Perhaps my crying spells are a spilling over from chronic suppression? I don't know, but I do know that a better way is to be genuine as much as possible. Even occasional public crying, if need be. CBT agrees.

The following techniques are all derived from a cognitive behavioral model. They are not intended to change an individual's God-given personality. No amount of self-help, therapy, or knowledge will transform an introverted person into an extrovert, and that is not the goal of CBT. The following truths represent what is good. Only Jesus was all good. So we will let Him make up the difference when we fall short (which we decidedly will).

Thought Monitoring

Thought monitoring begins with the observation of one's automatic thoughts (Wood 2010). Automatic negative thoughts (also called ANTs) are self-critical, frequent, repetitive, and rigid. These are the voice of the corpse, and they are rules/judgment based.

Many people are unaware of the content of their automatic thoughts. Some common examples in social anxiety are: "Everyone is always judging me," "I'm no good at making friends," and "There's something wrong with me" (Wood 2010, 58). We often do not even realize these thoughts are swimming around in our beautiful heads.

ANTS= *Automatic Negative Thoughts. Tiny biting creatures.*

One simple way to begin thought monitoring is to keep a thought journal. The goal is to discern who is speaking the thought: the corpse or our new identity. The journal can be divided into four columns: situation, feelings, automatic thoughts, and corpse/new me.

I have created a thought monitoring journal page for you to use (in the Appendix). Feel free to record specific anxiety-provoking situations, along with the feelings and thoughts that accompanied them. Once you have identified unhealthy or unbiblical thought-patterns, the next step is to directly challenge those thoughts. We cannot go down without a fight.

Oh No You Di'n't: Thought Challenging

The following are questions designed to directly challenge untruthful, unbiblical, ungraceful thoughts. If you ever find yourself obsessing over some painful thought (like I do) ask yourself the following:

1. Is this thought focused on a rule or on grace?
2. Is this thought helpful?
3. Is it realistic?
4. What is the evidence for/against my thought/belief?
5. Am I focusing on the negatives and ignoring other information?
6. Is this thought an opinion or fact?
7. Can I find biblical support for this thought?
8. Am I jumping to conclusions?
9. What would others think if they were in my situation?
10. Am I being rigid in my thinking (i.e., thinking in black and white terms)?
11. Am I thinking of the worst-case scenario?
12. Would God argue against this thought?
13. Am I magnifying/minimizing important aspects of the situation?
14. Am I personalizing something, making it more about me than it is?
15. Am I assuming I know what someone else is thinking?
16. Are my thoughts based on my emotions rather than on actual facts?
17. Do my thoughts represent judgment or God's unconditional love towards me?
18. Is this thought coming from my old nature or my new identity in Christ?

Cognitive Restructuring

Cognitive restructuring is reforming our thought-patterns. To do that we examine and challenge our thoughts as well as the deep core beliefs that linger in our old nature. For example, a Christian who worries frequently about money may have an underlying core belief that God is not paying attention to his finances.

Here's a guarantee: The deeper we dig into the ugliness of our old nature, the more evil we will find there. Please do not be surprised if you become appalled while examining your thoughts and beliefs. That is the nature of the corpse. That is its job. It is there to be ugly. It is there to remind us that we do not deserve God's complete love. Yet we get it anyway. All that darkness just serves to highlight the Light of the world (John 1:5).

Faulty core beliefs usually represent either that our view of God is too low or our view of ourselves is too high. For example, in the above scenario, the Christian worried about money is placing far too much pressure on himself to be the provider. There really is only one Provider. The Christian can only do his little bit and then trust God to arrange circumstances in such a way as to provide the exact amount of money God intends—whether it is a lot or a little. We can take the pressure off of ourselves (mere humans) and trust God to provide.

Looking inward... oooh, my corpse is ugly!

In social anxiety, a common core (corpse) belief is: "There's something wrong with me, so it's best to stay away from other people so they won't discover my faults" (Wood 2010, 82). A belief centered on our new identity is: "There is something wrong with everybody, but we are covered by the grace of Christ." Which belief will we choose to put on, embrace, walk around in?

Next, we will look at three specific strategies CBT uses to change thinking patterns.

1. LOOK... A SQUIRREL!
ATTENTION BIAS MODIFICATION

Attention bias is the tendency to pay extra attention to perceived threats in the environment (Sportel et al. 2013). SAD individuals also seem to ignore or pay less attention to positive stimuli. For example, in a crowded room, the socially anxious person might notice someone who has not greeted him as expected.

My attention loves the negative

> I sidle into the room and give Joe a wave. (OK, for the record, I never sidle in...so let's say, I slink in). Joe gives me a nod but does not wave back. Fear pierces my heart. Is Joe mad at me? Have I offended him? Does he somehow know that I think his pants are way, way too short? Is this the beginning of a large church split? Oh, why did I even come here? I hate these events and someone is always side-eyeing me!

All of the attention is directed towards this perceived evidence of possible rejection. Meanwhile, little attention is given to a friend smiling and waving from another direction.

Why does Sue have to be so friendly? I wish she would just get out of the way. I can't even see if Joe's looking at me right now with her lurking around!

Cognitive bias modification is intent on changing both what individuals pay attention to and also how they interpret the things they give their attention to (Sportel et al. 2013). Basically, it is learning to pay more attention to the positive and recognizing when things *are* positive.

This is a newly emerging form of treatment for anxiety disorders based on cognitive models (Mobini, Reynolds, and Mackintosh 2012, 178). From a biblical perspective, we are encouraged to meditate on lovely, good, noble, just, pure, and praiseworthy things (Philippians 4:8-9). This just makes sense. Of course, doing what makes sense it not always so easy.

I am not sure why we frequently find the negative riveting while the positive goes unnoticed. I have read a certain amount of research that points back to that wacky old Brain Circus. All the major players in the brain seem to be primed to "protect" us from harm. To do so, they are hypersensitive to threat. There is a place for that skill. We would make wonderful lookouts during bank robberies. But in everyday life (i.e., trips to Walmart) noticing the negative rather than the positive can be rather draining.

But, just how much control do those with social anxiety have over what holds their attention? Can you teach us to be different? Please? There is some evidence that SAD individuals have reduced attentional control, compared to healthy subjects (Moriya and Tanno 2008, 1353). That means, bluntly, what triggers our attention is largely beyond our control.

When it comes to the message of Christianity, I certainly see in myself the tendency to pay attention to the negative and forget all about the positive. My eyes fix on every rule there is to find in the Bible. I mourn my inability to do and be. Yet, grace is waving at me from the corner. Always. If I would only pay attention to it.

2. CLEARLY EVERYTHING IS BAD: INTERPRETATION BIAS MODIFICATION

The premise of interpretation bias in social anxiety is that we often interpret totally neutral social events as threatening (Mobini, Reynolds, and Mackintosh 2012). According to researchers, "Individuals with social anxiety tend to perceive innocuous comments or behaviors by others as indicating criticism or rejection, and to interpret their own behaviors as poorer than the behaviors of other people" (174).

Researchers have studied interpretation bias by presenting people with ambiguous social scenarios and then having them come up with an interpretation. For example, individuals in one study were given the scenario of a fictional blind date (Constans et al. 1999, 643–651). In the fictional scenario, a blind date partner states, "You're certainly not

You're certainly not what I expected..?!

what I expected." The subjects of the study then had to explain what this statement probably meant. Guess what kind of interpretations socially anxious people came up with?

First of all, I want to congratulate the researchers for picking the most awful, ambiguous, threatening sentence ever known to man: "You're certainly not what I expected." Imagine stating that to your newborn baby, your boss, your pastor, your spouse. In fact, I dare you to say that to someone you know today. It really could go either way. And by either way I am thinking bad or badder. But that could be my interpretation bias talking.

Some techniques used to change interpretation biases include brainstorming, the "pie method," and worst-case scenarios (Voncken and Bogels 2006, 59–73). For brainstorming, individuals are asked to interpret a scenario from the viewpoint of various other individuals. For example, a counselor might ask us to imagine having our boss call us into the office. I would then interpret the scenario from the perspective of my mother, the president, and Jesus. Interpretations can range from rational to absurd.

My mother would assume I am about to get a raise because I am so awesome (thanks, Mom!). The president would assume it is time for a security evaluation (I look dangerous). And Jesus would assume my boss wants to confess how awful he has been lately (or how awful I have been lately?).

My perspective is colored by my corpse (kind of a greenish color)

The goal of brainstorming is to widen perspective. Obviously, my own interpretation would be a calm: *I'm done for! I've been found out! I had better start scrambling to pick up the pieces RIGHT NOW!* My perspective is...uh...slightly paranoid (thank you, corpse).

The "pie method" consists of taking all the various interpretations from brainstorming, and assembling them into a probability pie (Voncken and Bogels 2006, 65). For example, I would give my mom's interpretation a 1% likelihood of being correct. She thinks way too highly of me (thanks, Mom!). This exercise is designed to reality check probabilities and interpretations. It involves some math, which is misleading and disappointing since it is named after a bakery item.

Finally, worst-case scenarios are explored from various perspectives (Voncken and Bogels 2006, 68). For example, what if one of my friends thought something I had said was very stupid? What would I do? Hide. What would Mohammed Ali do? Knock him out. What would my mom do? Knock him out. Exploring worst-case scenarios from different vantage points is supposed to increase our ability to think flexibly.

All these perspective exercises are well and good, but in my mind, it really comes down to two perspectives: the Old Me and the New Me. The Old Me is under rules, always failing, always losing. The New Me is viewed through the lens of God's adoring love. He is understanding, compassionate, loving, forgiving, all knowing, and merciful vs. judgmental, angry, condemning, or aloof. An accurate Jesus perspective is based on a biblical description of who Jesus is.

Yet, we can even read the Bible with a skewed interpretation bias. An individual who is still enslaved by rules will read Matthew 5:48 (NKJV), "Therefore you shall be perfect, just as your Father in heaven is perfect" as a personal, obtainable command. A person utilizing a grace-based interpretation will read this portion of scripture and understand that Jesus was describing what it would take for a human to earn her way into Heaven… apart from His grace.

A grace-based perspective does not come naturally, but we do grow into it. This is the kind of growth we are seeking, growth in grace. 2 Peter 3:18a says, "But grow in the grace and knowledge of our Lord and Savior Jesus Christ…" (NKJV). Never does the Bible say to grow in righteousness (right thinking and behavior). Grow in grace. Grace is the ultimate in perspectives.

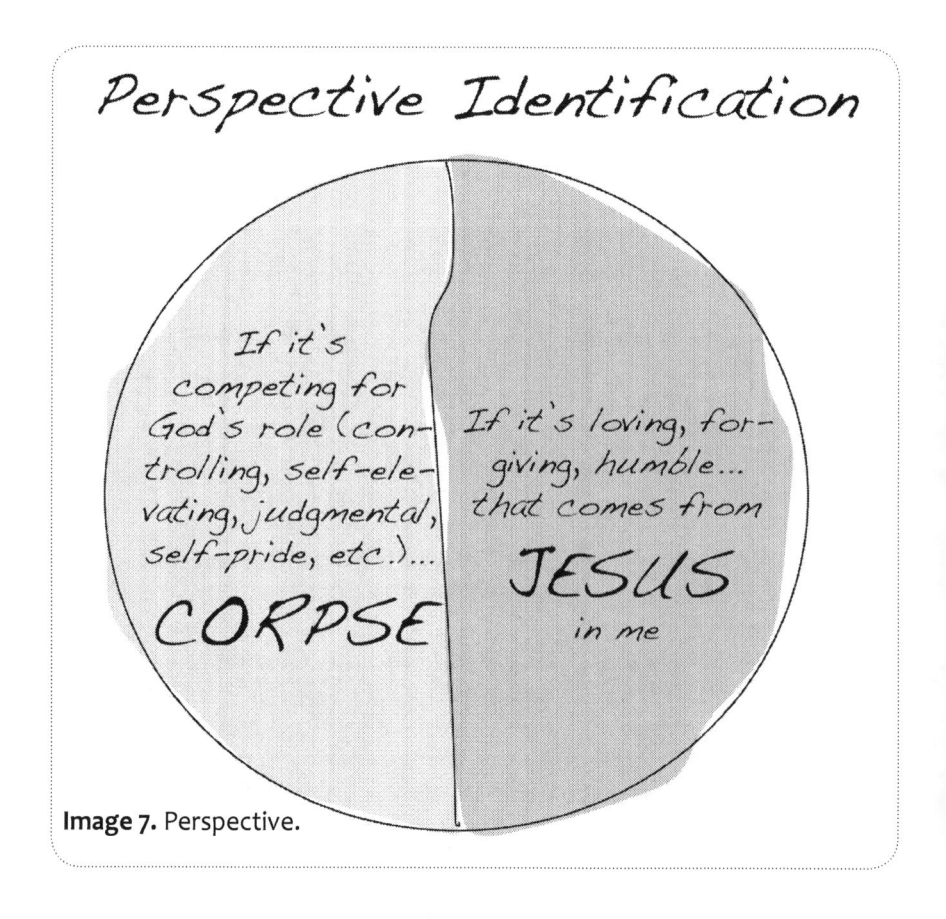

Image 7. Perspective.

3. Social Cost Bias: On Point?

The third type of cognitive bias is social cost bias (Mobini, Reynolds, and Mackintosh 2012, 176). It is an overestimation of the probability and detriment of a negative event. In other words, we are *certain* that things will turn out very badly. And we are *certain* that things will turn out very badly very often. We are the quintessential pessimist for all things social.

In social anxiety, these overestimations only occur in relation to social events (Mobini, Reynolds, and Mackintosh 2012, 176). For example, the socially anxious does not overestimate the risk of injuries from a drive to the local park. He would only overestimate his likelihood to be *socially awkward* at the park. And his estimate might not be all that far off. I have always had a theory that pessimism might actually be realism. But, of course, that might be my social cost bias talking. Read on.

This negative bias towards social events is not related to depression (Mobini, Reynolds, and Mackintosh 2012, 176) even though depression and social anxiety often occur together. In depression, negative views span both social and non-social scenarios. Social cost bias seems to be a core feature of social anxiety itself.

There is the possibility that the high social cost estimates found in social anxiety don't reflect an overestimation, but the reality that social events really *are more costly and are more negative*. If socially anxious individuals do not experience the same sense of pleasure from social interactions that others do, what's the payoff? It seems like all-cost/few-benefits.

The following excerpt is an example of social cost bias from a socially anxious blogger contemplating getting a job:

> I am so inadequate in almost every way when it comes to work. I don't feel confident at all in my own abilities and I can say with 100% honesty that I cannot see why anyone would want to hire me over anyone else who happened to apply for the same position... I am immediately taken back to my first job where I could not cope at all with the demands of working there and I dread (and I really do mean dread) having to be in that position again...All of this and more comes to me in a flood of sickening anxiety. Needless to say this makes job hunting quite a daunt [sic] task.[1]

This man truly did experience deep discomfort in the past, with no evidence of increased coping since then. What if he is right?

Unfortunately, he is generalizing his inadequacy to all lines of work. Every person God created (which would be, um, every person) has a unique life purpose. For us socially anxious people, it is often a challenge

---

[1] The Social Phobic: Living with Social Anxiety and Depression. 2013. https://socialphobic.co.uk/2013/07/04/describing-anxious-feelings/

to find just where and how we fit. But fit we do because we are a vital part of God's creation.

Perhaps the problem of social cost bias is rooted in an accurate assessment of poor fit. Choosing social scenarios that are a good fit for the individual might lead to great improvements in the areas of work, relationships, and worship. For the blogger above, a job that is less socially taxing and better utilizes his strengths would surely lead to greater success. Less anxiety. Rest.

One of my most idiotic mistakes was putting faith into God *changing* me rather than putting faith into God *replacing* me. I would go ahead and commit to a job or ministry position that I knew would be too taxing. The social costs would be too high for me to handle. I had burned out enough times to recognize this. But I believed God would change me and sustain me. If He wanted me to do good for Him, He would have to step up! So, in faith, I would embark on a new commitment.

God better STEP UP!

Somehow, I neglected to recognize that the only faith I can really, truly invest in is faith in Jesus Christ as the one perfect, capable, inexhaustible human. I did not realize I could rest in His perfection...and be myself. That is what true faith is all about. It is not about trusting God to change us, or sustain us, but to love us. It is not even about doing good for Him but rather embracing the good He has done toward us.

These days, I am well aware of my flaws—the ones that have caused me the most trouble, anyway. I accept them. I do not deny that they are there. I do not expect God to remove them. I work around them as best I can. And I rest in God.

Social costs are no joke, people.

DO BIAS MODIFICATION STRATEGIES WORK?

Now let's get down to the nitty gritty. Do the three CBT strategies listed above actually help? Can we change what we pay attention to, how we interpret events, and our negative skew on social interactions? Maybe a tiny bit, but is it enough to truly make a dent in our social anxiety?

Treatment is not so successful

Bias modification strategies have certainly enjoyed a tremendous surge in popularity over the last 10 years. Unfortunately, a recent review of 49 studies (from 2005 to 2013) showed very little, if any, significant effect of these strategies on mental health problems (Cristea, Kok, and Cuijpers 2015, 9-10). Ten of those studies used cognitive bias strategies specifically for SAD and demonstrated no significant benefits. So, the short answer on effectiveness appears to be...not so much.

Ironically, the studies on cognitive bias often contain their own cognitive bias—a tendency to over-estimate positive treatment outcomes (Cristea, Kok, and Cuijpers 2015, 10). Many of the positive effects reported could be traced to factors not related to cognitive bias modification. Likewise, the quality of many of the studies was found to be low. The highest quality studies showed the lowest levels of benefit from cognitive bias modification (14). Not good.

Researchers concluded that cognitive bias modification strategies have very limited, if any, effectiveness, casting doubt on the future of this type of therapy. Trying to strong-arm our attention, interpretation, and social cost estimates may only increase their power. I am convinced that the less we *try*, and the more we *rest* in Christ, the better these things get. You can quote me on that.

I Feel Bad for Mini-Me: Imagery Rescripting

A completely different approach to reducing social anxiety symptoms is called imagery rescripting. We socially anxious people tend to experience distorted, excessively negative images of selves (Wild, Hackmann, and Clark 2008, 47). In my mind's eye, I see myself as a hunched, green-haired hag standing in the corner. In real life, I don't have that much style.

For some, these negative self-images can be traced back to a triggering event, such as being bullied as a child. Past imagery rescripting focuses on an early negative image that resulted in a negative core belief (Morrison and Heimberg 2013, 251, 255). For example, a client may remember being humiliated in a classroom as a child. This memory is a recurring mental image that undergirds his belief that humiliation is likely to occur in any social setting.

Imagery rescripting addresses the early memory and inserts corrective beliefs, based on compassion towards self. The client is invited to imaginatively relive the early traumatic event but from a different perspective. For instance, the client may envision his childhood classroom humiliation, but compassionately step in as an adult to comfort his childhood self. This past self-compassion is hypothesized to create more positive views of self in the future.

One very small study (only 11 participants) found imagery rescripting effective in reducing anxiety about social events (Wild, Hackmann, and Clark 2008, 52). It was a fast-acting treatment; patients exhibited positive change in as little as one session. The key to successful imagery rescripting seems to be a stance of self-compassion. Imagery rescripting conducted in most clinical settings is devoid of spiritual connotations.

Christians have long been skep-

> The only spirit guide I trust is the Holy Spirit

tical of the use of imagery, and for good reason. On one extreme, author David Hunt observes that visualization has been at the heart of witchcraft and shamanism for centuries.[2] In a New Age context, individuals believe that inner visualization has the power to provide healing, create wealth, manipulate reality, and contact spirits. Guided imagery may invoke the use of a spirit guide for advice and direction. These practices are, to be frank, no bueno. In this context, the use of imagery is an individual's attempt to be a god (i.e., to control, create, and manipulate circumstances). That makes it an act of the flesh (corpse).

That said, however, the use of images to rewrite unbiblical core beliefs is not, in and of itself, evil. Theophostic Prayer Ministry, founded by Dr. Ed Smith, is a Christian oriented program that uses methods similar to imagery rescripting.[3] The first step of theophostic prayer is to re-imagine an early, painful life experience. Then, Jesus is prayerfully invited to enter the early memory, rewriting the painful experience with an expression of His unconditional love.

For example, a client might remember being scared as a child when his parent was drunk and violent. The client would then visualize Jesus hugging the child version of himself, protecting him from harm. Thus, Theophostic Prayer is a means of connecting with the very real compassion of God. It is less an act of imagination (compared with traditional imagery rescripting) and more a request for genuine healing from God.

Dr. Smith has received a tremendous amount of criticism regarding Theophostic techniques, for various reasons. In my opinion, the biggest risk in imagery rescripting is the potential of twisting the imagination to serve human (corpse-based) desires. Although this is not what Smith advocates, unfortunately some have misused his techniques to visualize God condoning their desires of the flesh (the corpse).

> ## Not-So Fun Fact
>
> Many years ago, I tried Theophostic Prayer Healing (inviting Jesus in to heal past memories) as a treatment for panic attacks. It did not alleviate my symptoms. In fact, it increased the physical symptoms tremendously. So, while it may be useful for some, it didn't help me.

---

2 Hunt, David, quoted in Weldon, John and John Ankerberg. 2009. "Visualization (Part One)." Christian Research Journal. Read more @ http://www.equip.org/article/visualization-part-one/#christian-books-1

3 Read more about Smith's ministry at http://www.theophostic.com/

Authors Stanton L. Jones and Richard E. Butman wrote about a client who felt trapped in his loveless marriage (2011). The client imagined God comforting him and supporting his decision to leave his wife. The use of imagination here is self-serving and not true to the nature of God. As with any counseling technique, straying from the heart of God will only cause additional pain.

Anyone interested in using imagery rescripting will need to use great discernment, focusing on the biblical ideal of God's compassion over our past traumas.

ME, MYSELF, AND I: SELF-FOCUSED ATTENTION

Another (surprise!) problem area we socially anxious people have is self-focused attention. I am my favorite subject—particularly when it comes to what is going on inside of me. Look, I have basically written a whole book about me and my problems!

Self-focused attention is an awareness of internal physical states, thoughts, emotions, beliefs, attitudes, and memories. It has long been proposed that socially anxious individuals are highly attuned to their own physical and emotional states. This may be due to unusually strong internal sensations. We may experience life more intensely than others and have trouble ignoring this intensity.

Interoceptive awareness is the degree of sensitivity one has towards one's own bodily state (Terasawa et al., 2012). I am painfully aware of when I am blushing, trembling, and sweating. Research indicates that a greater self-awareness of one's bodily state contributes to the development of intense emotions and anxiety disorders (259). I am aware, and I dislike.

The magnitude of bodily sensations for a highly interoceptive person exceeds normal sensation (thus causing discomfort and distraction). Researchers using brain-imaging techniques were able to pinpoint the role of the anterior insula (the Mysterious Island of Feels!) in interoceptive awareness (Terasawa et al. 2012, 265). The more active the insula was, the more exaggerated bodily sensations were, along with levels of anxiety.

Here's a fun little story to illustrate my high level of self-focused attention. Once upon a time, I managed to pick up an angry stalker on social media. I discovered that he had flooded his social media account with threats directed at me. As a rather sheltered farm wife, I was horrified. I had a full body reaction...a flood of adrenaline, burning in my heart, and shaking. For someone with social anxiety, public judgment is a pretty powerful trigger.

> **Public judgment triggers a self-focused war**

My internal state was on high alert for danger. There was no ignoring my discomfort. No refocusing. No distracting. No controlling it or working myself out of it. My hurt felt real, powerful, intense, and overwhelming. I don't think everyone reacts like this. But that's me. I suspect an MRI of my brain might have shown it bursting into flames.

And that, my friends, is what being overly aware of one's inner state feels like. My physical reaction was completely out of proportion to the actual threat. Internet insults? Come on!

Heightened self-focus has led to treatments aimed at distracting the individual from self (Morrison and Heimberg 2013, 269). The goal is to direct attention to outer, environmental stimuli and ignore inner sensations. Basically, they want us to forget about all those icky feelings happening inside of us and tune in to our surroundings. Good luck with that.

One small study of 29 social phobia patients revealed that changing focus from self to external stimuli led to improvements in anxiety within one week (Mortberg et al. 2013, 63–73). In fact, in this study, changing self-focused attention was effective at lowering social anxiety symptoms, whereas trying to change automatic negative thoughts did not help.

Well, maybe this is a good idea. The idea of "other-focus" vs. "self-focus" is, of course, a biblical ideal. Even if I manage to turn my focus outward just a touch, that is good stuff.

Even more helpful, in my opinion, is to allow ourselves to feel what we feel. It may be out of proportion. It may be a little wacky. But it's honest... It is what's inside of us. And while we are feeling what we feel, we can remember some important truths. People-judgment is irrelevant. God-judgment is settled. (P.S. my social media stalker only stalked me for one day. And God's grace calmed me, soothed me, and allowed me to move on in less than an hour.)

So far we have focused mostly on the thought elements of CBT. There is a battle in our mind between the old and new nature. The Old Us will fail often at CBT techniques. The New Us is credited with perfect thoughts and behavior. Counseling methods and effort did not give us credit, Jesus did.

The next section is all about additional counseling methods. We will learn to pick out good rules, bad rules, and apply grace to each one. Grace, after all, trumps all.

* * *

Reflection

1. In your opinion, what role do thoughts play in social anxiety?

2. Is it possible to eliminate social anxiety by changing your thinking?

3. Do you frequently suppress your emotions? If so, are you willing to try being more authentic (with a gentle spirit)?

4. What are your biggest fears? What core beliefs are at the root?

5. What is God's perspective on social anxiety?

6. Take a moment to notice something positive in your environment right now.

7. Is there a good fit between you and your home, work, church, and community environments? Are there changes you would like to make?

8. Read Philippians 4: 6-7. Who do you know who seems to have this type of peace? Why do you think that is?

11

COMMITTED
(AND NOT TO A MENTAL INSTITUTION)

A newer counseling method born from CBT digs a little deeper. It is called Acceptance and Commitment Therapy (ACT), and the title gives a clue to its focus. ACT is all about accepting yourself while remaining committed to your values.

ACT has been around since the late 1980s.[1] Steven Hayes has been credited as the founder of ACT. It is a third generation offshoot of behavior therapies. Before ACT, most treatments for SAD focused largely on symptom reduction. The goal was always some manner of change, which was held to bring relief. ACT is much different.

With ACT, neither change nor symptom reduction are primary or even necessary. One of the main goals of ACT is to live a life in accordance with one's deepest held values, *regardless of symptoms.* The emphasis is on "accepting social anxiety as it is, not needing it to be any different, while still pursuing valued life goals" (Kocovski, Fleming, and Rector 2009, 287).

At first glance, that would seem like a pretty major disappointment. Who wants to go to all the trouble of attending therapy without expecting change or relief? Nobody, that's who. And yet, there is something about *taking off the pressure to change* that unexpectedly produces both change and

**Not change.
Not improvement.
*Values.***

---

[1] Dewane, Claudia. 2008. The ABCs of ACT- Acceptance and Commitment Therapy. *Social Work Today*, 8(5): 34. http://www.socialworktoday.com/archive/090208p36.shtml

symptom relief. Does that not sound a little like grace?

ACT appears to be an effective treatment for disorders including anxiety, depression, pain, work stress, smoking, substance use, psychosis, and borderline personality disorder (Hayes et al. 2006). A recent review of 39 studies using ACT showed that it was as effective as other traditional treatment models (Davis et al. 2015, 30-36). This is particularly interesting since the focus of ACT is not reducing symptoms. Because that is exactly what it does, at least as successfully as any other treatment.

One recent study examined the usefulness of ACT for social anxiety delivered via videoconferencing (Yuen et al. 2013, 389-397). It went like this: 24 clients agreed to Skype with a therapist for 12 weekly one-hour sessions. Therapists used something called Acceptance Based Behavior Therapy for Social Anxiety Disorder. This treatment focused on role play and exposure exercises.

By Skyping with their therapists, individuals were taught to "view anxiety as less threatening, to engage in behaviors consistent with personally derived values, and to weaken the influence of thoughts on behavior" (Yuen et al. 2013, 392). After treatment, 54% no longer met the diagnostic standard for social anxiety disorder. What that probably means is that they experienced some symptoms but not enough to significantly affect quality of life.

54% no longer met the diagnosis for SAD

Thirty-three percent were rated very much improved, and an additional 38% were rated as much improved (Yuen et al. 2013, 393). Seventeen percent were rated as minimally improved. Overall, those are pretty impressive statistics.

Now, granted, this was a very small study. It does not (I know, you have heard me say this a million times) provide evidence that we have found a magic bullet for social anxiety. But it does provide clues that ACT may prove useful for social anxiety. I am hopeful that future research will back this up. I promise you, if someone ever does find the magic bullet (apart from __GRACE__), I will put it in all caps, bold, italics, and underline it so you cannot miss it.

ACT is traditionally delivered as a secular or generically spiritual model.

Of all the methods I have researched, this one seems particularly suited to molding itself to the gospel. Turns out, I am not the only one who thinks so. Therapist and author Ingrid Rhea Ord's ACT manual (*Act with Faith, Acceptance and Commitment Therapy for Christian Clients: A Practitioner's Guide,* 2014) is designed to help therapists make grace the center of ACT with their clients.

Ord believes that a major reason why ACT works, and why it jibes with Christianity, is that it directly addresses the nature of suffering. Individuals who attempt to avoid pain often unintentionally increase long-term suffering. Yet, suffering is a part of the human condition and can bring with it an increase in faith, character, patience, etc. Ord states: "Grace theology can promote flexibility by encouraging willing acceptance of unpleasant experiences" (2014, 42).

Further, Ord says, "As a Christian who prays, reads and studies the Bible, and who has experienced my belief in God as life-changing, I am confident that ACT is acceptable to mainline Christian teaching and can be underpinned by Scripture" (2014, 21). Ord believes that ACT can be a grace-based therapy that encourages endurance of suffering for the achievement of eternally-focused goals. Ord has carefully included the theology of grace (vs. religion or rules) in every step of the ACT process.

Unlike many other theoretical models, biblically oriented ACT lays the responsibility for change directly in God's hands. The client has the responsibility of making value-oriented choices, but God produces transformation through His own devices (i.e., circumstances, divine intervention, comfort, encouragement, etc.). If suffering persists, it is considered His will, and for His glory and our own eternal benefits.

> **God alone is the producer of change**

Traditional ACT includes six core processes: present moment awareness, defusion, acceptance, perspective of self, values, and committed action. Each is explored below, through the lens of grace (relying heavily on the work of Ord 2014).

1. Present Moment Awareness
God, are you there? Its me, Julie

This process builds on the platform of mindfulness (or mindfulness meditation). Mindfulness is a big word for simply paying attention to what is going on upstairs (as in, up in our minds and around us). Apparently, a lot of us have a whole Broadway show going on up there, but we never really follow the plot line. Researchers put it a little more elegantly: "paying total attention to the present moment with a non-judgmental awareness of inner and outer experiences" (Chiesa and Serretti 2011, 442).

Mindfulness meditation has been around for a very long time.

Some of us Christians might have a little red flag pop up when we hear the term. It sounds a little New Agey. It is actually older than New Agey. It's Old Agey: Mindfulness originated in the East and has only recently become of interest in Western culture. The red flag probably pops up because mindfulness can be traced back ultimately to Zen Buddhism (Tan 2011, 243). And, let's be honest, Buddhism and Christianity do not play well together (nor should they).

But if we strip Buddhist influences from mindfulness, we end up with a mindset that simply recognizes the inner workings of the mind *without* being swept away by them (Seigel 2010, 91). Mindfulness requires the thinker to take a step back from one's thoughts. The goal is to observe inner thought processes "without overtly identifying with them or without reacting to them in ways that further distress" (Vøllestad, Nielsen, and Nielsen 2012, 240). The client is taught that thoughts do not define self. Thoughts are just thoughts.

> Get to know the plot, dialogue, and characters in your Broadway show

Kevin Tupper, founder of christiansimplicity.com, states:

> Mindfulness is paying attention. It is noticing what you are doing, feeling and thinking at the time you are actually doing, feeling and thinking it. Because God is part of our everyday lives, paying attention to God and focusing on God's kingdom is a fundamental practice of Christian mindfulness.[2]

I have very little experience with mindfulness (but a ton of experience with mindlessness). But here is a demonstration of what mindfulness might look like in my own life:

> *I feel down in this moment. Something's bugging me, tugging at my heart. What is it? What am I feeling right now, and why? Ah... I spy guilt. And a liberal dose of shame. I am thinking about my general selfishness. I recognize shame. I call it what it is. I remind myself that I am completely forgiven by God. But the feeling might remain...perhaps enduring for a few moments, hours, days. But for now, in this moment, that is what I am experiencing. That is what's in my mind.*

Unlike secular mindfulness, my experience would also include taking thoughts captive to Christ (applying grace; 2 Corinthians 10:5). I recog-

---

[2] Read more at http://christiansimplicity.com/christian-mindfulness/

nize that no matter how I feel, or what I experience, I am loved by God, through Christ alone. My healthiest, truest thoughts are *captivated* by God's unconditional love. Still, I do not fight what I am feeling. I do not deny my feelings, try to stuff them, banish them, or change them. I honestly experience what I experience, soaking up grace all the while.

Mindfulness also relies on the act of being present. This translates into paying attention to the current moment, ignoring both the future and the past (Tan 2011, 243). It is a surrendering of our past and future to God. Mindfulness-based therapy also emphasizes self-acceptance and compassion. For the Christian, this is more a sense of God-compassion and God-derived acceptance through Christ. Ord writes: "The practice of mindfulness promotes flexible sensitivity to self-judgment, and the development of compassion for self and others" (2014, ix).

Unlike traditional cognitive therapy, there is no effort to correct faulty thought-patterns (Vøllestad, Nielsen, and Nielsen 2012, 240). The goal is simply to increase well-being, not to combat thoughts.

Present moment awareness also celebrates the sacredness of each moment, in relationship with God (Tan 2011, 246). This encompasses a constant surrendering to His will, of "letting go and letting God" take control. *This is what I am experiencing, God; do with it what You will.* We are advised biblically to forget the past (Philippians 3:13-14) and not to worry about tomorrow (Matthew 6:33-34). We actively and honestly experience the present, in God's presence.

Ord (2014, 35) includes the following helpful aims of being present in the moment from within a grace-based worldview:

- Teaches you to just be, right here and now
- Notice and let go
- Especially let go of judgment

To set the stage for mindfulness meditation (connecting to God), Ord (2014) recommends sitting in a private place—allowing silence and blocking possible disturbances. To develop mindfulness into a habit, spend perhaps 5 minutes a few times a week. If desired, bring a Bible or study aids. You can use music as a tool for simple worship. The overarching goal is to become aware of one's mind and experience connection with God. There is power in resting in our relationship.

Please do not make this into a performance-based law for spiritual growth or holiness. It is really just a tool to help us recognize our constant connection to God. We are connected whether we meditate or not. Here is a Bible verse that proves it: "Be strong and of good courage, do not fear nor be afraid of them; for the Lord your God, He is the One who goes with you. He will not leave you nor forsake you" (Deuteronomy 31:6, NKJV).

The mind can be trained to practice mindfulness at all times. The heart purpose is a life of continual awareness of our connection with God, which is what it means to "pray without ceasing" (1 Thessalonians 5:17, NKJV). I find that I go long stretches of time forgetting that God is with me (this does not surprise or horrify Him). The more I remember He is near, and loving me, the healthier I am.

God, are you there? my heart whispers.

Yes... always.

Mindfulness has also been practiced and researched as a treatment of its own (independent from ACT). We will examine the results in the next chapter.

2. DEFUSION
Be a mental gymnast!

The second element of ACT is called **defusion.** According to Ord, defusion is the "ability to 'unstick' from rigid personal rules and to renew the mind" (2014, p. 128). The term comes from the word "defuse," as in dismantling a bomb. To implement defusion, an individual must step back (create some distance) between strong emotions or thoughts. Strong emotions are a bomb that we observe from a distance. They are there, but we leave them be because they pose no real threat from a distance. Defusion includes a detachment from strong emotions, recognizing them for what they are, without accepting them as absolute truth.

Rigid thinking (or fused thoughts) include making global judgments about self/others, refusing to change an opinion, unreasonable demands, inability to admit fault, aversion to change, etc. (Ord 2014). The highly religious or performance-oriented person may resort to rigid (fused) rule observance.

The goal of defusion is to introduce flexibility into thought-patterns and decrease rigid and rule-based thinking. I have found that rigid thinking has gotten me into a lot of trouble. For instance, I used to measure my personal worth by how well I did as a wife/mother. Under this rigid thinking, if I screwed up (e.g., didn't get dinner done on time, failed to keep the house clean) I felt condemned. I was a failure. The rules were set, and there was no wiggle room. That is a nasty, unrelenting way to live.

I once traveled on a mountain highway during a severe windstorm. We had purchased a new vehicle the day before, and gusts pitched the vehicle noticeably. Beside the road ahead of me, a lovely, mature pine bent in the wind. To my astonishment, it bowed further, further, until it cracked explosively and sprayed across the road. I was able to stop my vehicle sharply, just before hitting it. The splintered remains of the tree blocked the entire highway, halting traffic. It took the efforts of five other travelers to clear the road before I could continue.

I spent the rest of my drive marveling at the image of that pine snapping. It was not one of the young, more vulnerable trees that had snapped. Rather, the tallest, strongest, most regal tree of the forest had gone down in a splash of bark and dust. It was all about flexibility.

> **The wind blows where it wishes, and you hear the sound of it, but cannot tell where it comes from and where it goes. So is everyone who is born of the Spirit** (John 3:8, NKJV).

Life never turns out quite how we expect it to. We must bend and curve to survive the tempests. God's unconditional love provides the flexibility for the storm.

So just how can we increase our mental flexibility? *That* is a great question. The first step is to incorporate the perspective of grace into our thoughts. I might observe myself thinking, "I am so lazy. All I did was watch TV today." I have made a harsh, rigidly defined self-judgment. A grace-based perspective reminds me that even though I spent a lot of time resting today, God still treasures me, all thanks to Jesus.

3. ACCEPTANCE
Just relax, man!

Acceptance includes embracing all experiences (even suffering) as a part of the human journey. ACT, according to researchers Dalrymple et al. (2014) views "emotional pain…as a natural result of living, and unnecessary suffering is created when repeated efforts to escape from or avoid emotional pain are undertaken" (p. 519). The acceptance of the reality of suffering can lead to growth, peace, and triumph.

Evangelist Billy Graham wrote:

Suffering in life can uncover untold depths of character and unknown strength for service. People who go through life unscathed by sorrow and untouched by pain tend to be shallow in their perspectives on life. Suffering, on the other hand, tends to plow up the surface of our lives to uncover the depths that provide greater strength of purpose and accomplishment. Only deeply plowed earth can yield bountiful harvests (Graham and Graham 2011, p. 337).

Ord states that many people who convert to Christianity believe it will be a life-enhancement (2014). The reality is that suffering happens to Christians just as much as to others, "sometimes even more so…if there is persecution" (75). Yet, for Christians, acceptance of suffering is a submission to God's will. Even the experience of social anxiety can fulfill God's purposes and further His Kingdom. Social anxiety does not feel good. But it can *do* good. It can keep us humble, dependent on God's undeserved love, and put us in the right places at the right times.

Whether symptoms flare or fade, nothing can stop the good that God has planned for His people. Oftentimes, pain is the very instrument God uses to highlight His unconditional love (Ord 2014, 78). It is during times of pain that we are the most human, and the most unworthy of divine favor. Yet, we have it in full measure.

It is important to note that acceptance of difficult life circumstances does not mean pretending all is well or remaining helpless. Genuine acceptance gives the person permission to both feel and act. The apostles of the early church were hard-pressed on every side, and they admitted it. Jesus Himself wept in grief. Even within intense negative emotions, trusting in God's loving will provides a vast measure of peace.

Humans, Christians included, have little control over the experience of suffering. Suffering comes to us all. It cannot be prevented or avoided. Likewise, painful thoughts and feelings cannot be controlled (Ord 2014, 81). But accepting our errant thoughts and feelings, while remaining committed to our values, is possible. During difficult times, I often imagine an ox with his head down, plodding steadily forward. "Head down, keep going," I whisper to myself.

4. Perspective of Self
Just who am I?

The "perspective of self" element of ACT is seeing one's self from a new, more compassionate perspective (Ord 2014). It involves refusing judgment because of the covering of grace. For the Christian, the perspective of self all comes back to the topic of Chapter 7: am I really the New Me (in Jesus) or the corpse?

Learning to see ourselves and others through the lens of grace, regardless of our performance, is counterintuitive. It takes practice, which is growing in grace (2 Peter 3:18). It is the only type of spiritual growth that is important and eternally worthwhile.

5. VALUES
Oh, I love that! I really, really love that!

And now we come to my favorite part of ACT: values! Guess who gets to choose your values? That's right—you do! A value is a strongly held ideal. You can probably think of a few top values right now. Maybe, like me, these are a few of your favorites: family, love, hard work, nurturing, faithfulness. Or maybe creativity, artistry, fellowship, or solitude are the keys to your heart. Any value that mirrors a God-value is a good value. Individual values might be as different as snowflakes, but together they add up to a dazzling blizzard.

We get in trouble when we absorb other people's (or organizations') unique values. I don't know if all people with social anxiety are like this, but I can almost *feel* the values of a place when I walk in. There are clues everywhere. The way people talk, dress, are organized, etc. And I have to resist the temptation to begin morphing my values to the group's, which tends to be another form of "people-pleasing" for me.

> "It's not hard to make decisions when you know what your values are."
> — Roy Disney

I think many people in faith communities are intent on pleasing, or rather *not displeasing*, fellow believers (Ord 2014, 108). This is particularly true for judgment-sensitive socially anxious people. Thus, our values are easily absorbed from other people. Some churches emphasize fellowship activities. Others emphasize adoption, financial giving, missions, organized ministry, humility, intellectual prowess, etc. Families do the same thing. Some families value dependence on one another while others idealize freedom and independence. We can (and will) get lost trying to achieve and maintain the values of others.

One goal of ACT is to allow the client to develop his own unique values apart from others' influences. This is very, very important because God designed each individual with a unique role to play in His Kingdom. Nobody can do what you do. Nobody loves what you love. Your unique values are worthwhile.

Personal values come in all shapes and sizes. Some deeply value education; others, marriage, parenthood, hard work, rest, big family gatherings, children, careers, art, farm life, cultural experiences... The list is infinite. Every unique value can be infused with God's love. The person who loves his job at plumbing can work as if working for God. The person who loves art can use it to display praise for God's creation.

And on and on and on.

A frequent problem is people forcing their values on those around them. For instance, the person who values education may insist that everyone needs a college degree. Although education may have played a pivotal role in one person's life journey, it could be irrelevant to someone else. As a universal rule, therefore, it makes no sense.

Another problem occurs when we face adversity while in pursuit of our values. One goal of ACT is to reduce the tendency to avoid all forms of suffering. We don't go to the party because we know it will make us terribly nervous and uncomfortable. We avoid so as not to suffer. But living a life that aligns with our values actually embraces *some* suffering—though not all the time, of course. We will be forced to carefully, intentionally prioritize our time/energy/suffering in relation to our values. Perhaps we will choose to refuse party attendance our whole life, except that one party at which we know our presence is clearly a pivotal extension of God's love.

Take some time to identify your own values. Be really honest with yourself, and with God, about what you deeply care about in life. Don't try to make your values sound good, religious, or deep. Values should be specific (rather than broad or too open-ended). For instance, don't write down loving people—too general. Instead write something like: *making people laugh by telling silly jokes.*

Once you identify your personal values, you will typically write them out as a part of ACT therapy (starting with the most important). I have provided a values worksheet for you in the Appendix of this book. You may want to tear it out, write down your values, and tape it somewhere as a frequent reminder.

Now ask yourself: How do these values help express God's love? How can your identified values help make decision-making easier for you?

Do you feel excited and energized when you look at your list of values?

The client will then use his God-given values to formulate a plan of committed action. Goals spring from values. And in order to achieve your goals, you will need to be a superhero. Read on.

6. Committed Action
I'm a Superhero!

Committed action is any purposeful step that gets one closer to living out a cherished value. Values, in effect, create the path towards something. Committed action is taking a step down that path. I like the analogy of a hiker on a hiking trail. Obviously, there will be times when the hiking is vigorous and difficult (times of suffering or anxiety). The hiking may go slow. Still, continued plodding forward, no matter how insignificant, will eventually complete the hike. God's grace provides the shade, drinking water, and walking stick that make the hike do-able. Not only do-able, but also deeply enjoyable.

The Bible certainly places an emphasis on acting in accordance with one's beliefs. The best way to have a life of committed action is to start with very, very small steps. For example, a man who feels isolated has identified the goal (value) of being in a caring community. He is far too intimidated to simply attend a church service. So his first tiny step would be to join a church Facebook page. In doing so, he has successfully inched down the path. Every step, no matter how small, is successful movement forward.

Traveling the path towards fulfilled values entails a certain amount of risk. Listen to James' words: "For we all stumble in many things. If anyone does not stumble in word, he is a perfect man, able also to bridle the whole body" (James 3:2, NKJV). Stumbling is a natural part of the human condition. Yet, even stumbling is a form of travel. Clumsy traveling is better than no traveling at all! And rest is permitted whenever necessary.

> **Obstacles are sure to come**

The table on the next page shows the ACT steps beginning with defining values and leading all the way to purposeful living. Taking committed action based on values is actually a very simple way to live.

Still, obstacles are sure to come up. Ord believes that loss is actually built into committed action (2014, 121). Often, the people around us are somewhat alarmed by movements of growth. Common obstacles for socially anxious people include displeasing/disappointing others, going against expectations, tolerating conflict, and triggering our physical anxiety symptoms.

Still, each obstacle has the potential to drive us right back to the truth of who we are in God's eyes (rather than other people's). That is a good thing. That is growing in grace.

ACT STEPS

Step	Instruction	Example
1.	Define values	Love others through baking.
2.	Take small steps towards that value.	Bake a cake for my neighbor.
3.	Identify what behavior is goal oriented.	Using my baking skills to bless someone.
4.	Identify obstacles.	I will dread giving it to her in person. My social anxiety will be triggered.
5.	Use flexibility and non-judgmental attitude.	I will drop it off with a note. It might seem odd to not give it to her in person, but I accept my social anxiety for what it is and want to love her anyway.

Table 9. Steps of ACT

In the table above, dropping off the cake would be classified as avoidance by several counseling models. With ACT, however, there is no self-judgment, and the offering is seen for what it is—a simple gift of love. Whether fear or social anxiety is overcome or not, the gift of love remains. The critical point is that the value is being acted upon: loving others through baking.

One recent study examined the use of ACT (with medication) to treat SAD with comorbid depression (Dalrymple et al. 2014, 516–548). The results showed significant decreases in the severity of both conditions. In the study, one participant provided the following feedback, "Feeling more in control of my emotions, developed ways of dealing with feelings, my mood is on average better, I stopped having feelings of being a failure or ruminations of the past" (p. 536).

For individuals interested in trying ACT, or who already have an ACT therapist, I highly recommend getting a copy of Ord's *ACT with Faith, Acceptance and Commitment Therapy for Christian Clients: A Practitioner's Guide* for your therapist (2014). Most therapists are more than willing to include the faith-based values of their clients (and are required to do so by all major counseling ethics codes).

ACT is my favorite counseling method simply because acceptance, compassion, and commitment to values all share the perfume of grace.

* * *

Reflection

1. Are you aware, on a moment by moment basis, of God's presence? How? (i.e., a feeling, Bible promise, creation, etc.)

2. Does learning to be more mindful seem useful?

3. Can you think of someone who is very rigid in his or her thinking and behavioral patterns? Does it interfere with well-being?

4. In what areas do you tend to be a rigid thinker?

5. Have you ever considered accepting your social anxiety as it is and not trying to change it? What would that look like?

6. What are your top three values?

7. Do you have life goals related to your values?

8. What obstacles might get in the way of achieving your goals?

9. Have you ever endured suffering in order to pursue a deeply held value? Describe the situation.

12

MORE IN THE TOOL BOX

A number of additional treatments are available for social anxiety. These include: psychoeducation, exposure therapy, emotion regulation strategies, video feedback, relaxation training, psychodynamic therapy, mindfulness, and social skills training. Let's explore...

BACK TO SCHOOL SALE: PSYCHOEDUCATION

The good news is that you can check psychoeducation off of your list. You have already started the journey! **Psychoeducation** is the process of gaining knowledge about a mental health condition. This is a broad term that may incorporate the use of books (hi there!), videos, audio recordings, online education, support groups, etc., as tools for learning. If anyone asks, you can say you are thoroughly psycho-educated, thanks to this awesome book you are holding!

Psychoeducation is included in nearly all social anxiety interventions. For example, the first session of CBT is usually psychoeducation-related. Therapy starts by learning about the nature of SAD, available treatments, symptoms, etc. Books and online courses are inexpensive and non-threatening ways to receive psychoeducation.

Personally, books are my *very favorite* way to learn. I am so glad God left us with a long love letter (the Bible) rather than a video game. Not everybody is a purely visual learner, though. Some prefer listening, watching videos, or hands-on activities. Any and all of these add up to psychoeducation.

Knowledge helps to create a certain amount of distance between the disorder and the individual, resulting in a shift in identity. No person is just a sufferer of SAD. SAD is actually relevant only to our Old Nature. The New Us is so much more: creative, artistic, determined, brave, loving, quirky, etc. Being able to say "That's my SAD acting out" is very freeing. And being able to say "That's my corpse acting out, but I am securely loved" is the Ultimate in Freedom.

Learning how to divide SAD from the real us is important. In one study, participants found that group psychoeducation helped reduce the stigma of social anxiety (Lohr, Rosenvinge, and Wynn 2011, 317). How? Well, first, participation in a group created a sense of community. The knowledge that "I am not alone" is a tremendously powerful encouragement.

> *My corpse is acting up, but I'm securely loved*

Second, understanding the nature of social anxiety helped to normalize the participants' experiences. One participant stated, "Why didn't we learn this in school? If everyone had learned this – my life would have been different" (Lohr, Rosenvinge, and Wynn 2011, 315).

God basically begs us to obtain knowledge. "Wisdom is the principal thing; therefore, get wisdom. And in all your getting, get understanding" (Proverbs 4:7, NKJV). "When wisdom enters your heart, and knowledge is pleasant to your soul, discretion will preserve you; understanding will keep you…" (Proverbs 2:10-11, NKJV). Knowledge is protective, pleasant, and more valuable than gold. Knowledge enables us to better understand who God is, who we are as humans, and who we are in Christ. What could be more important than that?

> *Understanding doesn't always solve the problem*

Still, knowledge is not *everything*. In the counseling world there is something known as "Insight Fallacy." This is the false belief that understanding something will cure us of it. Understanding the problem does not necessarily solve it. So, if you get to the end of this book and still have social anxiety, please do not be shocked (and again, no refunds!). You will have a lot of information, some new tools, and (I hope) a deeper understanding of grace. And maybe, still, some anxiety.

A Form of Torture: Exposure Therapy

Exposure therapy is a pretty common treatment used for SAD (for a review read Ougrin 2011). Most of us have heard the phrase "You just need to face your fears!" and shivered in dread…. Facing fears is the cornerstone of exposure therapy.

The exposure process includes coming into contact with the feared situation (or a simulation of the feared situation). During exposure, the client experiences heightened anxiety, which gradually eases as the client sticks with the exercise.

> After months of practice, my therapist insists I give a speech in front of an audience. I get ridiculously panicky and transfixed with helplessness. I sweat, nearly vomit, and shake like a California earthquake. I get a few words out, embarrassingly soft. A few more. Somehow, I stick with the exercise. I notice it gets slightly less terrifying as I keep speaking, one awkward word at a time. By the time it is over, I will have either calmed down just a hair or passed over the Rainbow Bridge. In either event, I am definitely a winner!

The end goal of exposure therapy is the ability to master a previously avoided activity with a much lowered or nonexistent sense of fear. Exposure is usually used after significant cognitive behavioral techniques have been mastered. A therapist might ask us to imagine a scary situation, looking for negative automatic thoughts, and then challenge them. Some examples of first gradual exposures for social anxiety are holding a conversation with a stranger, reading aloud from a book, or telling about a recent experience to a casual group of people (Hope, Heimburg, and Turk 2010).

The next step is to role-play the situation with someone safe (such as a therapist, spouse, parent, etc.). We are asked to set an achievable behavioral goal, such as "I will say three things in a conversation" (Hope, Heimburg, and Turk 2010, 131). This should not be a feeling-based goal, such as "stay calm," "be liked by others," "make a good impression," etc. The best goals are concrete, behavioral, and measurable.

Finally, after repeated practice and preparation, the real-life exposure is performed. And as far as I can tell, most people live to tell about it.

Systemic Desensitization: easing into it.

Systematic desensitization is a very gradual form of exposure therapy (Ougrin 2011, 2). It typically begins with relaxation training followed by an imaginary exposure...that eases gently towards the fear.

Just the act of imagining public speaking is enough to induce anxiety in most of us. As we begin to overcome anxiety with an imagined exposure, the level of the exposure exercises increase. Maybe next time (instead of just imagining) we will actually perform a speech in front of a video camera. And then in front of our spouse. And so on, gradually increasing the levels of achievement.

On the opposite end of the exposure spectrum is flooding. Flooding involves exposure to the most feared stimulus in a real-life application.

For example, a person with a spider phobia would be asked to directly handle a spider. Theoretically, flooding would initially induce extreme anxiety, which would eventually taper off. The desired result of flooding is for a person to face a fear, survive it, and thus learn in a very hands-on, physical/emotional way that the fear was unfounded.

Flooding: AY-CARAMBA!!!!!!!

Learning how not to be afraid of something is called **fear extinction**. This type of learning seems tied to glutamate and the amygdala. One 2013 study found that the effectiveness of exposure therapy for social anxiety can be enhanced through the use of d-cycloserine (Smits et al., 1459). D-cycloserine is an antibiotic/amino acid that affects the glutamatergic receptors in the amygdala.

D-cycloserine increased the effectiveness of exposure sessions, but only when the individual ended the session with a low amount of fear (Smits et al. 2013, 1459-60). The participant had to reach a place of mastery over fear during the exposure in order for permanent learning to take place. Researchers continue to investigate the role of d-cycloserine in learning and fear extinction. I don't know about you, but I don't have any d-cycloserine just laying around. So for now, this is not a very practical source of help. But perhaps researchers are onto something useful for the future.

A pill for learning? Niiiiiice.

Virtual Reality Exposure therapy (VRE) is another form of exposure treatment for SAD. VRE involves exposing an individual to a targeted fear in a computer-generated environment (Anderson et al., 2013, 751-760). It is like a video game based on your worst fears! This reminds me of Tetris because I keep organizing and organizing but the de-organizing never stops!

Usually, VRE is done with a head-mounted display (a high-tech helmet) and multi-sensory input. In one experiment, researchers created a virtual conference room, classroom, and auditorium (with 5 to over 100 virtual people present for each scenario; Anderson et al. 2013). During the exposure therapy, participants were asked to speak in front of either virtual groups or real-life groups. The researchers were able to manipulate virtual audience reactions, making them look bored, hostile, distracted, etc. Imagine the power!

For whatever reason, people interpret these virtual environments as real enough to invoke anxiety, thus creating a genuine exposure experience. In a review of 23 studies (with 608 participants), VRE was found to be as effective as traditional real-life exposure therapy for anxiety disorders (Opris et al. 2011, 85–93). That is kind of amazing—that a virtual reality treatment can be as useful as in-person therapy. Not all video games are bad. Just Tetris.

How about a Video Game?

There is some concern that previous studies of virtual reality-based exposures may not have been high quality (McCann et al. 2014, 629). Thus, there is a need for more and better studies to support its effectiveness. Overall, however, the technique seems particularly promising for socially anxious people because it would be easily obtainable and affordable.

In general, exposure therapy does not seem particularly helpful if thought-patterns are not addressed. Dr. Dennis Ougrin conducted a meta-analysis of 3 studies examining CBT vs. exposure specifically for social anxiety (2011). The results indicated that exposure therapy alone was significantly less effective than CBT. These effects were true for both short-term and long-term outcomes. This may suggest that socially anxious individuals are not able to habituate, or get used to, feared social situations.

Slow, gradual, and "soft" exposures work best (of the systematic desensitization variety; Ougrin 2011). That's a relief to hear. For the socially anxious Christian, signing up for a week-long group retreat would not be a gentle, gradual exposure exercise for social anxiety. Instead, maybe start by having a small conversation with someone familiar at church. This is enough to invoke anxiety but will not be overwhelming. And onwards and upwards from there.

Exposure Therapy less helpful than CBT

I believe that God often empowers us to master social situations that are *important to Him*. He does this by planting a desire within us that is stronger than our fears. I registered for a several-day Christian writing conference all by myself and out of town. This is exactly the type of social activity I dread—all-new people, new environment, no moral support, and long hours of interacting. Even worse, I would be forced to *share meals with authority figures* (editors and publishers). The horror!

Because the subject matter was so utterly fascinating to me, however, I was willing—indeed sort of excited?—to go. My desire to attend was stronger than my fear. That doesn't happen often, but when it does, I know it is generally going to be something that strengthens me, from God.

Now if I were required to sign up for a week-long church retreat, fly-fishing camp, or nudist-colony getaway, I would probably give my social anxiety a little more say-so in event planning.

P.S. The conference was exhausting, nerve-wracking, inspiring, and wonderful! I was awkward, sweaty, smiley, and out of place. And in spite of all that God encouraged me deeply. Not because I overcame any fears but just because encouragement is always a part of His plan.

If Only I Could: Emotion Regulation

Oh, boy. This is a big one. I have already confessed that sometimes I have uncontrollable crying jags. Some people are good at controlling their emotions. Some are not. I am uncomfortable with nearly all emotions except bland. So I do a lot of stuffing, hiding, denying...internalizing. I bundle my emotions into a tiny little ball and bury them beneath layers of kidney, spleen, and liver. Internalizing is pretty common for women.

The ability to effectively manage emotions is (duh!) central to well-being. Healthy emotion regulation is the ability to experience a strong emotion, cognitively examine it, and then act in a goal-directed manner. Robot feel. Robot examine. Robot destroy (minus the robot part, and the destroy part was just for emphasis). Strong negative emotions/feelings include anger, sadness, jealousy, loneliness, shame, guilt, fear, and hurt.

> **Robot feel.**
> **Robot examine.**
> **Robot destroy.**

Here is an example of healthy emotional regulation:

> A man is traveling on a roadway and is cut off by another driver. He experiences intense anger. He imagines speeding up and ramming the car's bumper. Then he quickly imagines the consequences: either an accident or an arrest. Since he knows these actions will not achieve a positive result, he tells himself to calm down and take a deep breath. The anger fades.

This is effective emotion regulation. From a biblical standpoint it looks a lot like what the Bible calls "self-control" (Galatians 5:23). Except, self-control is a fruit of God's Spirit working in us. It is *not* a skill or strength that we possess. It is a skill/strength that He possesses (I always get that backwards) and gifts to us.

Many individuals, the socially anxious in particular, wish they could remove all negative emotions (such as fear) completely. But human emotions are not bad in and of themselves. They just *are*. It is how we manage those feelings that leads to consequences (good and bad).

Emotions are often an accurate warning sign that something is amiss. For instance, a fear of public speaking may reveal a deep-seated dread of judgment. Emotions tend to be honest, which we humans often dislike.

Emotion regulation is probably going to be more of a challenge for people with social anxiety than for most people. That seems to be how we are wired. Only the nerds reading this will appreciate the fact that the prefrontal cortex and dorsal anterior cingulate cortex are both vital in emotion control, trick-

> **Emotions tend to be honest**

ling down to the insula and amygdala (several studies cited in Koole, van Dillen, and Sheppes 2011). The rest of us are all...*what she said! Just great! Another thing wrong with me! My brain is outta control!!!*

All of these brain areas have been implicated as...er...sketchy for those with SAD (Brühl et al. 2014, 260–280). Indeed, research has linked social anxiety directly to a lowered ability to regulate emotions (Jazaieri et al. 2014). You do realize what the good news is here, right? Once again, we have an excuse! It's my brain, it's my brain...sometimes I just can't help it. (Just try not to hurt anybody with that excuse, OK?)

Social anxiety disorder has been characterized by emotional hyper-reactivity as well (Morrison and Heimberg 2013, 259). Emotions are not only more difficult to control, they are also experienced with greater intensity. Really. Intense. Less. Controllable. Double whammy. So not fair.

Socially anxious individuals also report a greater use of emotional suppression (hiding emotions) as well as negative beliefs about expressing emotions (Morrison and Heimberg 2013, 259-260). They report feeling the need to control emotions tightly and the belief that expressing emotions may lead to rejection or communicate personal weakness. Has someone been reading my journal?

Many socially anxious individuals display a poor understanding of their own emotions (Morrison and Heimberg 2013, 260). We have difficulty describing in words what we are feeling. We tend to direct anger inwards more often than healthy people. Ironically, SAD individuals also display discomfort with even positive emotions and experiences (Teal Sapach et al. 2014, 63-73). This may be due to the "in the spotlight" effect. We would rather just be invisible. Socially anxious people tend to dampen positive moods, savor them less, and do not pursue activities likely to generate a positive mood (several studies cited in Morrison and Heimberg 2013). We mostly like the emotion of "neutral."

> *I don't know exactly what I am feeling, but it's fierce*

Emotional processing generally follows a 4-step pattern (Koole, van Dillen and Sheppes 2011). See the table on the next page.

Emotion regulation strategies target any of these four steps. Individuals may avoid the emotionally triggering situation in the first place, distract themselves from it, reshape their ideas about it, or alter their behavior.

Theorists believe that emotion regulation strategies are more successful and easier to use when they target the earlier steps in emotional processing (Koole, van Dillen, and Sheppes 2011). Avoiding the trigger in the first place would be the most effective strategy for preventing intensely negative emotions.

4 Steps of Emotional Processing

Step	Action	Example
1.Trigger	A trigger produces an emotion	My mother criticizes me. I feel hurt and angry.
2. Attention	Attention is given to the trigger	My attention rivets to my mother.
3. Thoughts	Thoughts are formed about the trigger	"She always sees the worst in me."
4. Behavior	Emotions are translated into behavior	I storm out angrily.

Table 10. Emotional Processing

As it turns out, emotion regulation is really important to the success of CBT (Jazaieri et al. 2015, 530). In other words, if you are fairly good at emotional regulation, CBT will help. If you are not so good, CBT might not be quite as successful. This is a good thing to know before investing time, energy, and money into CBT.

Very few studies investigate emotional regulation strategies for social anxiety specifically (Morrison and Heimberg 2013). Cognitive reappraisal (rewriting the meaning behind experiences) was shown in one study to be helpful for building a belief is one's ability to regulate emotion for social anxiety symptoms. But as we discussed before, individuals with SAD may not be all that great (from a brain point of view) at cognitive reappraisal.

Cognitive reappraisal: rewriting meaning

Take, for example, that one time I was visiting a new church (this really happened). The pastor paused his sermon, looked directly at me, and said, "I spiritually sense that you are too stressed out." All eyes turned on me. I sank down in my seat, mortified to have been pinpointed. My thoughts included: *"What does he see in me that is so bad?" "What am I doing wrong as a Christian?" "Does God think I am too stressed out? 'Cause if this is how He is letting me know, He is really stressing me out."*

The meaning I created from the event was that I was a failure for drawing negative attention to myself. Cognitive reappraisal would have helped me to say, "Maybe this has more to do with the pastor than with me." Or: "He must be trying to make a point for the audience." And: "If God thought I was too stressed out, would He make a public spectacle of me?" I really do not think so. I think maybe He would have inspired the pastor to quietly give me a week-long beach vacation.

Another emotion regulation technique for SAD is **positive-affect-enhancing treatment** (Morrison and Heimberg 2013, 262). That is a convoluted way of saying: Be More Happier! As it turns out, one way to be happier is to be kind to others. In one study, socially anxious people were asked to engage in three acts of kindness over a 4-week period (Alden and Trew 2013, 64–75). The results showed an increase in positive mood, greater satisfaction in relationships, and less concern with self-protection. It would appear that being kind to others makes us happier! I am pretty sure this is something God wrote into our spiritual DNA.

CAN WE REALLY GET BETTER AT EMOTION REGULATION?

Most methods for teaching better emotion regulation have not yet been scientifically evaluated for success (Koole, van Dillen, and Sheppes 2011). A recent study found that people with social anxiety seem to have greater difficulty in "calming" their emotions due to brain activity (again, related to the amygdala; Burklund et al. 2014, 199–208). This difficulty was even more pronounced if the SAD individuals also had depression. Clearly, emotion regulation is very much tied to brain function.

The Greek word for our English term "self-control" is *egkrateia*, and it appears in the Bible seven times. Paraphrased, it means strength to master one's desires. Again, it is a fruit of God's Spirit. It is a beautiful, desirable skill and is often added in increasing measures as we blossom under God's love and care (2 Peter 1:5-9). We probably all start out with a certain amount (a little or a lot) of brain-based self-control and emotional regulating abilities. God helps us grow from there. We can totally trust Him.

Beneath many negative emotions lurks a faulty belief. I am often angry because I am sitting in judgment over someone (taking over God's role). I am often afraid because I doubt God is paying attention to me. I am filled with shame because I have fallen short of God's perfection. Yet, when I return to the truth of the gospel, each of those thoughts is neutralized, blasted to pieces within the glory of His love. When I rest in the truth, my emotions tend to follow. Not always, though, because (wretch that I am!) I sometimes remain unjustly angry for days! And God still loves me.

When you are facing strong negative emotions, see if any of the following sources might be at play.

> **Three Sources of Negative Emotions**
>
> 1. Expecting another human to be more like God in a specific area.
> 2. Expecting self to be more like God in a specific area.
> 3. Expecting God to respond in a human manner.

A Club for Misfits: Social Skills Training

Ah, the dreaded social skills! Most of us believe we are particularly lacking in this area. If we could just go to a class and come out extroverted and charming! I would pay a lot of money for that type of class—maybe even trade my husband (just kidding, honey!).

Turns out, there really is something called social skills training. I imagine a boot camp for awkward people. Everybody would be tripping over each other and blushing in embarrassment.

But real social skills training is designed to "decrease social anxiety, improve interpersonal skill, improve social performance (i.e., public speaking skill), and increase participation in social activities" (Beidel et al. 2014, 911).

Social Skills Training: bootcamp for awkward people

Although social skills training has been shown to provide some benefit for social anxiety, it is not as successful as other techniques (several studies cited in Bögels et al. 2010, 180). You can still go to Awkward People Boot Camp if you want. At the very least, you will probably come out the other side with some awesome and awkward new friends.

Hey... I'm a Star! Video Feedback

Imagine being the star of your own movie...good hair and makeup, perfect lighting, and dramatic, eloquent lines. Well, that is really nothing like video feedback therapy. Video feedback therapy involves being recorded while being yourself, often in an uncomfortable situation. I do not need to have myself recorded while sweating and trembling. Or, do I?

Leaving the movies to the stars

Video feedback is designed to correct overly negative self-perceptions (Morrison and Heimberg 2013, 256). One thing we socially anxious people often do is judge ourselves like power-drunk dictators. Seeing our own behavior on video might take some of the wind out of our inner dictating selves. We watch the video and realize...we look almost normal. It is hard to even see the blushing and sweating. And no one else seems to notice it either.

Studies have shown mixed results regarding how effective video feedback therapy is for social anxiety. A combination video and audience feedback experiment resulted in lowered anxiety and self-perception of performance (Chen, Mak, and Fuhita 2015, 721–739). It did not, however, improve how nervous participants felt during the actual speech. We might need to let the movie stars do their thing (movies), while we do our thing (solitude).

FREUD UN-FAN CLUB: PSYCHODYNAMIC THERAPY

According to Leichsenring et al. (2013), "Psychodynamic therapy is frequently used, both in social anxiety disorder and in clinical practice in general" (759). It is partly derived from the work of Sigmund Freud.[1] It is based upon the idea that unconscious processes are manifested in a person's present behavior. Got that? Past, unresolved conflicts (particularly with early caregivers) are believed to lead to current dysfunction (Bogels et al. 2014, 363). Insight into unresolved conflicts is seen as central to healing.

Most Christians have long rejected Freud-based therapies, due largely to Freud's antagonistic approach towards a relationship with God. Freudian psychoanalytic theory viewed belief in God as an unhealthy illusion. Most modern psychodynamic approaches, however, have moved away from a stringent, atheistic view. A psychodynamic therapist can incorporate a biblical worldview, and in fact some practicing Christian psychodynamic therapists do.

Most of the research shows that psychodynamic therapy for anxiety disorders is better than nothing (i.e., versus being on a waitlist for treatment; Fonagy 2015, 137–150). A large meta-analysis of the various types of therapy for social anxiety found psychodynamic therapy to be less effective than individual CBT, and just a hair better than nothing (Mayo-Wilson et al. 2014, 373). In fact, psychological placebo (in which the client receives a mishmash of therapeutic techniques) had roughly the same effect rate as psychodynamic therapy for SAD (369). Thus, psychodynamic therapy is recommended only as a third-line option, after CBT and SSRIs have been tried (374).

I am afraid Freud ends up at the bottom of the pile for SAD. If you currently have a great psychodynamic counselor (or are one) that doesn't mean the end is near. Just be sure that the grace and truth of the gospel are central. You really cannot lose with that.

---

1 Haggerty, Jim. 2006."Psychodynamic Therapy." *PsychCentral.* http://psychcentral.com/lib/psychodynamic-therapy/

Eyes Peeled for God: Mindfulness

I previously covered mindfulness as an important part of ACT. But mindfulness is also used on its own. Of all the different flavors of mindfulness, Mindfulness-Based Stress Reduction (MBSR) had been studied the most (Goldin et al. 2012, 65). It has been used to treat anxiety and mood disorders as well as medical conditions such as cancer and chronic pain (Tan 2011, 244).

Awareness of breathing to get distance

One MBSR exercise is called **awareness of breathing** (Vøllestad, Nielsen, and Nielsen 2012, 240). When the client begins to feel distracted by outer stimuli or inner thoughts, he redirects his attention to the physical sensation of breathing. The point is to be aware of the present; calm, centered, and non-judgmental towards self.

This exercise is supposed to allow distance from feelings and fears, lowering stress. I think there is a risk, however, of increased attention to breathing being difficult for individuals prone to panic attacks. A hyper-focus on breathing patterns may increase the sensation of not getting enough oxygen. For those of us prone to panic attacks, our breathing is a bit of a hot button.

MBSR is traditionally an 8-week psychoeducational program in which participants learn traditional Buddhist meditation techniques, presented in a non-religious format (Vøllestad, Nielsen, and Nielsen 2012, 241). It is usually conducted in small groups of 12 or fewer participants (Tan 2011, 244).

The **body scan** is another MBSR exercise, which includes "slowly attending to one's immediate experience or sensations from the feet up to the head, with attitudes of reverence, awe, kindness and acceptance without being judgmental" (Tan 2011, 244).

The body scan to relax

One study found that MBSR improved mood, functionality, and quality of life for socially anxious individuals (Koszycki et al. 2007, 2524). Another study compared MBSR to aerobic exercise (Jazaieri et al. 2015). In this study, aerobic exercise and MBSR showed equal amounts of a reduction of anxiety symptoms.

When applied specifically to social anxiety, researchers explain:

> Mindfulness practice in SAD patients involves focusing not just on how one is coming across in the situation, but to the full range of experience in the moment. Instead of judging one's experience, mindfulness practice encourages an attitude of acceptance and allowing towards physical sensations, feelings, and thoughts (Kocovski,

Fleming, and Rector 2009, 277).

A review of mindfulness based therapy for SAD found that although it provided benefits, they were not as strong as those seen in CBT (Norton et al. 2015). It is certainly not among the current recommended first-line treatments for SAD. Do I think being still and communing with God is valuable? Yes. Do I think mindfulness is that ever-elusive magic bullet? You can probably guess.

And now, you know literally everything there is to know about social anxiety. You know the counseling methods, techniques, and self-help tools. I bet you could outsmart a therapist right about now. But guess what? There are a few things I have not quite revealed yet. A few...mini-gifts that come along with social anxiety. And also, one big therapy technique that not too many therapists are actively recommending.

Despite the fact that it is the most powerful one of all.

* * *

Reflection

1. Have you ever forced yourself to face a fear (exposure) and been disappointed that it did not seem to produce a cure? Explain.

2. How would you rate your ability to manage your emotions—anywhere from poor to ninja?

3. Do you believe you experience emotions more strongly than most people?

4. Have you ever held someone else's behavior up to the perfect standard of Jesus? How did it make you feel?

5. Have you compared your own behavior to Jesus'?

6. Have you ever imagined that God is unjustly angry, petulant, thoughtless, distracted, or another human-based characteristic?

7. Are you uncomfortable with the Buddhist roots of mindfulness? Explain your opinion.

8. Have you ever experienced a panic attack? What helped or aggravated symptoms?

9. Take a moment to try out "The Body Scan." Focus on relaxing, starting with your feet and moving slowly up to your head. The goal is to become a wet noodle.

13

Extra Mini Gifts

As a writer, I tend to be repetitive! As a writer, I tend to be repetitive! As a writer, I tend to be... OK, you get the point. Throughout these pages, I have repeated the message of grace over and over again. The gift of grace is truly everything. The unconditional love of God releases us from the power of judgment. It enables us to love others in ways we could never accomplish on our own. Grace creates simple values and the strength to pursue them. Grace takes all the pressure off. Grace is rest and peace.

The overall message of this book is that social anxiety is a gift because it forces us to fail at the rules. And when we fail, we realize that we need love apart from the rules. Love without conditions. And that is when grace walks in the door, shiny and perfect and breathtaking.

Ah, but there is even more! I know, right? How can there be more? Well, I am happy to tell you that with the gift of social anxiety come several mini-gifts. Here you go... Merry Christmas (and no extra charge!).

Grace **is everything**

A Sensitive Spirit: Judgment Antennas

Social anxiety is a sign of a sensitive spirit. We seem to have super-antennas for picking up on judgment. And while we may read judgment into places when it is not always there, I am convinced that God gave us this hyper-sensitivity for a reason. And that reason is pretty darn important.

Of all the people in the church, WE will be the first to notice when the message of grace has been diluted. We will pick up on clues that judgment is creeping back into the gospel. We will feel uncomfortable when grace has just a tiny condition (or 20 big conditions) added to it. It will eat at us, hurt us, haunt us. And this is for the protection of the church.

So what do you do if you notice someone teaching something that is not really the gospel? Our first gut instinct will be...to judge. *How can he not understand the perfection of grace alone?* we may think. *How can he have gotten grace so wrong?* We will want to correct that false teacher, reject him, be impatient with him, or angry and offended by him. Well, maybe that's just me. But, that really is me.

I find that the more I treasure grace, the more I have to rethink judgment. A mere two years ago, I was a committed Christian who understood maybe 2% of the gospel. The other 98% was all law. How, then, can I justify being offended by someone else who understands the gospel partially, but not completely? I cannot. Justify it, that is. Because I was that person just a few years ago.

I want to be patient with others as they grow in grace. I want to love them purely, without an agenda to change them. But when I do have red flags warning of legalism, two very simple actions come next.

Pray. Love.

Pray, pray, and pray some more. Asking God to deepen someone's spiritual understanding of God's unconditional love is (in my estimation) the loveliest of prayers to pray. I cannot personally deepen anyone's understanding. I do not have the power to change anyone's heart, ideas, or beliefs. God might choose to use me (usually I am oblivious when He does), but it all comes back to Him and to what He is doing.

The second thing to do when we discern that the gospel of grace has been altered is to... love. Like, patiently love. Without needing the other person to change. Yeah, we cannot actually do this one unless God powers it. But how else do you teach someone about love without conditions besides loving him or her without conditions? God thought up that strategy. I think it is a really good one.

Now, please don't get me wrong. If you are attending a church, or are in a community, that emphasizes the law over grace, you have the freedom to leave. We all desperately need to be reminded about grace, and grace alone. We have terrible memories. And we have the freedom to seek fellow grace-lovers wherever we want. After all, we are not going to displease God by wanting more and more of His grace. Right?

So, don't get puffed up about this, but we socially anxious are kind of protectors of the Kingdom of God, defending the sufficiency of grace. Super heroes. Grace Protectors. But in really raggedy human clothing.

A Forced Strength: Creative Solitude

Another gift comes in the form of *requiring* time alone to recharge. Time alone is time with God, and it waters our souls. If we are the types who are easily drained, we need more solitude than most. And in that solitude, many of us are driven to be creative as well. Flowing from our souls are worshipful works of art, music, carpentry, baking, etc. Not all of us are artistic, but an unusually large number are. If you happen to be one of those creative, solitude-seeking individuals, do not ever feel guilty for your private time. Soak up God's love and let it flow out in whatever unique method of loving is yours.

American culture does not generally value stillness or private worship. Oh, but God does.

Always with the Red Flags!

Social anxiety makes it really hard to get too far from grace. We are judgment sensitive, so we are the first to notice when something is off. Anything that makes us feel troubled, condemned, or inferior is a flashing red light that we have somehow forgotten our loved position in God's eyes. Social anxiety gently keeps us on track—tenaciously committed to freedom.

Red flags do not feel good. But they are little ruby warning lights reminding us that we are loved. Regardless of our failures. That we must never forget we are loved. That being loved by God is everything.

The Power Play

Finally, I told you there was one super secret therapy technique that you don't hear much about. It is the one thing everyone looking for relief from suffering can do *easily*. It may be simple, but it's fantastically powerful. I may have mentioned it a little earlier. OK, I definitely mentioned it earlier.

Pray.

What? It's that simple? Why yes. Yes it is.

I want you to go on a journey with me for just a moment. We are on the moon. As we try to step out of our spaceship, we can barely get the door open. It bumps into a grain silo. For you awesome city slickers... a grain silo is a really, really tall round building used for... well... storing grain. Grains like wheat, rye, and oats are poured into silos after harvest.

Anyway, we gingerly get out, and put our hand against the wall of the grain silo. We look up, and it reaches into the sky are far as we can see. And right beside it is another one. In fact, there is just enough room to walk between the silos. And there are hundreds, thousands of them.

Amazingly, the whole entire surface of the moon is covered in grain silos, with a little squeezing space to walk between them.

Now, imagine that the grain inside the silos is not grain, but rather, shimmering, golden seeds of God-power. And not only is the moon full of silos brimming with kernels of God-power, but every star and planet is filled with silos spilling over with God-power.

When we knock on the door of the nearest grain silo, it's just enough force to shake loose one tiny seed of God-power. This seed slips beneath the door and falls to earth. It hits the earth with such force it turns the Grand Canyon inside out.

These seeds of God-power are at our fingertips. We need only knock (ask) to release them. The tremendous amount of God-power, through grace and at our disposal... is astonishing.

This verse spells it all out perfectly: "If you ask anything in My name, I will do it" (John 14:14, NKJV). What sort of prayers are guaranteed? The ones that incorporate God's will being done on earth: "Your kingdom come. Your will be done on earth as it is in heaven" (Matt. 6:10, NKJV). When you pray for God to do as He wants, that prayer is GUARANTEED to be successful. Guaranteed. It's truly astonishing how much power we have... by simply joining in God's work via prayer.

So when it comes to social anxiety, or really anything, ask God constantly for help. In the simplest of ways. There is no secret, fancy knock required to unleash God's power. It's as simple as breathing out "Help" or "Thank you" or "I'm afraid." Because through grace, we have access to all the power in the world. And virtually everything we pray (in God's will) is guaranteed a favorable answer. By asking for God's help, we can change the world. That is not an exaggeration.

And now, my gifted fellow sojourner, you have all the keys to the Kingdom. You have permission to just be you. Now go.

* * *

As the Father **loved** Me,
I also have **loved** you:
abide in My love
--Jesus

John 15:9, NKJV

Acknowledgments

To my handsome college sweetheart, Gavin: you are full of grace, gentle, and deliriously funny. You are, in most ways, my polar opposite. You have patiently supported me through the trials and the triumphs. You generously financed my schooling, gave me the gift of being a stay-at-home mom/writer, and also ate a lot of leftovers. Without God's grace working through you, this book would not have come to be. I love you and thank you!

To my children: my life's dream has always been to have a family to nurture. I didn't know that a beautiful, pink-cheeked daughter and a chubby baby boy would nurture me. Your arrivals introduced me to the splendor of unconditional love, revealing the nature of our heavenly Father's love.

And to my parents… you taught me how to love a family, just by being you. This is your legacy. You made loving easy, because great love is all I've ever known from you. I absolutely treasure you, and continue to need you at every step of the way.

And to my grandparents, you have always been on my side, rooting and praying me on! I will never forget summers spent at your house, reading Reader's Digest Condensed Books. Or the amazing road trips we took together. You helped to build that foundation of love that every child needs and deserves. Grandma Virginia, when I grow up I want to be the official family gatherer, just like you.

I also want to thank my aunts, who generously allowed me the use of their homes as writing retreats. These loans included a swimming pool, silence, and an unhinged violent kitten… all of which were vital in completing this manuscript.

REFERENCES

Ahadi, B. and S. Basharpoor. 2010. "Relationship Between Sensory Processing Sensitivity, Personality Dimensions and Mental Health." *Journal of Applied Sciences 10* (7): 570-574. doi:10.3923/jas.2010.570.574

Ahn, Roianne R., Lucy Jane Miller, Sharon Milberger, and Daniel N. McIntosh. 2004. "Prevalence of Parents' Perceptions of s Among Kindergarten Children." *The American Journal of Occupational Therapy 58:* 287–293. doi:10.5014/ajot.58.3.287

Alden, Lynn E. and Jennifer L. Trew. 2013. "If it Makes You Happy: Engaging in Kind Acts Increases Positive Affect in Socially Anxious Individuals." *Emotion 13* (1): 64–75. doi:10.1037/a0027761

Alonso, J., M. C. Angermeyer, S. Bernert, R. Bruffaerts, T. S. Brugha, H. Bryson, G. de Girolamo, et al. 2004. "The European Study of the Epidemiology of Mental Disorders (ESEMeD) Project: An Epidemiological Basis for Informing Mental Health Policies in Europe." *Acta Psychiatrica Scandinavica* 109, no. s420: 38-46. DOI: 10.1111/j.1600-0047.2004.00327.x

American Psychiatric Association. 2013. *Diagnostic And Statistical Manual Of Mental Disorders.* 5th ed. Arlington,Va.: American Psychiatric Association.

Anderson, Page L., Matthew Price, Shannan M. Edwards, Mayowa A. Obasaju, Stefan K. Schmertz, Elana Zimand, and Martha R. Calamaras. 2013. "Virtual Reality Exposure Therapy for Social Anxiety Disorder: A Randomized Controlled Trial." *Journal of Consulting and Clinical Psychology 81* (5): 751–760. doi:10.1037/a0033559

Aron, Elaine N., Arthur Aron, and Jadzia Jagiellowicz. 2012. "Sensory Processing Sensitivity: A Review in the Light of the Evolution of Biological Responsivity." *Personality and Social Psychology Review 16* (3): 262–282. doi: 10.1177/1088868311434213

Asghari, Parvaneh, Ali Mashhadi, Zohreh Sepehri Shamloo. 2015. "Effect of Group Cognitive Behavioral Therapy Based on Hofmann Model on Anxiety Symptoms and Brain Behavioral Systems in Adults Suffering from Social Anxiety Disorder." *Journal of Fundamentals of Mental Health,* 17 (1): 38-45. http://jfmh.mums.ac.ir/pdf_3797_bb4e2f107d491d5d82064f3a0c66fe92.html

Azar, Beth. 2011. "Oytocin's other side." *American Psychological Association,* 42 (3). Online Article. Accessed February 3, 2015. http://www.apa.org/monitor/2011/03/oxytocin.aspx

Backus, William. D. 1994. *Learning To Tell Myself The Truth.* Minneapolis, Minn.: Bethany House Publishers.

Bakermans-Kranenburg, M. J. and M. H. van IJzendoorn. 2013. "Sniffing Around Oxytocin: Review and Meta-Analyses of Trials in Healthy and Clinical Groups with Implications for Pharmacotherapy." *Translational Psychiatry* 3(5): e258. doi:10.1038/tp.2013.34

Bauer, Elizabeth P. 2015. "Serotonin in Fear Conditioning Processes." *Behavioural*

Brain Research 277: 68–77. http://dx.doi.org/10.1016/j.bbr.2014.07.028
Baur, Volker, Annette Beatrix Brühl, Uwe Herwig, Tanja Eberle, and Michael Rufer, Aba Delsignore, Lutz Jäncke, and Jürgen Hänggi. 2011. "Evidence of Frontotemporal Structural Hypoconnectivity in Social Anxiety Disorder: A quantitative fiber tractography study." *Hum. Brain Mapp.* 34 (2): 437–446.
Beck, James H. 1999. *Jesus & Personality Theory: Exploring the Five-Factor Model.* Downers Grove, Ill.: InterVarsity Press. Kindle edition
Beidel, Deborah C., Candice A. Alfano, Michael J. Kofler, Patricia A. Rao, Lindsay Scharfstein, and Nina Wong Sarver. 2014. "The Impact of Social Skills Training for Social Anxiety Disorder: A Randomized Controlled Trial." *Journal of anxiety disorders* 28, no. 8: 908-918. http://dx.doi.org/10.1016/j.janxdis.2014.09.016
Beidel, Deborah C., Samuel M. Turner, Brennan J. Young, Robert T. Ammermn, Floyd R. Sallee, and Lori Crosby. 2006. "Psychopathology of Adolescent Social Phobia." *Journal of Psychopathology and Behavioral Assessment* 29: 47-54. doi:10.1007/s10862-006-9021-1
Bejerot, Susanne, Jonna M. Eriksson, and Ewa Mörtberg. 2014. "Social Anxiety in Adult Autism Spectrum Disorder." *Psychiatry Research* 220 (1-2): 705–707. http://dx.doi.org/10.1016/j.psychres.2014.08.030
Ben-Sasson, Ayelet, Alice S. Carter, and Margaret J. Briggs-Gowan, 2010. "The Development of Sensory Over-responsivity From Infancy to Elementary School." *J Abnorm Child Psychol* 38 (8): 1193–1202. doi:10.1007/s10802-010-9435-9
Benner, David G. and Peter Jensen Hill. 1999. *Baker Encyclopedia Of Psychology and Counseling.* 2nd ed. Grand Rapids, Mich.: Baker Books.
Berg, David Brandt. n.d. "Shyness and Timidity." *Deep Truths.* Webpage. Accessed October 30, 2014. http://deeptruths.com/daily-bread/shyness_timidity.html
Bergamaschi, Mateus M., Regina Helena Costa Queiroz, Marcos Hortes Nisihara Chagas, Danielle Chaves Gomes de Oliveira, Bruno Spinosa De Martinis, Flávio Kapczinski, João Quevedo, and et al. 2011. "Cannabidiol Reduces the Anxiety Induced by Simulated Public Speaking in Treatment-Naïve Social Phobia Patients." *Neuropsychopharmacology* 36(6): 1219–1226. http://dx.doi.org/10.1038%2Fnpp.2011.6
Bernstein, Rosemary E., Karyn L. Angell, and Crystal M. Dehle. 2013. "A Brief Course of Cognitive Behavioural Therapy for the Treatment of Misophonia: A Case Example." *The Cognitive Behaviour Therapist* 6. doi:10.1017/S1754470X13000172
Bethlehem, Richard A. I., Simon Baron-Cohen, Jack van Honk, Bonnie Auyeung, and Peter A. Bos, 2014. "The Oxytocin Paradox." *Front. Behav. Neurosci.* 8. http://dx.doi.org/10.3389%2Ffnbeh.2014.00048
Blanco, Carlos, Laura B. Bragdon, Franklin R Schneier, and Michael R. Liebowitz. 2012. "The Evidence-Based Pharmacotherapy of Social Anxiety Disorder." *Int. J. Neuropsychopharm.* 16(01): 235–249. doi:10.1017/S1461145712000119
Bögels, Susan M., Lynn Alden, Deborah C. Beidel, Lee Anna Clark, Daniel S. Pine,

Murray B. Stein, and Marisol Voncken. 2010. "Social Anxiety Disorder: Questions and Answers for the DSM-V." *Depress. Anxiety* 27 (2): 168–189. doi: 10.1002/da.20670

Bremner, Douglas J. 2006. "Stress and Brain Atrophy." *CNS and Neurological Disorders: Drug Targets* 5(5): 503–512. doi: 10.2174/187152706778559309

Briggs, A. 1975. *Victorian People: A Reassessment of Persons and Themes, 1851-67.* Rev. and illustrated ed.; Paperback ed. Chicago: University of Chicago Press.

Brozovich, Faith A., Philippe Goldin, Ihno Lee, Hooria Jazaieri, Richard G. Heimberg, and James J. Gross. 2014. "The Effect of Rumination and Reappraisal on Social Anxiety Symptoms During Cognitive-Behavioral Therapy for Social Anxiety Disorder." *J. Clin. Psychol.* 71(3): 208–218. doi:10.1002/jclp.22132

Brühl, Annette Beatrix, Aba Delsignore, Katja Komossa, and Steffi Weidt. 2014. "Neuroimaging in Social Anxiety Disorder—A Meta-Analytic Review Resulting in a New Neurofunctional Model." *Neuroscience & Biobehavioral Reviews* 47: 260–280. doi:10.1016/j.neubiorev.2014.08.003

Bryant, Richard A., Meaghan L. O'Donnell, Mark Creamer, Alexander C. McFarlane, C. Richard Clark, and Derrick Silove. 2010. "The Psychiatric Sequelae of Traumatic Injury." *American Journal of Psychiatry* 167 (3): 312-320. doi: 10.1176/appi.ajp.2009.09050617.

Buckner, R. L., J. R. Andrews-Hanna, and Schacter, D. L. 2008. "The Brain's Default Network: Anatomy, Function, and Relevance to Disease." *Annals of the New York Academy of Sciences* 1124 (1): 1–38. doi:10.1196/annals.1440.011

Buckner, Randy L. and Carroll, Daniel C. 2007. "Self-Projection and the Brain." *Trends in Cognitive Sciences* 11 (2): 49–57. doi:10.1016/j.tics.2006.11.004

Burklund, L. J., M. G. Craske, S. E. Taylor, and M. D. Lieberman, 2014. "Altered Emotion Regulation Capacity in Social Phobia as a Function of Comorbidity." *Social Cognitive and Affective Neuroscience* 10 (2): 199–208. doi:10.1093/scan/nsu058

Cain, Susan. 2012. *Quiet: The Power of Introverts in a World That Can't Stop Talking.* 1st ed. New York: Crown Publishers. Kindle edition.

Caner, Ergun Mehmet. 2005. *When Worldviews Collide: Christians Confronting Culture.* Member Book. ed. Nashville, Tenn.: LifeWay Press.

Carducci, Bernardo and Philip G. Zimbardo. 1995. "The Cost of Shyness." *Psychology Today* 1 November. http://www.psychologytoday.com/articles/200910/the-cost-shyness

Carey, Paul D., James Warwick, Dana J. H. Niehaus, Geoffrey van der Linden, Barend B. van Heerden, Brian H. Harvey, Soraya Seedat, and Dan J. Stein. 2004. "New Reference." *BMC Psychiatry* 4 (1): 30.

Cassimjee, Naseema, Jean-Pierre Fouche, Michael Burnett, Christine Lochner, James Warwick, Patrick Dupont, Dan J. Stein, Karen J. Cloete, and Paul D. Carey. 2010. "Changes in Regional Brain Volumes in Social Anxiety Disorder Following 12 weeks of Treatment with Escitalopram." *Metabolic Brain Disease* 25 (4): 369–374. doi:10.1007/s11011-010-9218-6

Cavanna, Andrea E. and Stefano Seri. 2015. Misophonia: Current Perspectives.

Neuropsychiatric Disease and Treatment 11:2117–2123. http://dx.doi.org/10.2147%2FNDT.S81438

Chaves, Cristiano, Clarissa Trzesniak, Guilherme Nogueira Derenusson, David Araújo, Lauro Wichert-Ana, JoÃo Paulo Machado-de-Sousa, Carlos Gilberto Carlotti Jr., and et al. 2012. "Late-Onset Social Anxiety Disorder Following Traumatic Brain Injury." *Brain Injury* 26 (6): 882–886. doi: 10.3109/02699052.2012.666373

Chen, Junwen, Ronald M. Rapee, and Maree. J. Abbott. 2013. Mediators of the Relationship Between Social Anxiety and Post-Event Rumination. *Journal of Anxiety Disorders* 27(1):1-8. http://dx.doi.org/10.1016/j.janxdis.2012.10.008

Chen, Junwen, Rebecca Mak, and Satoko Fujita. 2015. "The Effect of Combination of Video Feedback and Audience Feedback on Social Anxiety: Preliminary Findings." *Behavior Modification* 39 (5): 721–739. doi: 10.1177/0145445515587087

Chiesa, Alberto and Alessandro Serretti. 2011. "Mindfulness Based Cognitive Therapy for Psychiatric Disorders: A Systematic Review and Meta-Analysis." *Psychiatry Research* 187 (3): 441–453. doi:10.1016/j.psychres.2010.08.011

Clarke, Nat. 2009. "Is Shyness a Sin?" Nat Clark Blogspot 20 July. Blog entry. Accessed October 30, 2014. http://natclarke.blogspot.com/2009/07/is-shyness-sin.html

Coles, Meredith E., Cynthia L. Turk, Lauri Jindra, and Richard G. Heimberg. 2004. "The Path from Initial Inquiry to Initiation of Treatment for Social Anxiety Disorder in an Anxiety Disorders Specialty Clinic." *Journal of Anxiety Disorders* 18 (3): 371–383. doi:10.1016/S0887-6185(02)00259-1

Constans, Joseph I., David L. Penn, Gail H. Ihen, and Debra A. Hope. 1999. "Interpretive Biases for Ambiguous Stimuli in Social Anxiety." *Behaviour Research and Therapy* 37 (7): 643–651. doi:10.1016/S0005-7967(98)00180-6

Consumer Reports Best Buy Drugs™. 2013. *Consumers Union.* Online Document. Accessed February 2, 2015. http://www.consumerreports.org/health/resources/pdf/best-buy-drugs/Antidepressants_update.pdf

Cox, Brian J., Paula S.R. MacPherson, and Murray W. Enns. 2005. "Psychiatric Correlates of Childhood Shyness in a Nationally Representative Sample." *Behaviour Research & Therapy* 43, no. 8: 1019-1027. doi:10.1016/j.brat.2004.07.006

Crippa, J. A. S., G. N. Derenusson, T. B. Ferrari, L. Wichert-Ana, F. L. Duran, R. Martin-Santos, M. V. Simoes, and et al. 2010. "Neural Basis of Anxiolytic Effects of Cannabidiol (CBD) in Generalized Social Anxiety Disorder: A Preliminary Report." *Journal of Psychopharmacology* 25(1): 121–130. http://jop.sagepub.com/content/early/2010/09/08/0269881110379283

Cristea, Ioana A., Robin N. Kok, and Pim Cuijpers. 2015. "Efficacy of Cognitive Bias Modification Interventions in Anxiety and Depression: Meta-Analysis." *The British Journal of Psychiatry* 206 (1): 7–16. doi:10.1192/bjp.bp.114.146761

Cuncic, Arlin. 2012. "Shy Authors: A List of Shy Authors and How They Handle Shyness." *About.com.* http://socialanxietydisorder.about.com/od/celeb-

ritieswithsad/tp/Shy-Authors.htm
—— 2014a. "Which Celebrities Suffer With Social Anxiety?" *About.com.* http://socialanxietydisorder.about.com/od/celebritieswithsad/tp/celebritySAD.htm
—— 2014b. "Which Musicians Are Shy?" *About.com.* http://socialanxietydisorder.about.com/od/celebritieswithsad/tp/Shy-Musicians.htm
Dalrymple, Kristy L., Theresa A. Morgan, Jessica M. Lipschitz, Jennifer H. Martinez, Elizabeth Tepe, and Mark Zimmerman. 2014. "An Integrated, Acceptance-Based Behavioral Approach for Depression With Social Anxiety: Preliminary Results." *Behavior Modification* 38 (4): 516–548. doi:10.1177/0145445513518422
Davis, Michelle L., Jasper A. J. Smits, and Stefan G Hofmann. 2014. "Update on the Efficacy of Pharmacotherapy for Social Anxiety Disorder: a Meta-Analysis." *Expert Opin. Pharmacother.* 15(16): 2281–2291. DOI: 10.1517/14656566.2014.955472
Davis, M. L., N. Morina, M. B. Powers, J. A. J. Smits, and P. M. G. Emmelkamp. 2015. "A Meta-Analysis of the Efficacy of Acceptance and Commitment Therapy for Clinically Relevant Mental and Physical Health Problems." *Psychotherapy and Psychosomatics* 84, no. 1:30-36. doi:10.1159/000365764
DeWitt, David. 2009. "Brain: Shaped By Experiences." Web Article. Accessed November 6, 2014. https://answersingenesis.org/human-body/brain/brain-experiences/
Dolan, R.J. 2007. "The Human Amygdala and Orbital Prefrontal Cortex in Behavioural Regulation." *Philosophical Transactions of the Royal Society B: Biological Sciences* 362 (1481): 787–799. doi:10.1098/rstb.2007.2088
Draganski, Bogdan, Christian Gaser, Volker Busch, Gerhard Schuierer, Ulrich Bogdahn, and Arne May. 2004. "Neuroplasticity: Changes in Gray Matter Induced by Training." *Nature* 427, no. 6972: 311-312. Academic Search Premier, EBSCOhost (accessed November 19, 2014).
Duclot, F. and Kabbaj, M. 2015. "Epigenetic Mechanisms Underlying the Role of Brain-Derived Neurotrophic Factor in Depression and Response to Antidepressants." *Journal of Experimental Biology* 218(1): 21–31. doi: 10.1242/jeb.107086
Duman, Catharine H., Lee Schlesinger, David S. Russell, and Ronald S. Duman. 2008. "Voluntary Exercise Produces Antidepressant and Anxiolytic behavioral Effects in Mice." *Brain Research* 1199: 148–158. doi: 10.1016/j.brainres.2007.12.047
Edelstein, Miren, David Brang, Romke Rouw, and Vilayanur S. Ramachandran. 2013. "Misophonia: Physiological Investigations and Case Descriptions." *Frontiers in Human Neuroscience* 7. doi: 10.3389/fnhum.2013.00296
Eeles, Abbey L., Alicia J. Spittle, Peter J. Anderson, Nisha Brown, Katherine J. Lee, Roslyn N. Boyd, and Lex W. Wood. 2012. "Assessments of Sensory Processing in Infants: A Systematic Review." *Developmental Medicine & Child Neurology* 55 (4): 314–326. doi:10.1111/j.1469-8749.2012.04434.x
Ekern, Baxter. 2013. "Benzodiazepine Abuse Causes, Statistics, Addiction Signs,

Symptoms & Side Effects." *Addiction Hope*. Webpage. Accessed September 30, 2015. http://www.addictionhope.com/benzodiazepine

Eng, Winnie, Meredith E. Coles, Richard G. Heimberg, and Steven A. Safren. 2005. "Domains of Life Satisfaction in Social Anxiety Disorder: Relation to Symptoms and Response to Cognitive-Behavioral Therapy." *Journal of Anxiety Disorders* 19, no. 2: 143-156. doi:10.1016/j.janxdis.2004.01.007

Engel-Yeger, Batya and Winnie. Dunn. 2011. "The Relationship Between Sensory Processing Difficulties and Anxiety Level of Healthy Adults." *The British Journal of Occupational Therapy* 74 (5): 210–216. doi:10.4276/03080221 1X13046730116407

Farach, Frank J., Larry D. Pruitt, Janie J. Jun, Alissa B. Jerud, Lori A. Zoellner, and Peter P. Roy-Byrne. 2012. "Pharmacological Treatment of Anxiety Disorders: Current Treatments and Future Directions." *Journal of Anxiety Disorders* 26 (8): 833–843. http://dx.doi.org/10.1016/j.janxdis.2012.07.009

Farb, D. H. and M. H. Ratner. 2014. "Targeting the Modulation of Neural Circuitry for the Treatment of Anxiety Disorders." *Pharmacological Reviews* 66 (4): 1002–1032. http://dx.doi.org/10.1124/pr.114.009126

Foret, Blaise. 2014. *It Is Finished: Why You Can Quit Religion and Trust in Jesus*. Nashville, TN: Blaise Foret Ministries and Publications.

Fonagy, Peter. 2015. "The Effectiveness of Psychodynamic Psychotherapies: An Update." *World Psychiatry* 14 (2): 137–150. http://dx.doi.org/10.1002%2F-wps.20235

Fouche, Jean-Paul, Nic J. A. van Der Wee, Karin Roelofs, and Dan J. Stein. 2012. "Recent Advances in the Brain Imaging of Social Anxiety Disorder." *Human Psychopharmacology: Clinical and Experimental* 28 (1): 102–105. doi: 10.1002/hup.2281

Frei, Jacqueline and Lorna Peters. 2012. "Which Client Characteristics Contribute to Good and Poor Cognitive-Behavioural Treatment Outcome for Social Anxiety Disorder? A Survey of Clinicians." *Behaviour Change* 29 (04): 230–237. doi:10.1017/bec.2012.22

Frick, Andreas, Fredrik Åhs, Jonas Engman, My Jonasson, Iman Alaie, Johannes Björkstrand, Örjan Frans, and et al. 2015. "Serotonin Synthesis and Reuptake in Social Anxiety Disorder." *JAMA Psychiatry* 72 (8): 794. doi:10.1001/jamapsychiatry.2015.0125

Frick, Andreas, Malin Gingnelland, Andre F. Marquand, Katarina Howner, Håkan Fischer, Marianne Kristiansson, Steven C.R. Williams, Mats Fredrikson, and Tomas Furmark. 2014. "Classifying Social Anxiety Disorder Using Multivoxel Pattern Analyses of Brain Function And Structure." *Behavioural Brain Research* 259: 330–335. doi: 10.1016/j.bbr.2013.11.003

Fung, Lawrence K., Lovina Chahal, Robin A. Libove, Raphael Bivas, and Antonio Y. Hardan. 2012. "A Retrospective Review of the Effectiveness of Aripiprazole in the Treatment of Sensory Abnormalities in Autism." *Journal of Child and Adolescent Psychopharmacology* 22(3): 245–248. doi:10.1089/cap.2010.0103

Furmark, Tomas. 2009. "Neurobiological Aspects of Social Anxiety Disorder." *The*

Israel Journal of Psychiatry and Related Sciences 46 (1): 5-12.

Furmark, Tomas, Lieuwe Appel, Susanne Henningsson, Fredrik Ahs, Vanda Faria, Clas Linnman, Anna Pissiota, and et al. 2008. "A Link between Serotonin-Related Gene Polymorphisms, Amygdala Activity, and Placebo-Induced Relief from Social Anxiety." *Journal of Neuroscience* 28 (49): 13066–13074. doi:10.1523/JNEUROSCI.2534-08.2008

Gartlehner, Gerald, Richard A. Hansen, Laura C. Morgan, Kylie Thaler, Linda Lux, Megan Van Noord, Ursula Mager and et al. 2011. "Comarative Benefits and Harms of Second-Generation Antidepressants for Treating Major Depressive Disorder." *Ann Intern Med* 155 (11): 772-785.

Gasquoine, Philip Gerard. 2014. "Contributions of the Insula to Cognition and Emotion." *Neuropsychology Review* 24 (2): 77–87. doi:10.1007 /s11065-014-9246-9

Gelfuso, Érica Aparecida, Daiane Santos Rosa, Ana Lúcia Fachin, Márcia Renata Mortari, Alexandra Olimpio Siqueira Cunha and Rene Oliveira Beleboni. 2013. "Anxiety: A Systematic Review of Neurobiology, Traditional Pharmaceuticals and Novel Alternatives from Medicinal Plants." *CNS & Neurological Disorders - Drug Targets* 12(8). doi.10.2174/18715273113129990102

Gilbert, Sarah E. and Kristina C. Gordon. 2012. "Interpersonal Psychotherapy Informed Treatment for Avoidant Personality Disorder With Subsequent Depression." *Clinical Case Studies* 12 (2): 111–127. doi: 10.1177/1534650112468611

Giler, David. 1988. *The Money Pit*. USA: Universal Pictures. Film.

Goldin, Philippe, Michal Ziv, Hooria Jazaieri, Kevin Hahn, and James J. Gross. 2012. "MBSR vs. Aerobic Exercise in Social Anxiety: FMRI Of Emotion Regulation of Negative Self-Beliefs." *Social Cognitive and Affective Neuroscience 8* (1): 65–72. doi:10.1093/scan/nss054

Goldin, Philippe R., Ihno Lee, Michal Ziv, Hooria Jazaieri, Richard G. Heimberg, and James J. Gross. 2014. "Trajectories of Change in Emotion Regulation and Social Anxiety During Cognitive-Behavioral Therapy for Social Anxiety Disorder." *Behaviour Research and Therapy* 56: 7–15. http://dx.doi.org/10.1016/j.brat.2014.02.005

Goldin, Philippe R., Michal Ziv, Hooria Jazaieri, Justin Weeks, Richard G. Heimberg, and James J. Gross. 2014. "Impact of Cognitive-Behavioral Therapy for Social Anxiety Disorder on the Neural Bases Of Emotional Reactivity to and Regulation of Social Evaluation." *Behaviour Research and Therapy* 62: 97–106. doi:10.1016/j.brat.2014.08.005

Gorka, Stephanie M., Daniel A. Fitzgerald, Izelle Labuschagne, Avinash Hosanagar, Amanda G. Wood, Pradeep J. Nathan, and K. Luan Phan. 2014. "Oxytocin Modulation of Amygdala Functional Connectivity to Fearful Faces in Generalized Social Anxiety Disorder." *Neuropsychopharmacology*. doi:10.1038/npp.2014.168

Grandgeorge, Marine, Eric Lemonnier, Celine Degrez, and Nelle Jallot. 2014. "The Effect of Bumetanide Treatment on the Sensory Behaviours of a Young Girl with Asperger Syndrome." *Case Reports 2014* (jan30 2): bcr2013202092.

doi:10.1135/bcr-2013-202092

Graham, Billy, and Franklin Graham. *Billy Graham in Quotes.* Nashville, Tenn.: Thomas Nelson, 2011.

Grant, Bridget F., Deborah S. Hasin, Carlos Blanco, Frederick S. Stinson, S. Patricia Chou, Rise B. Goldstein, Deborah A. Dawson, Sharon Smith, Tulshi D. Saha, and Boji Huang. 2005. "The Epidemiology of Social Anxiety Disorder in the United States: Results from the National Epidemiologic Survey on Alcohol and Related Conditions." (Abstract) *Journal of Clinical Psychiatry* 66(11). 1351–1361

Hamilton, J. P., M. Siemer, and I. H. Gotlib. 2008. "Amygdala Volume in Major Depressive Disorder: A Meta-analysis of Magnetic Resonance Imaging Studies." *Molecular Psychiatry* 13: 993–1000. doi:10.1038/mp.2008.57

Hammer, Alan L. and C. R. Martin. 2003. Estimated Frequencies of the Types in the United States Population. *Center for Applications of Psychological Type.* 3rd Edition. Gainesville, Florida, cited in McHugh, Adam S. 2009. *Introverts In The Church: Finding Our Place in an Extroverted Culture.* Downers Grove, Ill.: Intervarsity Press.

Hansen, Brant. 2015. *Unoffendable: How Just One Change Can Make All of Life Better.* Thomas Nelson: Nashville, TN.

Hayes, S. C., J. B. Luoma, F. W. Bond, Akihiko Masuda, and J. Lillis. 2006. "Acceptance and Commitment Therapy: Model, Processes and Outcomes" *Psychology Faculty Publications.* Paper. http://scholarworks.gsu.edu/psych_facpub/101

Hedman, Erik, Gerhard Andersson, Brjánn Ljótsson, Erik Andersson, Christian Rück, Ewa Mörtberg, and Nils Lindefors. 2011. "Internet-Based Cognitive Behavior Therapy vs. Cognitive Behavioral Group Therapy for Social Anxiety Disorder: A Randomized Controlled Non-inferiority Trial." *PLoS ONE* 6 (3): e18001. doi:10.1371/journal.pone.0018001

Heimberg, R. G., M. R. Liebowitz, D. A. Hope, F. R. Schneier, editors. 1995. *Social Phobia: Diagnosis, Assessment, and Treatment.* New York: Guilford Press.

Henderson, Donna A., and Charles L. Thompson. *Counseling Children.* 8th ed. Belmont, CA: Brooks/Cole Cengage Learning, 2011.

Hilimire, Matthew R., Jordan E. DeVylder, and Catherine A. Forestell. 2015. "Fermented Foods, Neuroticism, and Social Anxiety: an Interaction Model." *Psychiatry Research* 228 (2): 203–208. doi:10.1016/j.psychres.2015.04.023

Hilton, Claudia L., Jacquelyn D. Harper, Rachel Holmes Kueker, Andrea Runz Lang, Anna M. Abbacchi, Alexandre Todorov, and Patricia D. LaVesser. 2010. "Sensory Responsiveness as a Predictor of Social Severity in Children with High Functioning Autism Spectrum Disorders." *Journal of Autism and Developmental Disorders* 40 (8): 937–945. doi:10.1007/s10803-010-0944-8

Hofmann, Stefan G. and Patricia M. DiBartolo. 2010. *Social Anxiety: Clinical, Developmental, and Social Perspectives.* Elsevier Science. Kindle Edition. (Kindle Locations 10997-11010)

Hollander, Eric and Nicholas Bakalar. 2005. *Coping with Social Anxiety: the Definitive*

Guide to Effective Treatment Options. 1st ed. New York: H. Holt.

Hook, Joshua N., Everett L. Worthington, Don E. Davis, David J. Jennings, Aubrey L. Gartner, and Jan P. Hook. 2009. "Empirically Supported Religious and Spiritual Therapies." *J. Clin. Psychol.* 66(1), 46--72. doi:10.1002/jclp.20626

Hope, Debra A., Richard G. Heimberg, and Cynthia L. Turk. 2010. *Managing Social Anxiety, Workbook: A Cognitive-Behavioral Therapy Approach (Treatments That Work).* 2nd ed. Oxford: Oxford University Press, USA.

Hsu, Al. 2013. "When Suicide Strikes in the Body of Christ." *Christianity Today.* Webpage. http://www.christianitytoday.com/ct/2013/april-web-only/when-suicide-strikes-in-body-of-christ.html?paging=off#bmb=1

Huppert, Jonathan D. Daniel R Strunk, Deborah Roth Ledley, Jonathan R. T. Davidson, and Edna B. Foa. 2008. "Generalized Social Anxiety Disorder and Avoidant Personality Disorder: Structural Analysis and Treatment Outcome." *Depress. Anxiety* 25 (5): 441–448. doi:10.1002/da.20349

Ipser, J. C., Kariuki, C. M., and Stein, D. J. (2008). "Pharmacotherapy for Social Anxiety Disorder: a Systematic Review." *Expert. Rev. Neurother.* 8, 235-257.

Irle, Eva, Mirjana Ruhleder, Claudia Lange, Ulrich Seidler-Brandler, Simone Salzer, Peter Dechent, Godehard Weniger, Eric Leibing, and Falk Leichsenring. 2010. "Reduced Amygdalar and Hippocampal Size in Adults with Generalized Social Phobia." *Journal of Psychiatry and Neuroscience* 35 (2): 126–131. doi: 10.1503/jpn.090041

Isomura, K., M. Boman, C. Rück, E. Serlachius, H. Larsson, P. Lichtenstein, and D. Mataix-Cols. 2014. "Population-based, Multi-generational Family Clustering Study of Social Anxiety Disorder and Avoidant Personality Disorder." *Psychological medicine* 1-9. doi:10.1017/S0033291714002116

Jagiellowicz, J., Xu Xiaomeng, Arthur Aron, Elaine Aron, Guikang Cao, Tingyong Feng, and Xuchu Weng. 2010. "The Trait of Sensory Processing Sensitivity and Neural Responses to Changes in Visual Scenes." *Social Cognitive and Affective Neuroscience* 6(1): 38–4. doi:10.1093/scan/nsq001

James, Katherine, Lucy Jane Miller, Roseann Schaaf, Darci M. Nielsen, and Sarah A. Schoen. 2011. "Phenotypes Within Sensory Modulation Dysfunction." *Comprehensive Psychiatry* 52 (6): 715–724. doi:10.1016/j.comppsych.2010.11.010

Janowsky, David S., Shirley Morter, and Manuel Tancer. 2000. "Over-representation of Myers Briggs Type Indicator Introversion in Social Phobia Patients." *Depress Anxiety* 11(3) 121-125. doi:10.1002/(SICI)1520-6394(2000)11:33.0.CO;2-9

Jazaieri, Hooria, Amanda S. Morrison, Philippe R. Goldin, and James J. Gross. 2014. "The Role of Emotion and Emotion Regulation in Social Anxiety Disorder." *Curr Psychiatry Rep* 17 (1). doi:10.1007/s11920-014-0531-3

Jazaieri, Hooria, Ihno A. Lee, Philippe R. Goldin, and James J. Gross, 2015. "Pre-treatment Social Anxiety Severity Moderates the Impact of Mindfulness-based Stress Reduction and Aerobic Exercise." *Psychol Psychother Theory Res Pract*: n/a–n/a. doi:10.1111/papt.12060

Jenkins, Trisha, Jason Nguyen, Kate Polglaze, and Paul Bertrand. 2016. "Influence of Tryptophan and Serotonin on Mood and Cognition with a Possible Role of the Gut-Brain Axis." *Nutrients* 8 (1): 56. doi:10.3390/nu8010056

Jones, Stanton L. and Richard Butman. 2011. *Modern Psychotherapies: A Comprehensive Christian Appraisal* (Christian Association for Psychological Studies Partnership). IVP Academic.

Katzelnick, David J., Kenneth A. Kobak, Thomas DeLeire, Henry J. Henk, John H. Greist, Jonathan R.T. Davidson, Franklin R. Schneier, Murray B. Stein, and Cindy P. Helstad. 2001. "Impact of Generalized Social Anxiety Disorder in Managed Care." *American Journal of Psychiatry* 158: 1999–2007. http://dx.doi.org/10.1176/appi.ajp.158.12.1999

Kawaguchi, Akiko, Kiyotaka Nemoto, ShutaroNakaaki, Takatsune Kawaguchi, Hirohito Kan, Nobuyuki Arai, Nao Shiraishi and et al. 2016. "Insular Volume Reduction in Patients with Social Anxiety Disorder." *Front. Psychiatry* 7(3).

Kelm, M. Katherine, Hugh E. Criswell, and George R. Breese. 2011. "Ethanol-enhanced GABA Release: A Focus on G Protein-Coupled Receptors." *Brain Research Reviews* 65 (2): 113–123. http://dx.doi.org/10.1016%2Fj.brainresrev.2010.09.003

Kessler, Ronald C., Patricia Berglund, Olga Demler, Robert Jin, Kathleen R. Merikangas, and Ellen E. Walters. 2005. "Lifetime Prevalence and Age-of-Onset Distributions of DSM-IV Disorders in the National Comorbidity Survey Replication." *Archives of General Psychiatry* 62 (6): 593-602. doi:10.1001/archpsyc.62.6.593

Kessler, Ronald C., Maria Petukhova, Nancy A. Sampson, Alan M. Zaslavsky, and Hans-Ullrich Wittchen. 2012. "Twelve-Month and Lifetime Prevalence and Lifetime Morbid Risk of Anxiety and Mood Disorders in the United States." *International Journal of Methods in Psychiatric Research* 21 (3): 169–184. http://dx.doi.org/10.1002%2Fmpr.1359

Kim, Eun-Jung. 2005. "The Effect of the Decreased Safety Behaviors on Anxiety and Negative Thoughts in Social Phobics." *Journal of Anxiety Disorders* 19 (1): 69–86. doi:10.1016/j.janxdis.2003.11.002

Klumpp, Heide, Daniel A. Fitzgerald, M. Angstadt, D. Post, and K. L. Phan. 2014. "Neural Response During Attentional Control and Emotion Processing Predicts Improvement After cognitive Behavioral Therapy in Generalized Social Anxiety Disorder." *Psychol. Med.* 44 (14): 3109–3121. doi:10.1017/S0033291714000567

Klumpp, Heide, Daniel A. Fitzgerald, and K. Luan Phan. 2013. "Neural Predictors and Mechanisms of cognitive Behavioral Therapy on Threat Processing in Social Anxiety Disorder." *Progress in Neuro-Psychopharmacology and Biological Psychiatry* 45: 83–91. http://dx.doi.org/10.1016/j.pnpbp.2013.05.004

Klumpp, Heide, Michael K. Keutmann, Daniel A. Fitzgerald, Stewart A. Shankan, and K. Luan Phan. 2014. "Resting State Amygdala-Prefrontal Connectivity Predicts Symptom Change After Cognitive Behavioral Therapy in Generalized Social Anxiety Disorder." *Biology of Mood & Anxiety Disorder.* 4 (14): 1-7. http://dx.doi.org/10.1186%2Fs13587-014-0014-5

Kocovski, Nancy L., Jan E. Fleming, and Neil A. Rector. 2009. "Mindfulness and Acceptance-based Group Therapy for Social Anxiety Disorder: An Open Trial." *Cognitive and Behavioral Practice 16*, no. 3: 276-289. http://dx.doi.org/10.1016/j.cbpra.2008.12.004

Koole, Sander L., Lottte F. van Dillen, Gal Sheppes. 2011. "The Self-Regulation of Emotion." In *Handbook Of Self-Regulation: Research, Theory, and Applications*, ed. R. F. Baumeister and K. D. Vohs. Second edition. New York/London: Guilford.

Kostev, Karel, Juliana Rex, Thilo Eith, and Christina Heilmaier. 2014. "Which Adverse Effects Influence the Dropout Rate in Selective Serotonin Re-Uptake Inhibitor (SSRI) Treatment? Results for 50,824 Patients." *German Medical Science 12* (doc15). doi:10.3205/000200

Koszycki, Diana, Melodie Benger, Jakov Shlik, and Jacques Bradwejn. 2007. "Randomized Trial of a Meditation-Based Stress Reduction Program and Cognitive Behavior Therapy in Generalized Social Anxiety Disorder." *Behaviour Research and Therapy 45* (10): 2518–2526. doi:10.1016/j.brat.2007.04.011

Kühn, Simone, Robert Lorenz, Tobias Banaschewski, Gareth J. Barker, Christian Büchel, Patricia J. Conrod, Herta Flor and et al. 2014. "Positive Association of Video Game Playing with Left Frontal Cortical Thickness in Adolescents." *PLoS ONE 9* (3): e91506. doi:10.1371/journal.pone.0091506

Kurita, Masatake, Satoshi Nishino, Maiko Kato, Yukio Numata, NS Tadahiro Sato (2012). "Plasma Brain-Derived Neurotrophic Factor Levels Predict the Clinical Outcome of Depression Treatment in a Naturalistic Study." *PLoS ONE 7*:e39212: 1-7. http://dx.doi.org/10.3389%2Ffnint.2013.00055

Labuschagne, Izelle, K. Luan Phan, Amanda Wood, Mike Angstadt, Phyllis Chua, Markus Heinrichs, Julie C. Stout, and Pradeep J. Nathan. 2010. "Oxytocin Attenuates Amygdala Reactivity to Fear in Generalized Social Anxiety Disorder." *Neuropsychopharmacology 35*(12): 2403–2413. http://dx.doi.org/10.1038/npp.2010.123

Laeger, Inga, Kati Keuper, Carina Heitmann, Harald Kugel, Christian Dobel, Annuschka Eden, Volker Arolt, Pienie Zwitserlood, Udo Dannlowski, and Peter Zwanzger. 2014. "Have We Met Before? Neural Correlates of Emotional Learning in Women with Social Phobia." *Journal of Psychiatry & Neuroscience 39* (3): E14–E23. doi:10.1503/jpn.130091

Lane, Roger M. 2014. "Antidepressant Drug Development: Focus on Triple Monoamine Re-Uptake Inhibition." *Journal of Psychopharmacology 29* (5): 526–544. doi: 10.1177/0269881114553252

Lane, Shelly J., Stacey Reynolds, and Levent Dumenci. 2012. "Sensory Overresponsivity and Anxiety in Typically Developing Children and Children With Autism and Attention Deficit Hyperactivity Disorder: Cause or Coexistence?" *American Journal of Occupational Therapy 66* (5): 595–603. http://dx.doi.org/10.5014/ajot.2012.004523

Lang, Russell, Mark O'Reilly, Olive Healy, Mandy Rispoli, Helena Lydon, William Streusand, and et al. 2012. "Sensory Integration Therapy for Autism Spectrum Disorders: A Systematic Review." *Research in Autism Spectrum Disor-*

ders 6 (3): 1004–1018. http://dx.doi.org/10.1016/j.rasd.2012.01.006

Lapidus, Kyle, James Murrough, and Laili Soleimani. 2013. "Novel Glutamatergic Drugs for the Treatment of Mood Disorders." *Neuropsychiatric Disease and Treatment 9*:1101-1112.

Lazar, Sara W., Catherine E. Kerr, Rachel H. Wasserman, Jeremy R. Gray, Douglas N. Greve, Michael T. Treadway, Metta McGarvey, and et al. 2005. "Meditation Experience is Associated with Increased cortical Thickness." *Neuroreport 16* (17): 1893–1897.

Leekam, Susan R., Carmen Nieto, Sarah J. Libby, Lorna Wing, and Judith Gould. 2006. "Describing the Sensory Abnormalities of Children and Adults with Autism." *Journal of Autism and Developmental Disorders 37* (5): 894–910. doi: 10.1007/s10803-006-0218-7

Leichsenring, Falk, Simone Salzer, Manfred E. Beutel, Stephan Herpertz, Wolfgang Hiller, Juergen Hoyer, Johannes Huesing, et al. 2013. "Psychodynamic Therapy and Cognitive-Behavioral Therapy in Social Anxiety Disorder: A Multicenter Randomized Controlled Trial." *American Journal of Psychiatry 170*: 759–767. http://dx.doi.org/10.1176/appi.ajp.2013.12081125

Liebowitz, Michael R., Ester Salman, Humberto Nicolini, Norman Rosenthal, Rita Hanover, and Louis Monti. 2014. "Effect of an Acute Intranasal Aerosol Dose of PH94B on Social and Performance Anxiety in Women With Social Anxiety Disorder." *AJP 171* (6): 675–682. doi:10.1176/appi.ajp.2014.12101342

Lightbody, Amy A. and Allan L. Reiss. 2009. "Gene, Brain, and Behavior Relationships in Fragile X Syndrome: Evidence from Neuroimaging Studies." *Dev Disabil Res Revs 15* (4): 343–352. doi:10.1002/ddrr.77

Liss, Miriam, Jennifer Mailloux, and Mindy J. Erchull. 2008. "The Relationships Between Sensory Processing Sensitivity, Alexithymia, Autism, Depression, and Anxiety." *Personality and Individual Differences 45* (3): 255–259. doi:10.1016/j.paid.2008.04.009

Løhr, Hildegard D., Jan H. Rosenvinge, and Rolf Wynn. 2011. "Integrating Psychoeducation in a Basic Computer Skills Course for People Suffering from Social Anxiety: Participants' Experiences." *Journal of Multidisciplinary Healthcare, 4*: 311-319. doi: 10.2147/JMDH.S23691

Lopez-Larson, Melissa, Piotr Bogorodzki, Jadwiga Rogowska, Erin McGlade, Jace B. King, Janine Terry, and Deborah Yurgelun-Todd. 2011. "Altered Prefrontal and Insular Cortical Thickness in Adolescent Marijuana Users." *Behavioural Brain Research 220* (1): 164-172. http://dx.doi.org/10.1016/j.bbr.2011.02.001

Luscher, B., Q. Shen, and N. Sahir. 2011. "The GABAergic Deficit Hypothesis of Major Depressive Disorder." *Mol Psychiatry 16*(4): 383–406. doi:10.1038/mp.2010.120

Lynam, Donald R., Abbey Loehr, Joshua D. Miller, and Thomas A. Widiger. 2012. "A Five-Factor Measure of Avoidant Personality: The FFAvA." *Journal of personality assessment 94*, no. 5: 466-474. http://dx.doi.org/10.1080/00223891.2012.677886

Lynum, L. I., T. Wilberg, and S. Karterud. 2008. "Self-esteem in Patients with Borderline and Avoidant Personality Disorders." *Scandinavian Journal of Psychology 49*, no. 5: 469-477. doi: 10.1111/j.1467-9450.2008.00655.x

Machado-de-Sousa, João Paulo, Flávia de Lima Osório, Andrea P. Jackowski, Rodrigo A. Bressan, Marcos H. N. Chagas, Nelson Torro-Alves, André L. D. DePaula, José A. S. Crippa, and Jaime E. C. Hallak. 2014. "Increased Amygdalar and Hippocampal Volumes in Young Adults with Social Anxiety." *PLoS ONE 9* (2): e88523. doi:10.1371/journal.pone.0088523

Marazziti, Donatella, Marianna Abelli, Stefano Baroni, Barbara Carpita, Carla E. Ramacciotti, and Liliana Dell'Osso. 2014. "Neurobiological Correlates of Social Anxiety Disorder: An Update." *CNS Spectr. 20* (02): 100–111. doi:10.1017/S1092852914000008X

Maren, Stephen, K. Luan Phan, and Israel Liberzon. 2013. "The Contextual Brain: Implications for Fear Conditioning, Extinction and Psychopathology." *Nat Rev Neurosci 14* (6): 417–428. doi:10.1038/nrn3492

Maresh, Erin L., Joseph P. Allen, and James A. Coan. 2014. "Increased Default Mode Network Activity in Socially Anxious Individuals During Reward Processing." *Biol Mood Anxiety Disord 4* (1): 7. doi:10.1186/2045-5380-4-7

Mayo-Wilson, Evan, Sofia Dias, Ifigeneia Mavranezouli, Kayleigh Kew, David M. Clark, A. E. Ades, and Stephen Pilling. 2014. "Psychological and Pharmacological Interventions for Social Anxiety Disorder in Adults: A Systematic Review and Network Meta-Analysis." *The Lancet Psychiatry 1*(5): 368–376. http://dx.doi.org/10.1016/S2215-0366(14)70329-3

McCann, Russell A., Christina M. Armstrong, Nancy A. Skopp, Amanda Edwards-Stewart, Derek J. Smolenski, Jennifer D. June, Melinda Metzger-Abamukong, and Greg M. Reger. 2014. "Virtual Reality Exposure Therapy for the Treatment of Anxiety Disorders: An Evaluation of Research Quality." *Journal of Anxiety Disorders 28*(6): 625–631. http://dx.doi.org/10.1016/j.janxdis.2014.05.010

McCarthy, Odhran, David Hevey, Amy Brogan, and Brendan D. Kelly. 2013. "Effectiveness of a Cognitive Behavioural Group Therapy (CBGT) for Social Anxiety Disorder: Immediate and Long-term Benefits." *tCBT 6*. doi:10.1017/S1754470X13000111

McDowell, Julie. 2010. *Encyclopedia of Human Body Systems* [2 volumes]. Santa Barbara: Greenwood. 379.

McHugh, Adam S. 2009. *Introverts In The Church: Finding Our Place in an Extroverted Culture*. Downers Grove, Ill.: Intervarsity Press.

Meda, Shashwath A., Jennifer R. Pryweller, and Tricia A. Thornton-Wells. 2012. "Regional Brain Differences in Cortical Thickness, Surface Area and Subcortical Volume in Individuals with Williams Syndrome." *PLoS ONE 7* (2): e31913. doi:10.1371/journal.pone.0031913

Merikangas, Kathleen R., Hagop S. Akiskal, Jules Angst, Paul E. Greenberg, Robert M. A. Hirschfeld, Maria Petukova, and Ronald C. Kessler. 2007. "Lifetime and 12-Month Prevalence of Bipolar Spectrum Disorder in the National Comorbidity Survey Replication." *Archives of General Psychiatry 64*

(5): 543-552. doi:10.1001/archpsyc.64.5.543
Miller, Scott R. and Elizabeth Coll. 2007. "From Social Withdrawal to Social Confidence: Evidence for Possible Pathways." *Current Psychology* 26(2): 86–101. doi:10.1007/s12144-007-9006-6
Mitchell, Melissa A. and Norman B. Schmidt. 2014. "General In-situation Safety Behaviors Are Uniquely Associated with Post-Event Processing." *Journal of Behavior Therapy and Experimental Psychiatry* 45 (2): 229–233. doi:10.1016/j.jbtep.2013.11.001
Mobini, Sirous, Shirley Reynolds, and Bundy Mackintosh. 2012. "Clinical Implications of Cognitive Bias Modification for Interpretative Biases in Social Anxiety: An Integrative Literature Review." *Cogn Ther Res* 37 (1): 173–182. doi:10.1007/s10608-012-9445-8
Moriya, Jun and Yoshihiko Tanno. 2008. Relationships Between Negative Emotionality and Attentional Control in Effortful Control. *Pers. Individ. Differ.* 44:1348–55. doi:10.1016/j.paid.2007.12.003
Morrison, Amanda S. and Richard G. Heimberg. 2013. "Social Anxiety and Social Anxiety Disorder." *Annual Review of Clinical Psychology* 9 (1): 249–274. doi:10.1146/annurev-clinpsy-050212-185631
Mörtberg, Ewa, Asle Hoffart, Benjamin Boecking, and David M. Clark. 2013. "Shifting the Focus of One's Attention Mediates Improvement in Cognitive Therapy for Social Anxiety Disorder." *Behavioural and Cognitive Psychotherapy* 43 (01): 63–73. doi:10.1017/S1352465813000738
Moscovitch, David A., Karen Rowa, Jeffrey R. Paulitzki, Maria D. Ierullo, Brenda Chiang, Martin M. Antony, and Randi E. McCabe. 2013. "Self-Portrayal Concerns and Their Relation to Safety Behaviors and Negative Affect in Social Anxiety Disorder." *Behaviour Research and Therapy* 51 (8): 476–486. doi:10.1016/j.brat.2013.05.002
Nathan, P. E. and J. M. Gorman. 2015. *A Guide To Treatments That Work*. Fourth edition. ed. OxfordNewYork: Oxford University Press.
Neal, Jo Anne, Robert J. Edelmann, and Martin Glachan. 2002. "Behavioural Inhibition and Symptoms of Anxiety and Depression: Is There a Specific Relationship with Social Phobia?" *British Journal of Clinical Psychology* 41: 361-371. doi: 10.1348/014466502760387489
Newport, Frank. 2012. "In U.S., 77% Identify as Christian." Website. Accessed Oct. 26, 2014. http://www.gallup.com/poll/159548/identify-christian.aspx
Norcross, John C. and Bruce E. Wampold. 2011. "Evidence-Based Therapy Relationships: Research Conclusions and Clinical Practices." *Psychotherapy* 48 (1): 98–102. doi:10.1037/a0022161
Norton, Alice R., Maree J. Abbott, Melissa M. Norberg, and Caroline Hunt. 2014. "A Systematic Review of Mindfulness and Acceptance-Based Treatments for Social Anxiety Disorder." *Journal of Clinical Psychology:* n/a–n/a. doi: 10.1002/jclp.22144.
Ohayon, Maurice M. and Alan F. Schatzberg. 2010. "Social Phobia and Depression: Prevalence and Comorbidity." *Journal of Psychosomatic Research* 68 (3): 235–243. doi:10.1016/j.jpsychores.2009.07.018

Opris, David, Sebastian Pintea, Azucena García-Palacios, Cristina Botella, Ştefan Szamosközi, and Daniel David. 2011. "Virtual Reality Exposure Therapy in Anxiety Disorders: A Quantitative Meta-analysis." *Depress Anxiety* 29 (2): 85–93. doi:10.1002/da.20910

Ord, Ingrid R. 2014. *Act With Faith. Acceptance and Commitment Therapy with Christian Clients: A Practitioner's Guide*. Sittingbourne: Compass Publishing.

Ostrove, Barbara, Nancy Egan, and Susan Higgins. 2012. "Sensory Interventions." In *Inpatient Psychiatric Nursing: Clinical Strategies & Practical Interventions*. L. Damon, and Butler Hospital, 335-348. New York: Springer.

Ougrin, Dennis. 2011. "Efficacy of Exposure Versus Cognitive Therapy in Anxiety Disorders: Systematic Review and Meta-analysis." *BMC Psychiatry* 11(1): 200. doi:10.1186/1471-244X-11-200

Parashar, Bharat, Pankaj Kumar Bhatoa, Asha Bhatoa and Virender Yadav. 2012. "Anxiety: A Common Problem with Human Beings." *The Pharma Journal* 1(5): 10-21. http://www.thepharmajournal.com/vol1Issue5/Issue_july_2012/2.2.pdf

Plasencia, M. Leili., Lynn E. Alden, and Charles T. Taylor. 2011. "Differential Effects of Safety Behaviour Subtypes in Social Anxiety Disorder." *Behaviour Research and Therapy* 49(10): 665-675. doi:10.1016/j.brat.2011.07.005

Polenick, Courtney Allyn and Stephen Ray Flora. 2012. "Sensory Integration and Autism: Science or Pseudoscience?" *Skeptic* 17(2): 28-36.

Pollack, Mark H., J. Eric Jensen, Naomi M. Simon, Rebecca E. Kaufman, and Perry F. Renshaw. 2008. "High-field MRS Study of GABA, Glutamate and Glutamine in Social Anxiety Disorder: Response to Treatment with Levetiracetam." *Progress in Neuro-Psychopharmacology and Biological Psychiatry* 32(3): 739–743. doi:10.10 16/j.pnpbp.2007.11.023

Pollack, Mark H., Michael W. Otto, Peter P. Roy-Byrne, Jeremy D. Coplan, Barbara O. Rothbaum, Naomi M.Simon, and Jack M. Gorman. 2008. "Novel Treatment Approaches for Refractory Anxiety Disorders." *Depress. Anxiety* 25 (6): 467–476. doi: 10.1002/da.20329

Rabin, Roni Caryn. 2013. "A Glut of Antidepressants." *NYTimes.com*. Accessed October 29, 2014. http://well.blogs.nytimes.com/2013/08/12/a-glut-of-antidepressants/?_php=true&_type=blogs&_php=true&_type=blogs&_r=1

Reynolds, Stacey and Shelly J. Lane. 2007. "Diagnostic Validity of Sensory Over-Responsivity: A Review of the Literature and Case Reports." *Journal of Autism and Developmental Disorders* 38 (3): 516–529. doi:10.1007/s10803-007-0418-9

Riaza Bermudo-Soriano, Carlos, M. Mercedes Perez-Rodriguez, Concepcion Vaquero-Lorenzo, and Enrique Baca-Garcia. 2012. "New Perspectives in Glutamate and Anxiety." *Pharmacology Biochemistry and Behavior* 100 (4): 752–774. doi:10.1016/j.pbb.2011.04.010

Richards, Thomas A. 2014a. My Social Anxiety and How I Overcame It - Julie. *Social Anxiety Institute*. https://socialanxietyinstitute.org/julie

—— 2014b. What is Social Anxiety? *Social Anxiety Institute*. https://socialanxietyinstitute.org/what-is-social-anxiety

Richey, John A., Alison Rittenberg, Lauren Hughes, Cara R. Damiano, Antionette Sabatino, Stephanie Miller, Eleanor Hanna, James W. Bodfish, and Gabriel S. Dichter. 2012. "Common and Distinct Neural Features of Social and Non-Social Reward Processing in Autism and Social Anxiety Disorder." *Social Cognitive and Affective Neuroscience* 9 (3): 367–377. doi:10.1093/scan/nss146

Rodger, Sylvia, Jill Ashburner, Elizabeth Hinder. 2012. "Sensory Interventions for Children: Where Does Our Profession Stand?" *Australian Occupational Therapy Journal* 59(5): 337–338. doi:10.1111/j.1440-1630.2012.01032.x

Ross, Carolyn C., M.D. 2012. "Do Anti-Depressants Really Work?" *Psychology Today*. Webpage. Accessed October 29, 2014. http://www.psychologytoday.com/blog/real-healing/201202/do-anti-depressants-really-work

Rowa, Karen, Jeffrey R. Paulitzki, Maria D. Ierullo, Brenda Chiang, Martin M. Antony, Randi E. McCabe and David A. Moscovitch. 2014. "A False Sense of Security: Safety Behaviors Erode Objective Speech Performance in Individuals With Social Anxiety Disorder." *Behavior Therapy* 46 (3):304-315. doi: 10.1016/j.beth.2014.11.004

Ruscio, Ayelet M., Timothy A. Brown, Wai T. Chiu, Jitender Sareen, Murray B. Stein, and Ronald C. Kessler. 2008. "Social Fears and Social Phobia in the USA: Results from the National Comorbidity Survey Replication." *Psychological Medicine* 38, no. 1:15-28. http://dx.doi.org/10.1017%2FS0033291707001699

Salat, David H., Randy L. Buckner, Abraham Z. Snyder, Douglas N. Greve, Rahul S.R. Desikan, Evelina Busa, John C. Morris, Anders M. Dale and Bruce Fischl. 2004. "Thinning of the Cerebral Cortex in Aging." *Cerebral Cortex* 14 (7): 721–730. doi: 10.1093/cercor/bhh032

Sanacora, Gerard, Graeme F. Mason, Douglas L. Rothman, Fahmeed Hyder, James J. Ciarcia, Robert B. Ostroff, Robert M. Berman, and John H. Krystal. 2003 "Increased Cortical GABA Concentrations in Depressed Patients Receiving ECT." *AJP 160* (3): 577–579. doi:10.1176/appi.ajp.160.3.577

Sanislow, Charles A., Ellen Bartolini, and Emma Zoloth. (2012). Avoidant Personality Disorder. In V. S. Ramachandran (Ed.), *Encyclopedia of Human Behavior*, 2nd Ed. (pp. 257-266) Academic Press: San Diego.

Sarris, Jerome, Erica McIntyre, and David A. Camfield. 2013. "Plant-Based Medicines for Anxiety Disorders, Part 2: A Review of Clinical Studies with Supporting Preclinical Evidence." *CNS Drugs* 27(4): 301–319. doi:10.1007/s40263-013-0059-9

Schifano, Fabrizio, Laura Orsolini, Duccio Papanti and John Corker. 2015. "Novel Psychoactive Substances of Interest for Psychiatry." *World Psychiatry* 14(1):15-26. doi:10.1002/wps.20174

Schmidt, Norman B. 2012. "Innovations in the Treatment of Anxiety Psychopathology." *Behavior Therapy* 43 (3): 465–467. doi:10.1016/j.beth.2012.03.003

Schneier, F. R., T. E. Foose, D. S. Hasin, R. G. Heimberg, S.-M. Liu, B. F. Grant, and C Blanco. 2009. "Social Anxiety Disorder and Alcohol Use Disorder Co-Morbidity in the National Epidemiologic Survey on Alcohol and Related Conditions." *Psychol. Med.* 40 (06): 977–988. doi:10.1017/S0033291709991231

Schreier, Sina-Simone, Nina Heinrichs, Lynn Alden, Ronald M. Rapee, Stefan G. Hofmann, Junwen Chen, Kyung Ja Oh, and et al. 2010. "Social Anxiety and Social Norms in Individualistic and Collectivistic Countries." *Depress. Anxiety* 27 (12): 1128–1134. doi:10.1002/da.20746

Schröder, Arjan, Nienke Vulink, and Damiaan Denys. 2013. "Misophonia: Diagnostic Criteria for a New Psychiatric Disorder." *PLoS ONE* 8(1):e54706. doi:10.1371/journal.pone.0054706

Schulz, Ava, Timo Stolz and Thomas Berger. 2014. "Internet-Based Individually Versus Group Guided Self-Help Treatment for Social Anxiety Disorder: Protocol of a Randomized Controlled Trial." *BioMed Central Psychiatry* 14(1):115. doi:10.1186/1471-244X-14-115

Schwarz, Alan. 2014. "Thousands of Toddlers are Medicated for A.D.H.D., Report Finds, Raising Worries." *NYTimes.com*. http://www.nytimes.com/2014/05/17/us/among-experts-scrutiny-of-attention-disorder-diagnoses-in-2-and-3-year-olds.html

Scutti, Susan. 2015. "Social Phobia Linked to High Levels of Serotonin: Time to Rethink SSRIs and Other Anxiety Drugs?." *www.medicaldaily.com*. Webpage. Accessed Sept. 28, 2015. http://www.medicaldaily.com/social-phobia-linked-high-levels-serotonin-time-rethink-ssris-and-other-anxiety-drugs-338608

Seedat, S. 2013. "Social Anxiety Disorder." *South African Journal of Psychiatry* 19, no. 3:192. http://link.springer.com/article/10.2165/00023210-200519050-00002

Seifert, Christian L., Stefano Magon, Kathrin Staehle, Claus Zimmer, Annette Foerschler, Ernst-Wilhelm Radue, Volker Pfaffenrath, Thomas R. Tölle, and Till Sprenger. 2012. "A Case-Control Study on Cortical Thickness in Episodic Cluster Headache." *Headache: The Journal of Head and Face Pain* 52 (9): 1362–1368.

Shankar, Rohit, Kathryn Smith, and Virupakshi Jalihal. 2013. "Sensory Processing in People with Asperger Syndrome." *Learning Disability Practice* 16 (2): 22–27. http://dx.doi.org/10.7748/ldp2013.03.16.2.22.e658

Siegel, D. J. 2010. *Mindsight: The New Science of Personal Transformation.* New York: Bantam Books.

Simonoff, Emily, Andrew Pickles, Tony Charman, Susie Chandler, Tom Loucas, and Gillian Baird. 2008. "Psychiatric Disorders in Children With Autism Spectrum Disorders: Prevalence, Comorbidity, and Associated Factors in a Population-Derived Sample." *Journal of the American Academy of Child & Adolescent Psychiatry* 47 (8): 921–929. doi:10.1097/CHI.0b013e318179964f

Sisodiya, S., S. Free, D. Fish, and S. Shorvon. 1996. MRI-Based Surface Area Estimates in the Normal Adult Human Brain: Evidence for Structural Organisation. *Journal of Anatomy* 188(Pt 2), 425–438.

Smits, Jasper A.J., David Rosenfield, Michael W. Otto, Luana Marques, Michelle L. Davis, Alicia E. Meuret, Naomi M. Simon, and et al. 2013. "D-cycloserine Enhancement of Exposure Therapy for Social Anxiety Disorder Depends on the Success of Exposure Sessions." *Journal of Psychiatric Research* 47 (10):

1455–1461. http://dx.doi.org/10.1016/j.jpsychires.2013.06.020
Snipes, Eddie. 2013. *"Abounding Grace: Dispelling Myths and Clarifying the Biblical Message of God's Overflowing Grace."* Exchanged Life Discipleship. Kindle Edition
Sportel, B. Esther, Eva de Hullu, Peter J. de Jong, and Maaike H. Nauta. 2013. "Cognitive Bias Modification versus CBT in Reducing Adolescent Social Anxiety: A Randomized Controlled Trial." *PLoS ONE* 8 (5): e64355. doi:10.1371/journal.pone.0064355
Sripada, Chandra Sekhar, K. Luan Phan, Izelle Labuschagne, Robert Welsh, Pradeep J. Nathan, and Amanda G. Wood. 2012. "Oxytocin Enhances Resting-State Connectivity Between Amygdala and Medial Frontal Cortex." *Int. J. Neuropsychopharm.* 16 (02): 255–260. doi:10.1017/S1461145712000533
Stahl, Stephen M., Clara Lee-Zimmerman, Sylvia Cartwright, and Debbi Ann Morrissette. 2013. "Serotonergic Drugs for Depression and Beyond." *Current Drug Targets* 14 (5): 578–585. doi:10.2174/1389450111314050007
Stanford University. 2007. "What is Your Reaction Time?" Tech Museum of Innovation. PDF. Accessed Dec. 6, 2014. http://virtuallabs.stanford.edu/tech/images/ReactionTime.SU-Tech.pdf
Stangier, Ulrich, Elisabeth Schramm, Thomas Heidenreich, Matthias Berger, and David M. Clark. 2011. "Cognitive Therapy vs Interpersonal Psychotherapy in Social Anxiety Disorder." *Archives of General Psychiatry* 68 (7): 692. doi:10.1001/archgenpsychiatry.2011.67
Stein, Murray B. and Yin M. Kean. 2000. "Disability and Quality of Life in Social Phobia: Epidemiologic Findings." *American Journal of Psychiatry* 157: 1606–1613. doi: 10.1176/appi.ajp.157.10.1606
Stein, Murray B. and Dan J. Stein. 2008. "Social Anxiety Disorder." *The Lancet.* 371: 1115-25. http://dx.doi.org/10.1016/S0140-6736(08)60488-2
Stephani, C., G. Fernandez-Baca Vaca, R. Maciunas, M. Koubeissi, and H. O. Lüders. 2010. "Functional Neuroanatomy of the Insular Lobe." *Brain Structure and Function* 216 (2): 137–149. doi:10.1007/s00429-010-0296-3
Stewart, John. 2012. *Bridges Not Walls: A Book About Interpersonal Communication*, 11th edition. New York: McGraw-Hill.
Storch, Eric A., Carrie Masia-Warner, Heather Crisp, and Rachel G. Klein. 2005. "Peer Victimization and Social Anxiety in Adolescence: A Prospective Study." *Aggressive Behavior* 31: 437-452. doi: 10.1002/ab.20093
Suliman, Sharain, Sian M. J. Hemmings, and Soraya Seedat. 2013. "Brain-Derived Neurotrophic Factor (BDNF) Protein Levels in Anxiety Disorders: Systematic Review and Meta-regression Analysis." *Front. Integr. Neurosci.* 7. doi 10.3389/fnint.2013.00055
Syal, Supriya, Coenraad J. Hattingh, Jean-Paul Fouché, Bruce Spottiswoode, Paul D. Carey, Christine Lochner, and Dan J Stein. 2012. "Gray Matter Abnormalities in Social Anxiety Disorder: A Pilot Study." *Metabolic Brain Disease* 27 (3): 299–309. doi:10.1007/s11011-012-9299-5
Szuhany, Kristin L., Matteo Bugatti, and Michael W. Otto. 2015. "A Meta-Analytic Review of the Effects of Exercise on Brain-Derived Neurotrophic Factor."

Journal of Psychiatric Research 60: 56–64. http://dx.doi.org/10.1016/j.jpsychires.2014.10.003

Talati, Ardesheer, Spiro P. Pantazatos, Franklin R. Schneier, Myrna M. Weissman, and Joy Hirsch. 2013. "Gray Matter Abnormalities in Social Anxiety Disorder: Primary, Replication, and Specificity Studies." *Biological Psychiatry* 73 (1): 75–84. http://dx.doi.org/10.1016/j.biopsych.2012.05.022

Tan, Siang-Yang. 2011. "Mindfulness and Acceptance-Based Cognitive Behavioral Therapies: Empirical Evidence and Clinical Applications from a Christian Perspective." *Journal of Psychology and Christianity* 30(3): 243-249.

Tavassoli, Teresa, Rosa A. Hoekstra, and Simon Baron-Cohen. 2014. "The Sensory Perception Quotient (SPQ): Development and Validation of a New Sensory Questionnaire for Adults with and Without Autism." *Mol Autism* 5(1): 29 doi:10.1186/2040-2392-5-29

Taylor, Bonnie P. 2012. "Differentiation of Social Phobia from High-Functioning Autism Spectrum Disorder." Psychiatric Annals 42 (8): 296–298. doi:10.3928/00485713-20120806-07

Taylor, C. T., and L. E. Alden. 2010. "Safety Behaviors and Judgmental Biases in Social Anxiety Disorder." *Behaviour Research and Therapy* 48(3), 226-237. doi:10.1016/j.brat.2009.11.005

Tchividjian, Tullian. 2013. *One Way Love: Inexhaustible Grace for an Exhausted World.* Colorado Springs: David C. Cook.

Teale Sapach, Michelle J. N., R. Nicholas Carleton, Myriah K. Mulvogue, Justin W. Weeks, and Richard G .Heimberg. 2014. "Cognitive Constructs and Social Anxiety Disorder: Beyond Fearing Negative Evaluation." *Cognitive Behaviour Therapy* 44 (1): 63–73. doi:10.1080/16506073.2014.961539

Terasawa, Yuri, Midori Shibata, Yoshiya Moriguchi, and Satoshi Umeda. 2012. "Anterior Insular Cortex Mediates Bodily Sensibility and Social Anxiety." *Social Cognitive and Affective Neuroscience* 8 (3): 259–266.

Thakur, Priyanka and A. C. Rana. 2013. "Anxiolytic Potential of Medicinal Plants." *International Journal of Nutrition, Pharmacology, Neurological Diseases* 3(4): 325. doi:10.4103/2231-0738.119838

Tillfors, Maria and Lisa Ekselius. 2009. "Social Phobia and Avoidant Personality Disorder: Are They Separate Diagnostic Entities or Do They Reflect a Spectrum of Social Anxiety?" *Israel Journal of Psychiatry & Related Sciences* 46 (1): 25–33.

Torgersen, Svenn, Einar Kringlen, and Victoria Cramer. 2001. "The Prevalence of Personality Disorders in a Community Sample." *Archives of General Psychiatry* 58 (6): 590. doi:10.1001/archpsyc.58.6.590

Türck, Patrick and Marcos Emílio Frizzo. 2015. "Riluzole Stimulates BDNF Release from Human Platelets." *BioMed Research International* 2015: 1–6. http://dx.doi.org/10.1155/2015/189307

Tupper, Kevin. 2016. "Christian Mindfulness: Behold, the Kingdom of Heaven is at Hand." christiansimplicity.com. Webpage. Accessed Jan. 11, 2016. http://christiansimplicity.com/christian-mindfulness/

Tyson, Katherine E. and Dean G. Cruess. 2012. "Differentiating High-Functioning

Autism and Social Phobia." *Journal of Autism and Developmental Disorders* 42 (7): 1477–1490. doi:10.1007/s10803-011-1386-7

Van Hulle, Carol, Kathryn Lemery-Chalfant, and H. Hill Goldsmith. 2015. "Trajectories of Sensory Over-Responsivity from Early to Middle Childhood: Birth and Temperament Risk Factors." *PLoS ONE 10* (6): e0129968. doi:10.1371/journal.pone.0129968

van Veen, J. Frederieke, Irene M. van Vliet, Roel H. de Rijk, Johannes van Pelt, Bart Mertens, Durk Fekkes, and Frans G. Zitman. 2009. "Tryptophan Depletion Affects the Autonomic Stress Response in Generalized Social Anxiety Disorder." *Psychoneuroendocrinology 34* (10): 1590–1594. doi:10.1016/j.psyneuen.2009.05.007.

Vøllestad, Jon, Morten Birkeland Nielsen, and Geir Høstmark Nielsen. 2011. "Mindfulness- and Acceptance-based Interventions for Anxiety Disorders: A Systematic Review and Meta-analysis." *British Journal of Clinical Psychology 51* (3): 239–260. do:10.1111/j.2044-8260.2011.02024.x

Voncken, Marisol J. and Susan M. Bögels. 2006. "Changing Interpretation and Judgmental Bias in Social Phobia: A Pilot Study of a Short, Highly Structured Cognitive Treatment." *Journal of Cognitive Psychotherapy 20* (1): 59–73. doi:10.1891/jcop.20.1.59

Wang, Yu, Shanshan Zhao, Xu Liu, Qunying Fu. 2014. "Effects of the Bedial or Basolateral Amygdala Upon Social Anxiety and Social Recognition in Mice." *Turkish Journal of Medical Sciences 44*: 353-359. doi:10.3906/sag-1301-2

Washington, Stuart D., Evan M Gordon, Jasmit Brar, Samantha Warburton, Alice T Sawyer, Amanda Wolfe, Erin R. Mease-Ference, and et al. 2013. "Dysmaturation of the Default Mode Network in Autism." *Hum. Brain Mapp.* 35 (4) 1284–1296. doi:10.1002/hbm.22252.

Weeks, Justin W., Richard G. Heimberg, and Thomas L. Rodebaugh. 2008. "The Fear of Positive Evaluation Scale: Assessing a Proposed Cognitive Component of Social Anxiety." *Journal of Anxiety Disorders 22* (1): 44–55. doi:10.1016/j janxdis.2007.08.002

Weeks, Justin W. 2014. *The Wiley Blackwell Handbook Of Social Anxiety Disorder* Chichester, WestSussex: Wiley-Blackwell.

White, Susan W., Bethany C. Bray and Thomas H. Ollendick. 2011. "Examining Shared and Unique Aspects of Social Anxiety Disorder and Autism Spectrum Disorder Using Factor Analysis." *Journal of Autism and Developmenta Disorders 42* (5): 874–884. doi:10.1007/s10803-011-1325-7

Wigton, Rebekah, Jocham Radua, Paul Allen, Bruno Averbeck, Andreas Meyer-Lindenberg, Philip McGuire, Sukhi S. Shergill, and et al. 2015. "Neurophysiological Effects of Acute Oxytocin Administration: Systematic Review and Meta-analysis of Placebo-controlled Imaging Studies." *Journal o Psychiatry & Neuroscience 40*(1): E1-E22. doi:10.1503/jpn.130289

Wild, Jennifer, Ann Hackmann, and David M. Clark. 2008. "Rescripting Early Memories Linked to Negative Images in Social Phobia: A Pilot Study." *Behavio Therapy 39* (1): 47–56. http://dx.doi.org/10.1016%2Fj.beth.2007.04.003

Williams, M. R., R. Chaudhry, S. Perera, R. K. B. Pearce, S. R. Hirsch, O. Ansorge

M. Thom, and M. Maier. 2012. "Changes in Cortical Thickness in the Frontal Lobes in Schizophrenia Are a Result of Thinning of Pyramidal Cell Layers." *Eur Arch Psychiatry Clin Neurosci 263* (1): 25–39. doi:10.1007/s00406-012-0325-8

Williams, Tracey A., Melanie A. Porter, and Robyn Langdon. 2014. "Social Approach and Emotion Recognition in Fragile X Syndrome." *American Journal on Intellectual and Developmental Disabilities 119*(2): 133–150. doi:10.1352/1944-7558-119.2.133

Wittchen, Hans-Ulrich and Frank Jacobi. 2005. "Size and Burden of Mental Disorders in Europe—A Critical Review and Appraisal of 27 Studies." *European Neuropsychopharmacology* 15 (4): 357–376. doi:10.1016/j.euroneuro.2005.04.012

Wittchen, H.U, M. Fuetsch, H. Sonntag, N. Müller, and M. Liebowitz. 2000. "Disability and Quality of Life in Pure and Comorbid Social Phobia. Findings from a Controlled Study." *European Psychiatry* 15 (1): 46–58. doi:10.1016/s0924-9338(00)00211-x

Wood, Jeffrey J. 2010. *The Cognitive Behavioral Therapy Workbook For Personality Disorders: A Step-by-Step Program*. Oakland, Calif.: New Harbinger Publications.

Yang, Xun, Keith Maurice Kendrick, Qizhu Wu, Taolin Chen, Sunima Lama, Bochao Cheng, Shiguang Li, and et al. 2013. "Structural and Functional Connectivity Changes in the Brain Associated with Shyness but Not with Social Anxiety." *PLoS ONE 8* (5): e63151. doi:10.1371/journal.pone.0063151

Young, Simon N. 2007. "How to Increase Serotonin in the Human Brain Without Drugs." *J Psychiatry Neurosci* 32(6):394-9.

Yuen, Erica K., James D. Herbert, Evan M. Forman, Elizabeth M. Goetter, Adrienne S. Juarascio, Stephanie Rabin, Christina Goodwin, and et al. 2013. "Acceptance Based Behavior Therapy for Social Anxiety Disorder Through Videoconferencing." *Journal of Anxiety Disorders*, 27(4), 389-397. doi:10.1016/j.janxdis.2013.03.002

Zhang, Wenjing, Xun Yang, Su Lui, Yajing Meng, Li Yao, Yuan Xiao, Wei Zhang, and Qiyong Gong. 2015. "Diagnostic Prediction for Social Anxiety Disorder Via Multivariate Pattern Analysis of the Regional Homogeneity." *BioMed Research International* 2015: 1-9. http://dx.doi.org/10.1155/2015/763965

Zou, Judy B., and Maree J. Abbott, M. J. 2012. Self-Perception and Rumination in Social Anxiety. *Behaviour Research and Therapy 50*(4), 250-257. doi:10.1016/j.brat.2012.01.007

APPENDIX A

THOUGHT MONITORING TABLE

Situation	Feelings	Automatic Thoughts	Corpse or New Me

APPENDIX B

VALUES

Make a list of the things you really care about, and be specific.
For example: *I really care about keeping my marriage strong and happy.*
Let your future goals and decisions be rooted in your values.

Index

A

Acceptance and Commitment Therapy (ACT)— 205
   acceptance— 211
   committed action— 215
   defusion— 210
   effective— 206
   fit with gospel— 206
   flexibility— 211
   perspective of self— 212
   present moment awareness— 207
   six core processes in— 207
   steps in— 216
   Table 9: Steps of— 216
   values— 27, 125, 129, 136, 137, 150, 155, 158, 164, 173, 178, 188, 205, 206, 207, 212, 213, 214, 215, 216, 217, 218, 233
Adam and Eve— 13, 30, 33, 44, 53, 122, 123, 155, 189
Alcohol— 26, 74, 106, 113, 114, 127
Aloradine IN— 111, 112
Assessments
   Infant/Toddler Sensory Profile— 94
   Liebowitz Social Anxiety Scale (LSAS).— 36
   Safety Behaviors— 174
   sensory assessment for children— 94
   Sensory Perception Quotient (SPQ)— 94
Attention— 193
   negative— 193
   positive— 193
   self-focused— 201
Autism— 7, 71, 79, 80, 87, 88, 89, 94, 110
   autism spectrum disorder— 79, 80, 89, 242
   linked to social anxiety— 79

Avoidance— 32, 33, 85, 87, 156, 173, 174
Avoidant Personality Disorder— 33
   symptoms— 34
      Table 3: APD Symptoms— 34

B

Book of Life— 143, 144
Brain
   amygdala— 61, 62, 63, 64, 65, 104, 106, 110, 143, 144, 222, 225, 227
   anterior cingulate— 62, 143, 144, 224
   capacity to change— 72
   cortical thickness— 66, 67, 260
   Default Mode Network— 70, 71, 72
   differences in SAD— 53, 61, 110
   fear circuit— 61
   functional magnetic resonance imaging (fMRI)— 61, 74
   gray matter— 39, 47, 66, 67
   hypothalamus— 63
   injury— 60
   insula— 61, 62, 63, 64, 84, 110, 201, 225
   intradiploic hematoma— 60
   neurons— 59
   our flesh— 60
   prefrontal cortex— 62, 65, 66, 71, 104, 224
   reward— 46, 79, 80, 110
   uncinate fasciculus— 70, 74
Brain Derived Neurotropic Factor (BDNF)— 108

C

Church— 93
   as a trigger— 25
   avoiding— 31, 161
   difficulty with— 28
   exposure to— 215
   freedom to leave— 234
   judgment— 139
   not fitting in— 161
   protecting— 234

rules in— 164
self-disclosure in— 173
sensory trouble— 78, 84, 92
values in— 214
views on mental illness— 99
Cognitive Behavioral Therapy (CBT)— 241
  as rules— 188
  attention bias modification— 193
  automatic negative thoughts— 191
  Christian— 188
  cognitive restructuring— 192
  gold standard— 184
  imagery rescripting— 199
  internet based— 185
  interpretation bias modification— 194
  non-responders— 185
  perspective exercises— 195
  pie method— 195
  self-focused attention— 201
  social cost bias— 197
  statistics— 184
  thought challenging— 192
  thought monitoring— 191
  Truth Therapy— 188
Cognitive reappraisal— 178, 179, 180, 226, 227
Confession— 90, 91, 92, 156, 173
Corpse— 130
  Image 3— 130
Counselor— 94
  avoidance of— 29
  modeling grace— 187
  psychodynamic— 229
  training manual— 42
Creativity— 235
  DMN— 71
  introvert— 160

D

Death— 51, 87
  of Jesus— 45, 51, 52
  of our flesh— 51, 74
Depression

ACT— 206, 216
BDNF— 108
CBT— 184, 187
comorbid— 186
electroconvulsive therapy— 106
failure— 99
insight— 143
isolation— 166
oxytocin— 110
sensory problems— 81
serotonin— 101
unmedicated— 63
Dopamine— 80, 84, 89, 106, 108

E

Emotion Regulation— 66, 73, 219, 224, 226, 227
  four steps in— 226
  prefrontal cortex— 65
  Table 10— 226
Escitalopram— 67, 102
Exhaustion— 16
Expectations— 28, 136, 137, 146
Exposure— 90, 220, 223
  flooding— 221
  systematic desensitization— 221
Expressive suppression— 190

F

Foods
  bread— 116
  cheese— 116
  chocolate— 116
  kefir— 116
  kimchi— 116
  kombucha— 116
  pickles— 116
  sauerkraut— 116
  yogurt— 116
Fragile X Syndrome— 61

G

Gamma-aminobutyric acid (GABA)— 106

Glutamate— 109
Goodness of fit— 92
Gospel— 44, 47, 54, 127, 141, 180, 206, 227, 229, 234
Grace— 5, 13, 17, 18, 19, 20, 21, 35, 36, 41, 42, 45, 47, 48, 49, 50, 51, 52, 53, 54, 55, 74, 87, 88, 91, 93, 97, 98, 99, 102, 109, 121, 122, 125, 126, 127, 131, 133, 137, 138, 139, 141, 142, 144, 149, 150, 154, 155, 157, 163, 164, 165, 166, 167, 169, 170, 173, 175, 177, 178, 179, 181, 183, 185, 187, 188, 189, 190, 192, 193, 194, 196, 202, 206, 207, 209, 211, 213, 215, 216, 217, 220, 229, 233, 234, 235, 236, 239

H

Hippocrates— 32
Holy Spirit— 141, 142, 199

I

Identity— 29, 32, 36, 51, 57, 122, 127, 128, 129, 131, 137, 141, 144, 163, 189, 192, 193, 219
Interoceptive processing— 201
Irritability— 86, 89, 105

J

Jesus— 45, 48, 51, 55, 94, 128, 129, 131, 144, 146, 160, 178, 200, 236, 242, 246
Jezebel spirit— 16, 18
Job— 49, 52
Judgment— 178, 209
　antennas— 234
　avoiding— 125, 174
　day of— 136, 142, 143, 144, 156
　fear of— 150, 153, 170, 171, 172
　of God— 122, 131
　of others— 137, 138, 140, 153, 154, 164, 177
　self— 210, 211, 213, 216, 230

L

Law— 41, 43, 48, 49, 50, 126, 127, 129, 131, 137, 138, 139, 140, 149, 154, 166, 167, 169, 177, 179, 190, 209, 234. *See also* **Rules**

M

Medications
　Abilify. *See* apripiprazole
　antidepressant— 14, 16, 17, 18, 19, 72, 98, 100, 102, 103, 105, 106, 108, 109, 118
　aripiprazole— 89, 246
　bromazepam— 107
　bumetanide— 89, 247
　Celexa. *See* citalopram
　Cipralex. *See* escitalopram
　Cipramil. *See* citalopram
　citalopram— 72, 102
　Clonazepam— 107
　controversy— 98
　discontinuation syndrome— 105
　Effexor ER. *See* venlafaxine
　escitalopram— 67, 102, 243
　fluoxetine— 102
　fluvoxamine— 102, 103
　Lexapro. *See* escitalopram
　Lustral. *See* sertraline
　Luvox. *See* fluvoxamine
　paroxetine— 103
　Paxil. *See* paroxetine
　Pexeva. *See* paroxetine
　Prozac. *See* fluoxetine
　serotonin and norepinephrine re-uptake inhibitor (SNRI)— 102, 103, 104, 105
　serotonin reuptake inhibitor (SSRI)— 101, 102, 103, 104, 105, 251
　sertraline— 97, 103
　side effects— 104
　statistics— 98
　Table 4.— 103
　venlafaxine— 102
　Zoloft. *See* sertraline
Meditation— 187, 207, 209, 230, 252
Memory— 65, 67, 101, 199, 200

Mindfulness— 184, 207, 208, 209, 210, 219, 229, 230, 231, 232, 250, 254, 259
  awareness of breathing— 230
  body scan— 230
Misophonia— 86, 242, 243, 245, 257
Moses— 31, 32, 45, 49, 162
  Image 6— 162

N

nature vs. nurture— 159
Neurogenesis— 108
Neurotransmitters— 72, 100, 106, 109

O

Oxytocin— 109, 110, 111, 241, 242, 247, 251, 258, 260

P

Panic— 23, 24, 25, 34, 62, 83, 86, 106, 230
Pet Therapy— 89
Post-Event Processing (PEP)— 7, 156, 176, 177, 178, 179
prayer— 200, 234
Psychodynamic Therapy— 229
Psychoeducation— 219

R

Religion— 45
  works— 48
Rules— 147
  about friends— 165
  face fears— 31, 156
  fear of judgment— 21, 24, 170
  God-created (good)— 17, 21, 35, 43, 47, 53, 148, 150, 202
  hide all flaws— 30, 150, 169, 170, 173
  love perfectly— 28, 126, 155
  man-made— 35, 150, 164
  master one's body— 24
  on being boring— 162
  on being introverted— 160
  on quietness— 157
  on selfishness— 165
  on shyness— 158
  pleasing God or man— 150
  purpose— 42
  religious— 16, 18
  rest from— 20, 47, 49, 52, 93, 95, 100, 137, 150
  Table 7.— 150
  top twelve— 147
Rumination— 176, 244

S

Safety Behaviors— 7, 169, 170, 173, 174, 175, 180, 256
  assessment— 174
  impression management— 171
  subtle avoidance— 171, 173, 174
Schizophrenia— 66, 71, 260
Self-disclosure— 166, 173, 174, 175
Sensory
  assessment for children— 94
  diet— 88
  gating— 80
  Infant/Toddler Sensory Profile— 94
  matchmaking— 92
  oversensitive— 49, 80, 84
  processing— 84, 85, 87, 89
  sensitivity— 78, 79, 84, 94
  Sensory Integration Disorder— 87
  Sensory Integration Therapy— 87, 88
  Sensory Modulation Disorder— 87, 249
  Sensory Perception Quotient (SPQ)— 94
  Sensory Processing Disorder— 87, 94
  symptoms— 81
  therapy equipment— 88
  threshold— 79, 80, 81, 183
  under-sensitive— 80, 84
Serotonin— 100, 101, 186, 241, 246, 249, 251, 257, 261
Shyness— 28, 49, 93, 152, 153, 158, 159, 160, 168
Sin— 124
Social Anxiety
  age of onset— 27
  authority figures— 25, 29, 30, 112, 223
  definition— 23

diagnosis— 27, 33, 61, 79, 87, 206
expectations— 20, 24, 28, 90, 91, 98, 104, 136, 137, 146, 161, 216
gift— 21
in adolescents— 28
in females— 30
puberty— 27
signs in infants— 27
statistics— 26, 29
treatment delay— 29
Social Skills Training— 219, 228
Suicide— 29, 249
Supplements
Cannabidiol— 115
Kava Kava— 113
Lavender— 114
Lemon Balm— 113
Passionflower— 113
Picamilon— 107
Rain of Gold— 114
Roseroot— 114
St. John's Wort— 114
Table 5— 115
Valerian— 114
Symptoms
blushing— 51, 123, 155
enduring— 25
eye contact— 24, 25, 29, 30, 61, 79, 83, 152, 170, 171, 173, 174, 175
heart racing— 24, 85
panic. *See* Panic
sweating— 24, 63, 103, 171, 201, 228, 229
Table 1: APA Symptoms— 25
tachycardia— 24, 113
trembling— 12, 21, 24, 37, 63, 85, 154, 157, 201, 228

T

Theology. *See also* **Grace**
antinomianism— 49
false teaching— 18
Theophostic Prayer Ministry— 200
Treatments
Table 8— 187
Triggers— 25

Table 2: Triggers— 26

V

Video Feedback— 228

W

Williams Syndrome— 60
Worry. *See* **Rumination**

About the Author

Julie Rajnus holds a Master of Arts degree in Human Services from Liberty University. She lives on a potato and wheat seed farm in rural Oregon, with her husband, two children, three dogs, and a collection of uninvited pack rats (as in... the actual animals... not hoarding humans).

Made in the USA
San Bernardino, CA
02 September 2016